JOEL GUTTORMSOW

SLAYING THE DRAGON

D0061879

SLAYING THE DRAGON

◆

Mythmaking in the Biblical Tradition

◆

BERNARD F. BATTO

Westminster/John Knox Press
Louisville, Kentucky

© 1992 Bernard F. Batto

All rights reserved. No part of this book may be reproduced or transmitted in any form or by any means, electronic or mechanical, including photocopying, recording, or by any information storage or retrieval system, without permission in writing from the publisher. For information, address Westminster/John Knox Press, 100 Witherspoon Street, Louisville, Kentucky 40202-1396.

Book design by Kevin Raquepaw

First edition

This book is printed on acid-free paper that meets the American National Standards Institute Z39.48 standard. ∞

Published by Westminster/John Knox Press
Louisville, Kentucky

PRINTED IN THE UNITED STATES OF AMERICA

9 8 7 6 5 4 3 2 1

Library of Congress Cataloging-in-Publication Data

Batto, Bernard Frank.
 Slaying the dragon : mythmaking in the biblical tradition /
Bernard F. Batto. — 1st ed.
        p.   cm.
 Includes bibliographical references and index.
 ISBN 0-664-25353-9 (alk. paper)

 1. Myth in the Old Testament.   2. Bible. O.T.—Criticism,
interpretation, etc.   I. Title.
BS1183.B38 1992
221.6'8—dc20   91-38569

CONTENTS

PREFACE

This book has been many years in the making and reflects the author's own evolution in thinking about myth in the Bible. At its conception this project was envisioned as a history of the motif of sea in the exodus traditions. At that point I labored under the naive assumption that the principal issue was one of historicity: how to assess the reliability of the various accounts of the sea deliverance and how to account for obvious embellishments of the basic account in later tradition. But as each child has a way of asserting its own individuality, so my volume as it developed seemed to force upon me a reassessment of the nature of the project in which I was engaged. The more it matured the more obvious it became that my subject had as much to do with myth as history—if not more. Although I had not intended originally to produce a volume on myth in the Bible, I am very pleased with the outcome.

At the outset I acknowledge gratefully that the Revised Standard Version (RSV) serves as the basis of most translations of biblical texts cited in this book. My dependency upon the RSV extends beyond the few parenthetical acknowledgements to be found in these pages. Because the theses that I develop frequently are grounded in subtle nuances present in the Hebrew text—or the Greek text, in the case of the epilogue—I regularly alter the RSV wording to reflect a nuance that I wish to emphasize or else provide my own original translations. Even for the latter, however, my indebtedness to the RSV will be evident. Furthermore, biblical passages are cited according to the numbering of the RSV, unless otherwise noted.

This volume has benefited from discussion with many persons too numerous to be mentioned by name here. However, I would be remiss not to single out the following people for reading portions of this volume in earlier forms and offering valuable suggestions for amelioration: Richard J. Clifford, S.J. (chapters 2–3); John J. Collins (all chapters); W. W. Hallo (chapters 1–3); and Mark S. Smith (chapters 2–3). Finally, I wish to thank Dr. Jefferies M. Hamilton of Westminster/John Knox Press for numerous emendations, particularly in clarifying my thesis in chapter 5.

Special credit is due my wife, Teresa. Without her encouragement and help, this project would have taken even longer to come to fruition. But even more importantly, she has been my best and most relentless critic. Both in matters of style and of substance this volume bears her imprint on every page. It is therefore with loving acknowledgment of her role as ʿēzer that this volume is dedicated to her.

INTRODUCTION

This book is about myth and mythmaking in the Bible. Just a few short years ago such a book would have been unthinkable. Jews and Christians alike regarded myth as the antithesis of revealed religion. Myth was the stuff of pagan religion; it was false belief. By definition, then, myth could not exist within the revealed word of God in the Bible. In the last two decades, however, attitudes have begun to change. Since about 1970 myth has become increasingly recognized as an important theological medium in biblical tradition.[1]

Not so many years ago it was commonplace to claim that "history is the chief medium of revelation."[2] Biblical narratives are not as historical as once assumed, however.[3] Recent scholarship has emphasized the literary character of biblical narratives. At the same time scholars have gained a new appreciation for the ancient genres in which biblical authors wrote. Myth is one of those genres, although its centrality in biblical tradition has not yet been sufficiently recognized.

The thesis upon which this book is predicated is that myth is one of the chief mediums by which biblical writers did their theologizing. Rather than trying to read myth out of the Bible as many in the past have done, I intend to demonstrate that myth permeates virtually every layer of biblical tradition from the earliest to the latest. Texts from all periods and of virtually every literary genre reveal that biblical writers borrowed old myths and extended their meanings in novel ways for the purpose of expressing new theological insights.

1

THE STRUCTURE OF THE PRESENT VOLUME

Although this volume is about mythmaking in the Hebrew Bible, chapter 1 is a study in the development of myths from Mesopotamia, and for good reason. First, the development of Mesopotamian myths is well documented through multiple exemplars over a long time; it thus can serve as a control on our theories about the growth of biblical myths. Thanks to the scribal practice in Mesopotamia of writing upon clay tablets, which when fired are virtually indestructible, literally thousands of tablets from many different sites and periods have been uncovered by archaeologists. Accordingly, it is possible to reconstruct with a reasonable assurance of verisimilitude the various stages of development through which the major Mesopotamian myths passed during more than two millennia. Second, the so-called Primeval History (Genesis 1–11) is heavily dependent upon the mythic tradition of Mesopotamia. An acquaintance with the major myths of Mesopotamia is a prerequisite for appreciating the mentality and the creative genius of the authors of the opening chapters of Genesis in particular. Other portions of the Bible seem to be more dependent on Canaanite myth. However, the lessons learned from the study of Mesopotamian myth apply mutatis mutandis to Canaanite and biblical mythic traditions as well.

Chapter 2 concerns the first systematic attempt by an Israelite theologian to define the place of humans within creation. I argue for a radically new interpretation of the familiar story of the Garden of Eden (Genesis 2–3). It is not a story of "the Fall" as commonly interpreted. Rather it is part of a new primeval myth created by the Yahwist, the basic elements of which were borrowed from the older Babylonian myth of *Atrahasis*. Like *Atrahasis*, the Yahwist's primeval myth posits that the Creator's initial efforts at creating humans were more experimental prototypes than perfected designs. Partly divine, these human prototypes overreached their proper status by attempting to usurp prerogatives reserved for the deity, an act of hubris that eventually brought about the annihilating deluge of Genesis 6–8. The burden of the Yahwist's primeval myth is to produce a reconciliation of Creator to a flawed humankind; in the process the proper place of humankind within creation is defined and permanently secured.

Some centuries later the Priestly Writer found it necessary to rewrite the Yahwist's myth when the latter failed to answer the new doubts raised by the catastrophic events of the Babylonian exile (chapter 3). The common Semitic Combat Myth, which narrated how in primeval time the creator deity had slain the chaos dragon, functioned to provide assurance that meaningful existence was possible within this often chaotic world. Apparently borrowing from *Enuma elish*, the Babylonian version of the Combat Myth, the Priestly Writer rewrote the biblical primeval myth in such a way as to reaffirm Israel's traditional faith that their god Yahweh was indeed sovereign in heaven and earth and, at the same time, account for the ubiquitous presence of evil in a seemingly disintegrating world. The Priestly retelling of the creation myth (Genesis 1–9) provided assurance that evil, no matter how menacing, will never overwhelm the creator's benevolent design for the world in general and for Israel in particular.

The Combat Myth, whether in its Babylonian or Canaanite form, undergirds to some extent virtually every aspect of Israel's supposedly historically based faith. The exodus narrative, for example, is less a historical account than a mythic reinterpretation of this "event" as a second act of creation (chapter 4), the Egyptian host not so much an earthly enemy as an incarnation of the chaos dragon. The exodus is about the establishment of the kingdom of God through a slaying of the dragon anew; this was a theme that was promoted and even partially created within Israel's cult (chapter 5). The prophets also resorted to the Combat Myth to express their belief that behind seemingly historical threats to the people of God lies a suprahistorical evil power that must be overcome before the kingdom of God can become a reality. Ezekiel inverted the Combat Myth to say that the definitive victory of the Creator over chaos is not so much a primeval event as eschatological hope (chapter 6).

The theme of an eschatological victory over chaos or evil continued to develop in much fuller form later outside the canon of the Hebrew Bible both in Jewish apocalyptic and in the New Testament. Although these literatures lie outside the scope of this volume, it seems to me entirely appropriate to notice that the process of reappropriating "old" myths did not end with the closing of the Hebrew Bible canon. Accordingly, in the Epilogue I call attention to the manner in which apocalyptic writers, both Jewish and Christian, extended the Combat Myth as an eschatological myth. Similarly, the New Testament evangelists understood fully mythmaking as a method of "doing theology"; they applied it with great effect, for example, in the stories of Jesus walking on the sea and Jesus asleep on the storming sea.

This volume, then, is a case study in the methodology of biblical writers in using myth and mythmaking speculation to express their most profound theological insights. In view of the heavy negative connotations attached to the word "myth" in our culture, perhaps some sort of apologia for this project is in order.

THE DEFINITION OF MYTH

"Myth" is one of those words which in our society cause strong reactions. Mere mention of the word conjures up within most people negative images of falsehood, naïveté, superstition, or the like. In popular parlance myth implies something that is untrue. Politicians, economists, and historians alike frequently label as "myth" an opinion they oppose, as if this label were sufficient of itself to dismiss that opinion without further ado. Among many religionists the term "myth" has been used to characterize the beliefs of "primitive" peoples as inferior to their own and as "pagan" superstitions. This situation may be the result of the way the word "myth" entered our language and the history of its usage in Western tradition.

Originally the Greek term *mythos* referred to a tale or something spoken aloud; encompassed within its semantic range were phenomena as diverse as a public speech, a conversation, a proverb, a narrative, and even the plot of a story or play. Gradually, however, *mythos* became more restricted in meaning. From the time of the poet Pindar in the fifth century B.C.E. *mythos* acquired a connotation of fiction. The Sophists introduced a distinction between *mythos* and *logos*; the latter was identified with what was factual and the former with what was unhistorical. Similarly, Plato used *mythos* to refer to early Greek legends in which human and divine activity are often intertwined, with the suggestion that at best one is dealing with poetic metaphor rather than historical reality. This trend to denigrate myth climaxed in the third century B.C.E. with Euhemeros of Messene. In the course of his travels Euhemeros claimed to have discovered an ancient temple of Zeus in the Indian Sea where Zeus and other Greek gods were depicted as mere mortals, heroes to be sure, but mortals nonetheless. From this Euhemeros rationalized that deities originated in an exaggerated hero worship of famous kings and conquerors, resulting in their eventual deification. (Today we use "euhemerism" as a technical term referring to the attempt to discover human precursors for the various deities.) Accordingly, with the passage of time *mythos* came to mean primarily an imaginative or fictitious story, much like Latin *fabula*, "fable," a "fabulous (tale)."

Perhaps even more influential than the Greeks in establishing a pejorative view of myth was the attitude of New Testament writers. These writers sought to dismiss pagan and Jewish opponents by labeling their beliefs as myths, that is, as "cleverly concocted" fraud (2 Peter 1:16) and the antithesis of authentic Christian doctrine (1 Tim. 1:4; 2 Tim. 4:4; Titus 1:14). It is not surprising, therefore, that Christians were admonished to "have nothing to do with profane myths and old wives' tales" (1 Tim. 4:7). Later Christian apologists even employed euhemeristic arguments to show the human—and therefore inauthentic—origins of pagan deities. With some inconsistency of logic, they also argued that Jesus' nonlegendary and nonmythic, historical being confirmed his divinity. The outcome of all this was that as Christianity prevailed in the West, so did this identification of myth with pagan superstition and falsehood. This pejorative understanding of myth has remained characteristic of popular usage right down to our own day.

In view of such heavy negative connotations attached to the word, one may well question the wisdom of trying to rehabilitate "myth" as a positive term to describe one of the very common and important activities in biblical tradition. Nonetheless, that is exactly the goal of this book. In the chapters that follow I demonstrate that the presence of myth is a common phenomenon within the Bible. More specifically I show how biblical authors used mythopoeic or mythmaking speculation to do some of their most profound theologizing about their God and their relationship to that God.

Because of the possibility of being misunderstood, I would have liked to avoid using the term "myth" to characterize the phenomenon that is the topic of this volume. However, so far as I know, no other word is available in any modern language for use as an adequate substitute. That is because the term "myth" as used in this book is the invention of modern scholarship, which has been forged through some five centuries of laborious investigation into human religiosity and intensive searching of the human psyche. Although rooted in ancient Greek conceptions, myth has acquired a modern technical meaning that bears only slight resemblance to the original meaning. In this regard the situation is similar to "physics" or "politics"; although the Greek origin of these sciences is obvious, the modern conception of them is vastly different from their ancient counterparts. But unlike physics and politics, myth is not well understood in its modern technical meaning and therefore must be defined. While many agree on the existence and the importance of myth, there is considerable variation about both its definition and function among several competing schools of thought. In part this is the result of the history of intellectual thought in the West.

The Renaissance awakened a renewed interest in classical antiquity, including Greek and Roman mythology. But the modern study of myth began in earnest with the Enlightenment during the eighteenth and nineteenth centuries, when Europeans were first encountering new and exotic cultures of strange lands. From a comparative study of the religions of such far-flung lands as Persia, India, China, Africa, and the New World, many Enlightenment philosophers posited an evolutionary development of religion from primitive superstition to "revealed" religion to rational thought. Naturally their own "critical" philosophy, in which human reason is considered to be the supreme guide and arbitrator for all human activity, stood at the apex of this progressive evolution. The Rationalists held that religion and myth developed as the awed but mistaken response of ignorant savages to natural phenomena that were beyond their comprehension and control. Even Christian churchmen who had little sympathy with critical Enlightenment philosophy were persuaded that Christianity as revealed religion was far advanced beyond the level of myth, which they likewise identified with primitive superstition.

This view that myth is simply *precritical* thought continued into the twentieth century, aided in no small part by the popularity of evolutionary Darwinism[4] as the model for explaining the development of not only animal species but also humankind itself. For example, practitioners of the newly emerging science of anthropology claimed that myth and science developed out of the same basic human impulse to understand the causes of the natural world, with myth being merely a more primitive stage of understanding than science.[5] In the same vein, the great mythologist Sir James Frazer considered myth a kind of primitive science based on ignorance and misapprehension.[6]

Biblicists of that period shared this view that "myth is primitive science." One of the most influential of these was the French anthropologist Lucien Lévy-Bruhl. Lévy-Bruhl posited that a mythopoeic (or mythmaking) mind is characteristic of primitive peoples. Radically different from logical and rational thought, mythopoeic thought is expressive, poetic, and mystical. Rather than seeking to explain phenomena it encounters, the mythopoeic mind seeks active participation with phenomena.[7] Although Lévy-Bruhl later abandoned this theory himself, it was picked up and popularized by others.[8] As a result, mythopoeic thought was commonly assumed to be characteristic of "primitive" societies whose abilities to think had not progressed beyond a certain "prelogical" stage; supposedly the mythopoeic mind was incapable of rational or empirical thought. Fortunately, except in uninformed circles, this line of thought is now recognized for what it was, the product of a biased "first-world" mentality that regarded the rest of humanity as inferior in culture to itself.[9]

Meanwhile a more positive understanding of myth had been inaugurated in the early eighteenth century by the Italian philosopher Giambattista Vico. With great insight Vico posited that myth came from within man's own deepest inner nature: using the human faculty of imagination rather than reason the first men gave true, even if nonrational and prescientific, answers to the original human dilemmas. (In contemporary psychological jargon, one might say that Vico was making the case that our earliest forebears tended to use the right brain rather than the left brain in approaching the mysteries of life.)

Vico's influence upon the Romantics of the following century was considerable. For the Romantics myth is an authentic expression of the spiritual dimension of humankind. Myth, they affirmed, is an autonomous configuration of the human spirit, with its own mode of reality and a content that cannot be translated into rational terms without an irretrievable loss of inner force. In other words, myth is myth. Like music and art, myth must be understood in its own terms; it cannot be reduced to history or metaphor or any other substitute.[10]

Our own century has continued the search for the origin of myth within the human person. The psychological approach claims that myth is generated by the human unconscious to meet deep-seated psychological needs. According to Sigmund Freud, myths function much like dreams, to which they are related. Both proceed out of the human unconscious. The human unconscious is the repository for various instinctive drives; sexuality and power are but two of the more prominent. These drives demand expression but often are in conflict with the standards a society imposes for right order and acceptable behavior. Thus to give open expression to these drives would result in societal chaos (e.g., incest, the drive for absolute power, hostility toward one's kin). Through dreams a person can allow the unconscious to express itself in a form that society can tolerate. Myths are the collective dream of a people: "distorted vestiges of the wish-phantasies of whole nations—the age-long dreams of young humanity."[11] But just as dreams are a veiling or transformation of that which the dreamer's unconscious would find unacceptable, so too myths are a culturally infantile manifestation of the group unconscious. For Freud myth belongs to an early stage of human development that deserves to be transcended. Just as dreams represent childhood traumas that need to be worked through in order to arrive at a psychologically mature personhood, so the religion and myths of a nation must give way to science. At this point Freud's psychological theory of myth has joined hands with the "myth is primitive religion" school of thought, and suffers from the same deficiencies.

Carl Jung, however, developed the psychological theory of myth along a different—and more positive—vein. Like Freud, Jung found great similarities between dreams and myth; he also agreed that they both proceed from the unconscious. However, the human unconscious is not so much an infantile, aggressive drive seeking outlet as it is a spiritual desire for meaning. Dreams and myths reveal the very structure of the human psyche or soul. A central issue for Jung was how to explain the fact that certain symbols or images seem to be universally shared among all peoples. His answer was that such recurrent symbols and images are collective representations; they come from a universal substratum of humankind that Jung labeled the "collective unconscious." Hence, myths and symbols arise autochthonously, that is, independently, and yet are identical, in even the remotest parts of the world, because they are fashioned out of the same universal substrate of humankind. The primary symbols that thus arise are limited in number (e.g., The Mother, The Divine Child, The Trickster, The Spirit), and are essentially transpersonal and transhistorical. Hence Jung's name for them: "archetypes." Myth thus reveals the very structure of the soul and can provide a mechanism for reconnecting with the transpersonal. Religious myths provide valuable links to the eternal, such as cannot be had through logic or reason. Myth is therefore not to be abandoned lightly in favor of rationality.

Structuralism likewise seeks to find the origins of myth within the way the human mind works.[12] In contrast to those who look for the meaning of myth(s) in the storyline or in deciphering the meaning of individual components, structuralists posit that the meaning of myth is to be found in the underlying structure that unifies a myth. They cite the analogy of language: although individual phonemes produce sounds associated with language, true language is present only when the intellect comprehends meaning in the system of relationships underlying the individual sounds. Just so, myth is a relational phenomenon. The elements of myth (barren land, a garden, a snake, a piece of fruit, nakedness, the ocean, a body of water to be crossed, and so forth) are meaningless in themselves; they acquire meaning only when their relationship with other elements within a given social context is understood. In this view myth is a sophisticated and abstract mode of thought—exactly opposite the view of those who posited myth as a "primitive" mode of thought.

Other approaches to myth emphasize their social function within a given society.[13] Traditional stories serve the purpose of creating and cementing social bonds. These stories define the origins of the group and set forth acceptable behaviors (filial piety, honesty, patriotism, and the like), and at the same time proscribe unacceptable behaviors (murder, incest, cheating, etc.). In this way disparate people are united into a single group and their identity defined in relationship to other groups. This serves the purpose not only of promoting the welfare of the group by validating its institutions, but also of defending the group against external threat (foreign gods and cultures, the enemy).

The phenomenological approach to the history of religions seeks to provide an objective study of the actual religious experiences of humankind.[14] Phenomenologists have tended to link myth and ritual as complementary aspects of religious experience. Myths are sacred stories that are set in time outside of "profane" or secular time. The function of myth is to reveal the exemplary models for all human rites and significant human activities (diet, marriage, work, education, art, wisdom, and the like). Despite the multiplicity of forms that religious phenomena take in various cultures, they are all hierophanies or manifestations of the same basic religious impulse in humankind.

Even from such a brief survey of the history of myth scholarship it is obvious that no one theory about myth will ever be completely satisfactory.[15] The phenomenon of myth is multifaceted and can be approached from many angles: sociological, psychological, phenomenological, linguistic, literary, and so forth. The theses developed in this book do not depend upon any one definition of myth. Rather, the validity of myth as integral to the human experience is assumed, without attempting to specify precisely its origin(s) or to give a comprehensive account of its function(s) in society. Accordingly, myth is here defined very broadly as *a narrative (story) concerning fundamental symbols that are constitutive of or paradigmatic for human existence.*[16]

Myth is a universal human phenomenon. It attempts to express ultimate reality through symbol. Myth points to a reality beyond itself that cannot be directly symbolized, as it transcends both the capacity of discursive reasoning and expression in ordinary human language. Paul Ricoeur refers to this as a "surplus of meaning." Every society, ancient and modern, has its myths and is given to mythmaking.

In nonliterate or archaic societies participation in myth may be more immediate and less critical than in modern Western (post-Enlightenment) societies. Clearly in modern societies participation and perception normally are mediate and critical, resulting in what is sometimes referred to as "broken myth." That is, old myths are appropriated in new, "reduced" forms. In the new appropriation the original values are translated as symbols, in themselves not worthy of belief, but with sign value in that they point to a more ultimate reality that can be believed. A biblical analogue of this may be found in the practice of offering animal and cereal sacrifices to the deity. As is widely attested in the ancient Near East, this ritual originated in the belief that the gods required regular sacrifices as their food.[17] Even though the biblical tradition makes it quite clear that Yahweh did not really "eat" their offerings[18] and even contains violent prophetic attacks on sacrifice,[19] the ancient Israelites nonetheless continued throughout their history to practice this ritual as the central feature of their cult. The Israelites recognized that sacrifice "is a prayer which is acted, a symbolic action which expresses both the interior feelings of the person offering it, and God's response to this prayer."[20] I doubt that any society in the historical period—and this includes not only the ancient Israelites but also the ancient Babylonians, Canaanites, Egyptians, and Greeks—has been so unsophisticated that it accepted its myths in an unreflected and preconscious naïveté.

Myths die or are abandoned when they cease to function in

the community as a carrier of the community's values or when they cease to signify for a person the inner and outer realities that he or she discovers in the course of life. But as nonfunctional myths die, others arise to fill the vacuum, myths that provide new and better coherence of meaning. The biblical tradition witnesses to continual adaptation of myth over the course of more than a millennium to meet the changing needs of a dynamic faith community.

One of the ways in which the biblical community met the challenge of giving new expression to its faith was through what in this book will be called "mythopoeic speculation." As this expression is subject to misunderstanding, I should define precisely what I mean by the term. As used here the term "mythopoeic speculation" has little in common with the theory of the mythopoeic mind proposed by Lucien Lévy-Bruhl, discussed earlier. At least in the popular version of that theory, mythopoeic thought was assumed to be characteristic of "primitive" societies whose abilities to think have not progressed beyond a certain "prelogical" stage; supposedly the mythopoeic mind was (is) incapable of rational or empirical thought. Patently this theory of the mythopoeic mind should be rejected outright as a post-Enlightenment, "first-world" bias that proceeds from ignorance of the abilities of persons in premodern and simple societies to think abstractly or to reason logically.

"Mythopoeism" (from a combination of two Greek words, *mythos* and *poein*) literally means "myth-making." I use the term "mythopoeic" to refer to that process by which new myths are created or old myths are extended to include new dimensions. Mythopoeic is to be carefully distinguished from "mythopoetic," another term sometimes used to describe the metaphoric or symbolic use of mythic images in artistic literary compositions. In mythopoetic usage the mythic elements have lost their value as operative myths and survive only as literary symbols or images, that is, as mere vestiges of their original mythic function. Some would claim that "mythopoetic" is the correct term when describing mythic elements in the Bible, often because they exclude a priori the possibility of authentic myth within the Word of God. While some biblical passages may indeed be only mythopoetic, others are clearly mythopoeic.

I add the word "speculation" to mythopoeic because I want to emphasize that this new mythmaking process is a *conscious*, *reflected* application of older myths and mythic elements to new situations. I stress the conscious, reflective aspect because in some circles it has been fashionable to claim that authentic myth operates on a preconscious level; that is, myths are immediate or unreflective statements about reality in the minds of those persons for whom the myth is operative. Almost by definition, then, any literary composition would be excluded from the category of authentic myth. Every author—ancient or modern—deliberates over the material and makes conscious choices about what is to be included or excluded, and about how a statement is to be phrased so as to accomplish the author's purposes. If myth is defined as preconscious and unreflected thought, then obviously there is no authentic myth in the Bible, any more than in modern Western society. But this can hardly be an adequate definition of myth.

In so far as one admits the presence of myth in ancient Babylonian and Canaanite literature, then one must also admit the presence of myth in the Bible. Biblical myth, like all ancient myth, is preserved for us only in literary form. Any nonliterary, popular versions of such myths are no longer available to us. Likewise, much of the original socioeconomic and cultural context of these myths is also lost to us. Despite significant gains by historical critical scholarship, our ability to reconstruct the original ancient Near Eastern setting of the Bible is—and likely always will be—severely limited. Without wishing to deny the validity of other approaches to myth, the approach taken in this book will, perforce, stress the imaginative or literary aspects of myth. The primary witness for myth in the Bible is the biblical text itself.

The widespread assumption that myth is usually oral—and its corollary, that written myth is derivative and secondary—cannot be sustained either for the biblical tradition (see especially chapters 2 and 3) or for the classical Mesopotamian myths (see chapter 1). It likely was not the case for Canaan and Egypt either. In the final analysis, ancient Near Eastern myths seem to have been first and foremost literary phenomena, consciously crafted, which only after publication were vulgarized or popularized to such an extent that they eventually became their community's "national myth."

This book, then, is a series of case studies of mythmaking in ancient Israel, or to be more exact, in the biblical tradition. Any number of texts could have been chosen for study, since the mythopoeism is actually quite common throughout the Bible. The examples studied here, with one exception, all are adaptations of the common Semitic Combat Myth, whether in its Babylonian version (*Enuma elish*) or in its Canaanite version (the Baal cycle). The Priestly Writer (chapter 2) drew most heavily upon the Babylonian version, though other biblical writers seem to have been more dependent upon the Canaanite version. Such dependency was not always direct or immediate, of course, as there was a great deal of intertextual borrowing and mutual influence at work within the biblical tradition itself. The exception has to do with the Yahwist's primeval story, beginning in Genesis 2 and continuing intermittently through Genesis 8. Because the Priestly Writer incorporated this Yahwistic primeval narrative into his own primeval story (Genesis 1–9), the Yahwist's case could hardly be omitted from consideration. Now the Yahwist's primeval narrative is itself a marvelous example of mythmaking based upon prior Mesopotamian myths, notably *Atrahasis* and *Gilgamesh*. Interestingly, the reappropriation of mythic traditions and intertextual borrowing posited for biblical writers was already present within ancient Babylonia, and illustrates that biblical writers must be understood within the larger ancient Near Eastern literary and theological tradition. Accordingly, it is fitting that we begin this study of biblical mythopoeism with an examination of mythopoeic speculation in Babylon.

Chapter 1

◆

MYTHOPOEIC SPECULATION
IN BABYLON

◆

The process of mythopoeic speculation by which ancient Israel gave enduring and universal significance to her "stories" was substantially the same process by which other ancient Near Eastern societies gave a similar meaning to their own national stories. Babylon lacked a canonical story of its national origins and purpose comparable to that of Israel in the Pentateuch. Nevertheless, a case can be made that Mesopotamia did have a kind of literary canon, which was propagated through the scribal schools and which remained fairly constant through almost two millennia, until cuneiform writing ceased to be actively used in the Hellenistic period.[1] Sumerian literature received its "canonical" shape during the Neo-Sumerian period (2200–1900 B.C.E.) and served as the basis of the curriculum for the training of scribes in influential schools at Nippur and elsewhere. During the Old Babylonian period (1900–1600 B.C.E.) Akkadian replaced Sumerian as the dominant language in Mesopotamia. This linguistic development provided the impetus for composing major new literary works in Akkadian, perhaps partially to serve the new curriculum requirements in the schools. In any case, during the course of another millennium and a half aspiring scribes honed their scholarly skills by reading, copying, and imitating Sumerian and especially Akkadian "classics." It was likely through this channel that *Gilgamesh*, *Atrahasis*, and later *Enuma elish*—three of the major myths of Babylonia—acquired a kind of canonical function within Mesopotamia, albeit in different degrees in different periods of Babylonian history.

As in Israel, so also in Babylonia these "national myths" seem to have originated with certain individual writers, literary geniuses who created new epic stories out of older traditions. In both cases, in Israel and in Babylon, these new compositions were so resonant with the community's traditions and aspirations that they in turn became the quintessential expression of their respective community's traditional story, which is to say, they became authentic myth(s) for that community. And like all myths, to survive these myths had to undergo substantial modifications over time in order to continue to mirror that community's evolving self-identity.

Of course, a similar situation prevailed among other ancient Near Eastern neighbors of Israel. I have chosen Babylon as a control for my thesis about mythopoeic speculation in the Bible for good reason. For each of its three major myths there is an abundance of texts from different periods so that one can readily reconstruct the history of development for each myth. Furthermore, the history of the modern critical study of these Babylonian epics parallels biblical scholarship in important respects and thus offers a means of evaluating our hypotheses about developments in the Bible.[2]

Unlike the situation in biblical studies, where there is no autograph copy of any biblical book, much less any of the hypothetical sources for given books of the Bible, Mesopotamian literature is well attested in multiple ancient cuneiform copies of varying ages. Because the common writing materials used in Mesopotamia were durable clay tablets, actual documents from various historical periods have survived and are available for our perusal. The necessity of resorting to speculation about the content or shape of the composition at its various stages of development, or even about the sources used by the authors, is thereby considerably reduced.

With the rediscovery of cuneiform literature in the nineteenth century, and particularly with George Smith's startling announcement in 1872 of a Mesopotamian flood story similar to that in the book of Genesis, the attention of biblical scholars quickly turned to the decipherment and study of these new documents. By a quirk of fate, the first extensive finds had come principally from the seventh-century B.C.E. Assyrian king Ashurbanipal's library in Nineveh. Prominent among these cuneiform tablets were the literary texts of *Gilgamesh* and *Enuma elish*.[3] With benefit of hindsight and many additional discoveries, we now know those late Assyrian copies from Nineveh represented only the most recent recensions of these epics and that behind them lay a long history of growth and development. But very early on those first Assyriologists, trained as many of them were in the critical methodology of biblical scholarship, quickly realized that these literary compositions must be an end product of a long and complex history of development, analogous to the situation that had been postulated for the Pentateuch. Thus already in 1898 Morris Jastrow, Jr., published an analysis of the *Gilgamesh Epic* in which he posited that five originally distinct episodes, including the flood narrative, had been secondarily brought together around the popular figure of Gilgamesh. While Jastrow may have been off in the details of his hypothesis, subsequent discoveries of documents containing earlier forms of the Gilgamesh tradition have vindicated his approach. The recovered documents span more than two millennia and cover the main historical periods in Mesopotamia from ca. 2700 to 500 B.C.E. These allow us to reconstruct in broad outline the developmental histories of the major myths and literary texts of Mesopotamia. This felicitous situation provides a control by which to test our theory of mythopoeic speculation in the Bible.

GILGAMESH

Gilgamesh apparently was a historical person, the king of the city-state of Uruk (biblical Erech) sometime between 2700 and 2500 B.C.E. There is little historical kernel, however, to the epic by that name. Moreover, it is not evident just why Gilgamesh became a hero of such legendary stature in later periods. Already by the Fara period (c. 2500 B.C.E.) Gilgamesh was regarded as a god and offerings were made to him, according to certain nonliterary texts. In the Sumerian King List "the god Gilgamesh" is named among the postdiluvian kings as one who ruled over Uruk. Some traditions even identified Gilgamesh with one of the traditional Mesopotamian gods: with Dumuzi

(Tammuz), the annually dying and rising god; with Ningishzida, a tree god; or with Nergal, the supreme god of the underworld. Because of his association with the underworld, figurines of Gilgamesh were invoked at burial rites and used in the cult of the spirits of the dead and with incantations to ward off underworld demons.[4]

The origins of the literary traditions about Gilgamesh are unknown. Five, perhaps six, tales about Gilgamesh written in Sumerian were composed perhaps as early as the Third Dynasty of Ur (twenty-first century B.C.E.), though all known copies date only to the Old Babylonian period (1900–1600 B.C.E.). W. L. Moran summarizes these as follows:[5]

> (1) *Gilgamesh and Huwawa* [also known as *Gilgamesh and the Land of the Living*][6] (c. 190–240 lines, three versions) tells how Gilgamesh, disturbed at the sight of dead bodies and determined to achieve the immortality of fame, sets out, together with his servant Enkidu and other retainers, to fight the monster Huwawa. The versions, reflecting oral variants, differ on how Huwawa was tricked and killed and what followed. (2) *Gilgamesh and the Bull of Heaven* (very poorly preserved) tells how the goddess Inanna, for reasons that are unclear, sent the Bull against Gilgamesh and Enkidu, who then probably slew it. (3) In *Gilgamesh, Enkidu, and the Netherworld* (c. 330 lines) Inanna gives Gilgamesh as a reward for certain services two objects of still-uncertain nature. These somehow become instruments for the oppression of Uruk and then fall into the underworld. Enkidu goes to fetch them back, but since he ignores Gilgamesh's warnings (not to call attention to himself or to distinguish himself as an alien), he must remain there. Eventually he appears before his master and answers his questions about the fate of various categories of underworld inhabitants. (4) The *Death of Gilgamesh* (very poorly preserved, c. 450 lines) seems to be concerned, in part at least, with Gilgamesh's resentment that he must die. (5) There is another fragment of what appears to belong to a distinct composition. (6) *Gilgamesh and Agga* (115 lines) tells of the conflict with the ruler of Kish.

In addition there is a Sumerian version of *The Deluge*,[7] but it seems to have had no connection with the Gilgamesh tradition. In their Sumerian form these texts were independent episodes that had no literary connection one with another.

The epic tradition of *Gilgamesh* began only later. The so-called standard version of the epic with which we are all most familiar is a late Assyrian recension (seventh century B.C.E.).[8] However, to judge from earlier fragmentary tablets, the original epic was composed in Akkadian during the Old Babylonian period and differed significantly from both the earlier Sumerian tales and from the later Assyrian recension. Fortunately, I can be brief regarding the long and complex history of development by which the *Gilgamesh* epic reached its ultimate (Assyrian) form, since Jeffrey H. Tigay's excellent monograph on *Gilgamesh* examines this issue in detail.[9]

During the Old Babylonian period these Sumerian tales were brought together into a single, integrated Akkadian composition with episodes arranged in a meaningful sequence and the whole held together by recurrent themes, quite unlike the independent and unconnected Sumerian tales. "The plan of the integrated epic thus testifies to the working of a single artistic mind," according to Tigay, "and the work of this person is so creative that he deserves to be considered an author, rather than an editor or compiler."[10] This Old Babylonian author judiciously used his Sumerian sources to create an original and profound work about human mortality and man's search to escape it.

The deliberateness with which this Old Babylonian author worked is extremely enlightening. Combining the plots and themes of three or four of the Sumerian tales (*Gilgamesh and the Land of the Living*; *Gilgamesh, Enkidu, and the Netherworld*; *The Death of Gilgamesh*; and possibly *Gilgamesh and the Bull of Heaven*), he fashioned a grand new epic of at least a thousand lines, perhaps much more. Taking a theme that had been only adumbrated in the Sumerian tales, namely Gilgamesh's concern with death and his futile desire to overcome it, the Old Babylonian author made it the central focus of the new story.

In a radical departure from the Sumerian tradition, the author has transformed Enkidu from Gilgamesh's physically undistinguished servant into a hero in his own right, and Gilgamesh's friend, and perhaps lover. In order to introduce Enkidu, the author composed accounts of Gilgamesh's early oppression of Uruk as an excuse for the gods to create Enkidu, a shaggy primeval human (*lullû*) of exceptional strength who at first had more in common with the beasts of the steppe than with humankind. Humanized through his love of Shamhat, a harlot and his first teacher, Enkidu eventually made his way to Uruk, where the two mighty heroes clash in a battle in which Enkidu prevails over Gilgamesh. But Enkidu magnanimously extends his hand to Gilgamesh and soon the two become inseparable friends. Anxious for adventure, the two go about performing Herculean exploits. Relying heavily upon the Sumerian tale *Gilgamesh and the Land of the Living*, the author describes at great length how the duo journeyed to the Cedar Mountain and killed the terrible monster Huwawa. Among the changes, according to Tigay, were "a complete reshaping of Gilgamesh's plans for the expedition, a new understanding of the role of Shamash [the sun god and divine overseer of justice] and of the significance of Huwawa, and a new location for the Cedar Forest. Several of these changes reflected the new geographical orientation of Mesopotamian affairs in the Old Babylonian Period and the roles of Gilgamesh, Shamash, and Huwawa in Mesopotamian religion."[11]

At this point in the Assyrian version (Tablet VI) stand scenes drawn from another Sumerian tale, *Gilgamesh and the Bull of Heaven*; it is unclear, however, whether these are the work of the Old Babylonian author or of a later hand. Having arrived back in his own city of Uruk, Gilgamesh washes and dresses in fresh clothes. Thus arrayed in his royal splendor, this semidivine king of Uruk catches the eye of Ishtar, goddess of love and war and patron deity of Uruk. Ishtar finds Gilgamesh so attractive that she proposes marriage, which Gilgamesh spurns. The hostility between the goddess Ishtar and divine Gilgamesh is embellished from the Sumerian by adding themes drawn from the sacred marriage ritual[12] and by providing a new cause for the goddess's animosity, namely, Gilgamesh's spurning of the goddess's marriage proposal. The irate goddess prevails upon her father, Anu—the god of heaven, one of the four major deities of Mesopotamia and in some traditions even the highest ranking god—to let her have "the bull of heaven" to punish the disrespectful, proud human pair. Gilgamesh and Enkidu, however, kill the bull and taunt Ishtar with their deed. Whether this episode was the work of the Old Babylonian author or a later addition, it emphasized the pinnacle to which Gilgamesh had risen—and from which he must also descend.

Events now begin to catch up with Gilgamesh and Enkidu. The divine sovereign Enlil, who had appointed Huwawa to guard the Cedar Forest, demands the death of the two heroes. Shamash, in his role as the divine overseer of justice, intervened to allow only the death of Enkidu, the one who actually cut off the ogre's head.

The Old Babylonian author made Enkidu's death the pivotal event of his story. To increase its poignancy the author wrenched the themes of Enkidu's death and Gilgamesh's grief from their original setting in the Sumerian *Gilgamesh, Enkidu, and the Netherworld* and placed them after the friends' victory over Huwawa (and possibly the "bull of heaven"). Moreover, Enkidu's acceptance of death was made to presage Gilgamesh's own fate. Prior to this point Gilgamesh, himself two-thirds god and only one-third human, was oblivious of human mortality. But now, confronted with the reality of the human condition, he begins a frantic search for the transcendence of immortality, which the gods have reserved for themselves. Gilgamesh embarks on a journey beyond the fringes of the human world to seek out Utnapishtim, the Babylonian flood hero whom the gods blessed with immortality following the deluge. This was of course another innovation, as the Sumerian deluge story had nothing to do with Gilgamesh. During the course of this journey first a barmaid, next Utnapishtim's boatman, and finally Utnapishtim himself all try to counsel Gilgamesh on the futility of his quest. But Gilgamesh refuses their advice. At last Utnapishtim suggests that if Gilgamesh can conquer sleep, the younger brother of death, there may yet be hope for him.[13] The exhausted Gilgamesh, however, promptly nods off and sleeps for six days and seven nights. Thus defeated, Gilgamesh resigned himself to his mortal fate and returned to Uruk to live out his remaining days, fully human.

Tigay suggests that the author's message to his audience is

expressed in the advice offered Gilgamesh by the barmaid when she tried to dissuade him from pursuing his futile search for immortality.

> The life you pursue you shall not find.
> When the gods created mankind,
> Death for mankind they set aside,
> Life in their own hands retaining.
> As for you, Gilgamesh, let your belly be full,
> Make merry day and night.
> Day and night dance and play!
> Of each day make a feast of rejoicing.
> Let your garments be sparkling fresh,
> Your head be washed; bathe in water.
> Pay heed to a little one that holds on to your hand.
> Let a spouse delight in your bosom,
> For this is the task of [woman].

In sum, the barmaid's advice to Gilgamesh is, Embrace reality. Her advice is a typical wisdom topos frequent in ancient Near Eastern literature. Presumably this conventional philosophy of life is intended for the epic's audience as well.[14]

The consummate skill of the Old Babylonian author is much in evidence throughout: in his composition of an original hymnic introduction to the epic in the style of Sumerian hymns about kings, through his unifying use of recurrent thematic and verbal motifs, and in his use of conventional formulas and wisdom sayings.[15] Moreover, as W. Moran observes, the Old Babylonian author is to be credited with structuring the narrative around three periods of six or seven days and seven nights, each associated with a profound transformation of character and corresponding "rites of passage." In the *first period* Enkidu and the harlot Shamhat make love, with the result that Enkidu becomes human. The rites of passage here require Enkidu to eat and drink in a human fashion, to wash and anoint himself, and finally to put on clothes. During a *second period* Gilgamesh mourns over the body of Enkidu, resulting in Gilgamesh becoming the anti-hero, anti-human, would-be god. This is symbolized by Gilgamesh going about mourning and unwashed, clothed in animal skins, and dwelling outside the human community. In the *third period* a resolution is reached: Gilgamesh sleeps before the flood hero Utnapishtim, eventuating in Gilgamesh resigned and accepting his humanity. Accordingly, Gilgamesh once more washes and dons his human clothing, as he prepares to rejoin the human community.[16]

The Gilgamesh epic continued to develop after the Old Babylonian period, as later copies (Babylonian, Hittite, Hurrian, Syrian [Emar], and a fragment from Canaanite Megiddo) attest. By the end of the Middle Babylonian period (c. 1000 B.C.E.) the epic had attained a form that became standard thereafter, a kind of *textus receptus*, to use a biblical analogue. The late (Assyrian) editors did not feel free to introduce substantive changes. The three major additions found in the late, standard version are the prologue, the flood story, and Tablet XII. The last is a mechanical translation of the last half of the Sumerian tale *Gilgamesh, Enkidu, and the Netherworld*, and probably was considered an appendix for the use of ritual priests, rather than an integral part of the work. If so, it was not intended to alter significantly the meaning of the epic. It is impossible to treat these changes in detail. But I cannot pass over the addition of the flood story to *Gilgamesh* without at least a brief comment.

The flood story was popular long before the Old Babylonian period, as is evident from not only the Sumerian version of *The Deluge* but also the many references to it in various texts. The classical Akkadian version, *Atrahasis*, was even composed during the Old Babylonian period. However, the Old Babylonian author of *Gilgamesh* apparently did not choose to incorporate the story into his epic. In that version it appears that when Gilgamesh sought out the survivor of the flood for the secret of immortality, Utnapishtim advised Gilgamesh to first conquer Sleep, the younger brother of Death. Gilgamesh of course failed even this easier task and was forced to leave the isle of immortality, his mission failed. On his return to the land of mortals Gilgamesh carelessly let even his last hope for immortality, the plant of life, slip out of his grasp, to the benefit of the serpent.[17] But in a major departure from the Old Babylonian story, in the late Assyrian version of the epic Utnapishtim actually recounts the flood story itself to Gilgamesh. This flood story is clearly retold from *Atrahasis*, merely by changing the third-person account into the first person to better fit the narrative structure of the Gilgamesh epic.

Just why this flood story was added to the Old Babylonian version of *Gilgamesh* remains a matter of speculation. Perhaps the mere presence of Utnapishtim was enough to attract the complete flood story to it. Tigay suggests that a later editor wished to add a digression to the story so as to heighten suspense and also to better prepare the audience for Utnapishtim's disappointing answer and the subdued conclusion to the epic.[18]

I suggest, however, that the addition of the flood story is linked with the addition of the prologue, which also links Gilgamesh with the flood:

> [Him who] saw everything, let me [make kno]wn to the land,
> [Who all thing]s experienced, [let me tea]ch i[t] ful[ly].
> [He searche]d (?) the l[ands(?)] entirely,
> [Was granted al]l (?) wisdom, ex[perienced(?)] all things.
> [The hi]dden he saw, the undisclosed he discov[ered].
> He brought back information from before the flood,
> Achieved a long [j]ourney, exhausted, but at peace.
> All his toil he [engra]ved on a (stone) stela / an
>   inscription.[19]

The effect of the prologue is to elevate Gilgamesh to the ranks of the antediluvian sages from whom all current human knowledge and human institutions were said to come.

According to Mesopotamian tradition there were (normally) seven such semidivine sages, known as *apkallu*, who "administer the 'patterns' (*uṣurātu*) of heaven and earth."[20] The "patterns" are somewhat elusive of definition, but this word refers to the sum total of arts and sciences and the institutions by which civilized people live. (As we shall see, the term *uṣurātu* also occurs in *Atrahasis*, where an interpretation as the "laws" or "regulations" by which humans should live seems more appropriate; these "regulations" are the prescribed social patterns laid down at creation, e.g., birth and marriage rites.)[21] The *apkallu* taught these to humankind before the flood; supposedly there has been no substantial new knowledge added since.

The tradition is not in agreement as to how this knowledge was transmitted from the antediluvian to the postdiluvian generations. In some texts the *apkallu* are said to continue on earth for a short time after the flood. According to Berossus, a third-century B.C.E. priest of Babylon, before the flood a sage by the name of Oannes buried all literature for safekeeping in the city of Sippar, from where it was later recovered and disseminated. Most people, however, probably assumed that such knowledge survived via the flood hero. In the standard Babylonian version, the flood hero is patently a sage, as is evident from his name Atrahasis, "Exceedingly Wise," and from the fact that he is portrayed as a devotee of Ea (also known as Enki), the god of wisdom. By recalling that Gilgamesh had successfully searched out and learned from the flood hero all antediluvian wisdom, the late editor of the epic implies that Gilgamesh was the sage through whom the antediluvian knowledge was transmitted to postdiluvian generations.

This line of reasoning is supported by similarities between Gilgamesh and Adapa. Adapa, identified as a "son of Ea," was the most celebrated of the *apkallu*. Adapa was one of those semidivine primeval wisdom heroes whose career spanned the flood. Like Gilgamesh, Adapa too squandered an opportunity for immortality.

Despite the myth surviving in four different accounts, our knowledge of the myth of Adapa remains incomplete, especially the ending, due to the fragmentary condition of the cuneiform tablets. The myth seems to be a variant account of primeval human origins.[22] In other words, Adapa appears to be another "Adam," a progenitor of the human species.[23] He was a faithful priest and servant of Ea, who ran Ea's house (sanctuary) in Eridu. Adapa was a special creation of Ea, apparently intended as a prototype of humankind, whom Ea endowed with special wisdom. Once while Adapa was out fishing, the South Wind suddenly descended upon the hitherto calm sea and submerged his boat. In retaliation Adapa uttered a powerful spell and broke the wing of the South Wind. Subsequently Adapa was ordered to appear before Anu, king of the heavens, to account for his infraction of the divine design. At this point the wisdom god Ea counseled "his son" Adapa to appear before Anu duly contrite, robed in mourning garb. Moreover, on no account should Adapa accept any food or drink offered him, as these would be the "bread of death" and the "water of death." He should, however, put on the garments offered him. Adapa did as Ea advised. Apparently moved by Adapa's piety, Anu received Adapa as guest instead of a culprit. He offered Adapa new garments and oil with which to annoint himself. Anu also extended the "bread of life" and the "water of life" reserved for the gods. Adapa accepted the garments and oil but refused to eat or drink. In response to Anu's questioning, Adapa replied that he was only faithfully carrying out his patron god's instructions. Anu laughed at Adapa's choice, apparently because the latter had just forfeited the chance at immortality—both for himself and for humankind. In the end Adapa was returned to earth to his mortal task of serving his deity. The remainder of the myth is lost to us—and with it some of the keys to unlocking the meaning of this myth.

At this point, however, our interest is in the relationship of Gilgamesh to Adapa. Adapa's refusal of "the bread of life" and "the water of life" paralleled Gilgamesh's letting "the plant of life" slip away. There is perhaps some intention to suggest a correspondence between the sage Adapa and Gilgamesh.

In any case, through the prologue the author of *Gilgamesh* clearly intended to supplement Gilgamesh's mythic status. By projecting Gilgamesh into the ranks of those who possessed wisdom from "before the flood"—that boundary between primordial time and our own time—the epic of *Gilgamesh* takes on an additional didactic aura of ultimate significance. It explores the fact—if not the why—of human mortality and its implications for how we mortals should live out our earthly existence. By adding his prologue, the later editor hoped to undergird the truth claim of the epic. He implies that the epic is based upon Gilgamesh's own wisdom (inscribed upon the stela mentioned in line 8). By projecting the origins of this wisdom back to divine revelation in primordial time, its mythic (that is, ultimate) values cannot lightly be circumvented. Such deliberate reworking of religious tradition is a clear example of what I am calling mythopoeic speculation.

ATRAHASIS

Atrahasis has been called "the Babylonian story of the flood."[24] But it is much more than that. It deals with the issues of theogony and cosmogony; that is, it makes mythic statements about the origins of the gods and of the cosmos and humankind in primordial time, but which patently are believed to be the cause or source for present reality. In this regard it would be more appropriate to call *Atrahasis* a "Babylonian Genesis," if one wishes to appeal to a biblical analogue.

The interpretation of *Atrahasis* is still a matter of debate, especially because the ending of the myth is only poorly preserved. This situation may be ameliorated in the near future, however. In 1986 Iraqi archaeologists excavating at the site of ancient Sippar discovered an intact library dating to approximately the sixth century B.C.E. Among the tablets is reported to be a complete version of *Atrahasis*.[25] It is to be hoped that this new text will be published quickly. Meanwhile, the main contours of the myth are clear enough from previously published tablets.[26] The story begins with the situation before the creation of humankind and therefore before the creation of "the world." In that primeval period apparently there existed only gods. But as the opening scene makes clear, there was something inherently wrong with this situation:

> When gods were human[27]
> Bore the labor, carried the corvee-basket,
> The corvee-basket of the gods was immense
> The work heavy, the distress severe.
> The seven great Anunnaki
> Were making the Igigi suffer the labor. (I.1–6)

Only the high gods (the Anunnaki) were able to enjoy the privilege of "rest." As there was no one else to do the work, the high gods required the lesser gods (the Igigi) to bear the burden of providing food and provisions for all the gods. This sets the stage for a theomachy in the next scene. The Igigi-gods banded together and revolted against this tyranny of the Anunnaki. They set fire to their tools and refused to continue slaving in such a "human" manner. In the ancient Near Eastern conception one of the prerogatives or symbols of deity was leisure or rest. Thus the revolt of the Igigi was in essence a demand for full divine status. The high gods recognized the validity of the lesser gods' complaint. Their solution proposed in the divine assembly is illuminating for what it reveals of the Mesopotamian conception of the divine vis-à-vis the human realm. Together Enki (another name for Ea, the god of wisdom) and Nintu, the mother-goddess, decided upon a plan. The ringleader of the rebel gods was killed and from his blood mixed with clay Enki and Nintu fashioned a kind of primitive humankind (*lullû*, or *lullû-awīlu*), seven males and seven females. The idea was that henceforth humankind would bear the burden of provisioning the gods so that the latter might rest. Henceforth, humans would till the fields, maintain the irrigation works, and in general, provide all the labor necessary for maintaining the gods in their proper rank. In short, humans were created to be servants of the gods.

Subsequent events, however, reveal that the gods were naive in thinking that their inchoate creation was the perfect solution. They had merely traded one problem for another. As humankind rapidly multiplied on earth, so did the "din" that they raised on earth. The "cries" of humankind kept Enlil, the king of the gods, from sleep. Consequently Enlil and the other gods successively sent plague, drought, and famine to diminish humankind. But thanks to Enki, the god of wisdom and the fashioner of humankind, the efforts of the other gods were unsuccessful. Enki revealed to Atrahasis a method to circumvent the designs of the other gods. This "exceedingly wise" person, it must be remembered, was the faithful devotee of the god of wisdom. Presumably, then, the intention was to portray Atrahasis as a pious king (like his Sumerian counterpart),[28] the very model of what humankind should be. Meanwhile, the cries of humankind continued to disturb the sleep of the king of the gods. Finally, as a last resort, the divine council decided to send a flood so as to annihilate humankind once and for all from the face of the earth. Once again the god of wisdom thwarted the plan of the other gods by revealing to Atrahasis the impending flood and giving advice on how to save himself, his household, and representative animals by building a boat. At the conclusion of the flood the flood hero descended from the boat and offered a sacrifice to the gods. The gods, deprived of food during the duration of the flood, seemingly recognized a kind of mutuality in the divine-human relationship and that humankind has a legitimate place in the order of things. Only Enlil remained unconvinced. However, Enki remonstrated with the divine king for punishing the innocent along with the guilty. The text is broken at this critical point, but apparently Enki successfully made his point because in the end Enlil "blessed" Atrahasis and his wife—at least according to the parallel text in *Gilgamesh*. In *Gilgamesh* this is understood to mean that Atrahasis and his wife were granted immortality. Whether *Atrahasis* also attributed immortality to the flood hero and his wife is unclear. But in any case, immortality was clearly not to be the lot of their descendants. Enlil ordered Enki and Nintu to make certain adjustments to their original creation, which it will be recalled had been termed as "primitive humankind" (*lullû-awīlu*). The text is extremely fragmentary at this point but enough remains to discern that Enki and Nintu imposed additional "human designs" or "human regulations" (*uṣurāt nišī*) that would cause these creatures henceforth to die. Apparently no limits had been placed upon the vitality of primeval humans when the original "human regulations" were defined for humankind at their creation.[29] But with these limits upon their lives, the descendants of the *lullû* were destined to become ordinary humans (*nišū*). The divine spirit in humankind was diminished, and with it the din that had denied the divine sovereign his sleep. Clearly, a satisfactory resolution to the "human problem" had been obtained, for *Atrahasis* concludes at this point.

The meaning of this myth is disputed, in part due to its fragmentary condition at key junctures. One interpretation suggests that the noise that deprived Enlil of his sleep was generated by an overpopulated earth, and even that Enlil's actions in attempting to destroy humankind were wholly capricious.[30] It is most unlikely, however, that the myth was a metaphor for an overpopulation problem in ancient Mesopotamia, at least not as normally understood.

The key to interpretation, it is true, resides in the meaning of the "cries" (*rigmu*) and the "din" (*ḫubūru*) that disturb the sleep of the king of the gods. Both terms describe not merely noise but rather the cries of rebellion.[31] These are the same terms used earlier to describe the revolt of the lesser gods against the high gods. It is hardly accidental that this revolt came in the dead of the night, when Enlil was sleeping. These primeval humans are portrayed as carrying on the spirit of the divine rebel(s). Created with the blood of the slain divine ringleader, humankind is explicitly said to possess the slain god's ghost (*eṭemmu*) and his capacity to scheme or plot (*ṭēmu*). Moreover, as suggested earlier, divine sleep or rest in the ancient Near East was a metaphor for divinity. Accordingly, to disturb the sleep of the chief deity was symbolic of challenging the sovereignty of that god.[32] It would appear that these primeval humans—for whom the demarcation between deity and humankind was blurred because of their origin—were refusing their subordinate role as servants of the gods and were guilty of aspiring to divinity.

The high gods had recognized the justice of the lesser gods' demands. But a similar demand from the *lullû*, even though they could claim part divinity, was clearly an overreaching of humankind's legitimate status. Accordingly, the gods' decision to destroy the *lullû* population successively by plague, drought, famine, and eventually by a catastrophic flood, should be understood as divine punishment for transgression of the proper boundaries between deity and humankind. Some such interpretation is required by Ea's reproach of Enlil, preserved in the parallel passage in *Gilgamesh* (XI.80): "On the sinner lay his sin, on the transgressor lay his transgression." Part god, part human, these prototype humans transgressed by aspiring to divine status and refusing to feed the gods. As long as the *lullû* were few they posed little threat to their divine masters. But as the *lullû* population increased, so did the potential for revolution (as Pharaoh recognized in an analogous situation, when a growing mass of Hebrew slaves threatened the security of their

Egyptian masters [Ex. 1:8–14]). The problem, then, was not that the earth was in danger of becoming overpopulated, but that the divine domain was in danger of being overthrown by an expanding rebellious *lullû* population. Apparently no provision had been made for a natural death for these semidivine creatures, so the gods resorted to killing off the rebels by improvised means: plague, drought, famine, and a deluge.

At the conclusion of the great deluge, Atrahasis, the pious flood hero, emerged from the boat to offer sacrifice; that is, he assumed the correct posture for humankind. By accepting the sacrifice, the gods acknowledged the righteousness of Atrahasis. Only the divine sovereign Enlil, whose authority had been most threatened by a rebellious humankind, remained unreconciled to this pious survivor of the flood. However, with Ea's intervention, a compromise was reached. In the derivative version of the flood in *Gilgamesh* Tablet XI Utnapishtim and his household were granted immortality. But that does not appear to be the case in *Atrahasis*; at least the flood hero and his household are not allowed to remain in this world. In the *Atrahasis* myth Enlil was reconciled only after certain *uṣurāt nišī* ("regulations for people") were imposed upon humankind, which I understand to be limitations upon their vitality. That is, provisions were made for humans to die naturally.[33] Henceforth, the demarcation between deity and humankind would be clearly delineated so that humankind might never again transgress upon the divine realm. With the definition of humankind as mortals clarified, ·Enlil gave his blessing to the survivors. The mother goddess Nintu's fly necklace served as a perpetual reminder that humankind had its own function as servants of the gods and so was not to be destroyed. With this redefinition of humankind, the primeval period came to an end and the world of our human experience began.

With these considerations in mind we may return to *Atrahasis* as an example of mythopoeic speculation. *Atrahasis* was composed during the Old Babylonian period. All known Old Babylonian copies of this myth apparently derive from Sippar and appear to contain the same text.[34] (The newly discovered complete Late Babylonian copy, mentioned above, also comes from Sippar.) However, a scribal note (*ḫi-pi* "broken") in two Old Babylonian manuscripts indicates that these were copies of an older tablet, making it likely that the poem was more widely disseminated than in just this one city.[35] In any case, *Atrahasis* is representative of the standard Mesopotamian outlook during the Old Babylonian period. *Atrahasis*, much more so than *Gilgamesh*, stands solidly in the traditional understanding of that society in envisioning humankind to be servants of the gods. The theme of humankind created as substitute laborers for the gods is highlighted also in the Sumerian text "Enki and Ninmah,"[36] or as Thorkild Jacobsen entitles it, "The Birth of Man."[37] But this story knew nothing of a rebellion of humankind against the gods or of any attempt to diminish humankind by means of plagues or a flood. Likewise, the Sumerian story of the flood, *The Deluge*, follows roughly the same outline as *Atrahasis*, though it diverges widely in actual language and content. Nonetheless, *Atrahasis* is no mere paraphrase of prior tradition. The only extant tablet of the Sumerian flood story was written in the late Old Babylonian period. M. Civil[38] suggests that the theme of a universal flood does not seem to belong in earlier Sumerian literature. If true, *Atrahasis* may actually be older than the Sumerian flood story and the source of the latter, rather than the other way around, as generally supposed.[39] In any case, the author of *Atrahasis* was no mere stenographer for his culture. The grounding of the flood story within a story of human rebellion against the gods and so providing a theological reason for the flood was certainly innovative. The Akkadian author's genius was to forge the traditions into a new synthesis of Mesopotamian understanding of reality, such that his contemporaries recognized in his composition an authentic expression of their own beliefs.

Again this has been done by a kind of sophisticated mythopoeic speculation. The epilogue ends with the words "I have sung of the flood to all the peoples. Hear it!" But this is not just a story of the flood; the author has transformed the flood story into a story of origins. The flood is subordinated to the question of the proper relations between the gods and humankind. Men were created to serve the gods. Therefore they must keep their place and not encroach upon the divine realm. The poem therefore concludes with regulations for humankind that will assure humankind a right relationship before the gods. The command at the conclusion of the poem—"Hear it!"—clearly expresses the author's intention to make a statement of ultimate significance for his audience. Apparently he succeeded; his story became standard in succeeding generations. It was his version of the flood story that the editor of *Gilgamesh*, Tablet XI, utilized in recomposing that epic.

ENUMA ELISH

Enuma elish is more of a theogony than a cosmogony; that is to say, it is more concerned with the establishment of the divine order (the origins of the gods and the hierarchy among them) than with the establishment of the world and the origins of humankind.[40] More precisely, the purpose of *Enuma elish* is to promote Marduk, the patron deity of the city of Babylon, to the position of supremacy within the Mesopotamian pantheon, a position traditionally occupied by the older, established Sumerian deity Anu (or alternatively by Enlil, as in *Atrahasis*). Somewhat earlier the Akkadian myth of *Anzu*, upon which *Enuma elish* is partially patterned, had attempted to stake out a similar claim for Ninurta, the patron deity of the city of Girsu in central Mesopotamia, by having him defeat the demonic Anzu when the older gods proved unequal to the task. Similarly, *Enuma elish* tells how an older hierarchy of gods was first established but then became inadequate, necessitating the transfer of authority to a younger and more vigorous deity, the awesome Marduk. Indeed, it would appear that the author of *Enuma elish* consciously stole a page from the Anzu myth and attributed Ninurta's feats to Marduk, as will be discussed shortly.

The *Enuma elish* story begins in primordial time, before the creation of the world, with the mingling of the waters of Apsu (the sweet-water abyss) and of Ti'amat (the salt-water abyss).[41] From this union of waters evolved a series of divine pairs (Lahmu and Lahamu, Anshar and Kishar), with each new pair surpassing the previous one. Finally the traditional Sumerian high gods were generated. From Anshar was "born" Anu, the king of the gods (according to this tradition); and Anu sired Ea (Enki), the god of wisdom. In the first cycle of events, these Sumerian gods proved capable of ruling the "universe." By their activity they disturbed Ti'amat's rest. As in *Atrahasis*, to disturb the rest, or sleep, of the chief deity is to challenge that deity's authority.[42] Consequently, a theomachy or battle between the gods was inevitable. It was a contest between the forces of chaos represented by Ti'amat and Apsu, on the one side, and the forces of divine order represented by the high gods, on the other side. Ti'amat sent forth her husband Apsu to annihilate the mutinous gods. Ea, however, defeated and killed Apsu and built his own palace over Apsu's body. In keeping with the canons inherited from Sumerian times, this cycle affirmed the erstwhile rankings within the traditional Mesopotamian pantheon. But then the myth continues with a second cycle, which revealed the inadequacy of the traditional high gods and the necessity of a new supreme deity.

Within Apsu Ea sired a marvelous son, none other than Marduk. At his birth the gods rejoiced and their activities again disturbed the rest of Ti'amat. Ti'amat engendered eleven fearsome new monsters to add to her army. So awesome was her new power that even some from the ranks of the gods went over to her side. Ti'amat elevated one of these, Qingu, to be her new husband and commander of her forces. Anu and Ea both proved inadequate to this new challenge; they both tried to face Ti'amat but were unable to withstand her superior power. At this point the young deity Marduk stepped forward and offered to defeat Ti'amat on the condition that, if he succeeded, the other gods would make him their king. To this the others readily agreed, especially after Marduk demonstrated the power to control the destinies through his creative word by making entities disappear and reappear. Marduk constructed a powerful bow, gathered his lightning bolts and storm winds and, clothed in all of his divine splendor, marched out to meet Ti'amat and her hosts. The task was an awesome one even for Marduk, but in the end he proved equal to it. When Ti'amat opened her mouth to devour Marduk, the latter drove his winds into her mouth and distended her belly. Through her gaping mouth he shot a deadly arrow into her heart and killed her. Her fleeing army he gathered into his net.

The battle won, Marduk set about bringing order out of chaos. He cut Ti'amat's body in two. With one half he formed the heavens as a barrier to keep back the waters above. At the same time he established stations for the various gods, the sun and moon and constellations, to signify day and night and the seasons. Using various portions of Ti'amat's body, Marduk then fashioned clouds, rivers, springs, and mountains. When he had finished creating the heavens and earth, he fashioned humankind. He had Qingu killed and from the blood mixed with clay he formed primeval humans (*lullû-amēlu*) to do the work of the gods so that the latter might have leisure, or rest, as befitting gods. (This last theme is clearly drawn from *Atrahasis*, a matter to which we must return shortly.) The gods in gratitude and in acknowledgment of Marduk's kingship built him a palace in Babylon from which to rule the universe. This temple-palace was cosmic rather than local, however. Its name, Esagila, means "House [temple/palace] that raises its head (i.e., into the heavens)." Moreover its impressive zigurrat, or temple tower, bore the significant name of Etemenanki, "House [temple/palace] where the foundation of the heavens and earth is." With his rule (creation) thus firmly established, the divine sovereign retired his warbow by hanging it up in the sky where it would forever shine as the bow star (probably the star Sirius)—a clear sign that chaos had been completely subdued and there no longer existed any threat to the divine order. The story ends with all the gods enjoying their appropriate rest and singing the praises of Marduk through a litany of his fifty titles. An epilogue admonishes all people to meditate on the words of this poem and to rejoice in Marduk as divine sovereign and in the universal order that he has established (created).

The date of composition for *Enuma elish* is uncertain. The oldest known copies of the work come from Ashur, the old capital of Assyria, and date to approximately 1000 B.C.E. Virtually all scholars who have studied the issue have concluded that *Enuma elish*, like *Gilgamesh* and *Atrahasis*, was written in Babylon during the Old Babylonian period, likely near the end of that period, or early in the Kassite period (sixteenth century

B.C.E.). W. G. Lambert, however, argues persuasively that this myth was composed later, likely around 1100 B.C.E. in the reign of Nebuchadnezzar I.[43]

The Babylonian origin of the composition seems assured since *Enuma elish* tells of the elevation of Marduk, the patron god of Babylon, to the position of head of the pantheon, above Enlil, Anum, and Enki, traditionally the highest ranking gods of Mesopotamia. The elevation of Marduk had already begun in the Old Babylonian period when under Hammurapi the city of Babylon first gained hegemony over other Mesopotamian city-states. Hammurapi's success necessitated a new synthesis that justified Babylon's—or in the local religious idiom, Marduk's—ascendancy to a position of preeminence. The beginnings of this resynthesizing are already evident in the prologue to Hammurapi's Law Code:

> When lofty Anum, king of the Anunnaki, (and) Enlil, lord of heaven and earth, the determiner of the destinies of the land, determined for Marduk, the first-born of Enki, the Enlil functions over all mankind, made him great among the Igigi, called Babylon by its exalted name, made it supreme in the world, established for him in its midst an enduring kingship. . . . (*Codex Hammurapi*, i, 1–20)

In this new composition the traditional three great gods of the older Sumerian pantheon are said to have promoted Marduk, formerly an unimportant god of an unimportant city, to the position of a first-ranking god along with themselves. In the same vein, Marduk is made to be the first-born son of Enki—this despite the clear testimony of his name that he was originally thought to be the son of the sun god Utu (Shamash). Utu, however, was a god of the second rank behind the three great gods Anum, Enlil, and Enki. By making Marduk the son of Enki, Marduk was elevated to the ranks of the great gods.[44] Similar transfers of divine authority are evident in the Akkadian myths of *Labbu* and *Anzu*. In *Labbu* the god Sin invites Tishpak to kill the monster Labbu and to exercise kingship as a reward. Since Tishpak was god of Eshnunna, it is probable that this is an instance of mythopoeic theologizing from the Diyala region to exalt a local god by equating him with the mighty divine warrior Ninurta. Indeed, in some god lists Tishpak is explicitly equated with Ninurta, suggesting that such theological propagandizing did achieve its goal in at least some instances.[45] In the original Old Babylonian myth of *Anzu*, of course, Ninurta was the vanquisher of demonic Anzu (note Ninurta is also called son of Ea), but almost a millennium later in a hymn of Ashurbanipal, Marduk is celebrated as "the one who crushed the head of Anzu."[46] One can observe this same tendency to ascribe all important functions to Marduk still at work in later periods as well. The Neo-Babylonian poet Kabti-ilani-Marduk, author of the poem of Erra, made his patron deity Marduk, rather than Enlil, to be the king of the gods who decreed the great primeval flood as a punishment for the sins of humankind.[47]

The process of exalting Marduk begun in the Old Babylonian period reached its culmination in the Late Babylonian period, in which there was a powerful movement to consolidate the earlier multiplicity of gods into just a few popular ones. With an almost monotheistic impulse, one such text goes so far as to equate all the other gods with Marduk alone (with the possible exception of his spouse Zarpanitum and the demons):

Urash (is)	Marduk of planting.
Lugalidda (is)	Marduk of the abyss.
Ninurta (is)	Marduk of the pickaxe.
Nergal (is)	Marduk of battle.
Zababa (is)	Marduk of warfare.
Enlil (is)	Marduk of lordship and consultations.
Nabu (is)	Marduk of accounting.
Sin (is)	Marduk who lights up the night.
Shamash (is)	Marduk of justice.
Adad (is)	Marduk of rain.
Tishpak (is)	Marduk of troops.
Great Anu (is)	Marduk of . . .
Shuqamuna (is)	Marduk of the container.
[(is)]	Marduk of everything (CT 24, 50, BM 47406, obverse)[48]

While one may not wish to call this an example precisely of mythopoeic speculation, it seems obvious that the Babylonian theologians responsible for this text were engaging in theological speculation. Moreover, it confirms the conscious and deliberate theological thinking witnessed in the prologue to Hammurapi's Code and which we find again in *Enuma elish*.

Enuma elish goes beyond the prologue to Hammurapi's Law Code; there Marduk *shared* the top position with the three great gods. As was already stated, one of the functions of the epic is to establish the hegemony of Babylon over all of Mesopotamia. Thorkild Jacobsen[49] proposes an interesting twist to the epic's political function. He interprets *Enuma elish* as a mythopoeic metaphor for the establishment of a new political model (monarchy) in Mesopotamia. Marduk's victory represents the victory of the newly emerged monarchy in Babylon over the older powers of inertia and rest (Ti'amat = anarchy; Enlil, Anum, and Enki = primitive democracy of the older Sumerian city states). All of this is done through obvious mythopoeic speculation. The author acknowledged the former authority of the Sumerian order by allowing Ea (Enki) the ability to meet the first challenge of anarchy (Apsu, the husband of Ti'amat). But in the face of the latest and more serious assault of anarchy (Ti'amat herself), only a new and more powerful ruler (Marduk/Babylonian monarchy) proved equal to the task. All of this is, of course, projected back into primordial time and therefore given absolute and universal authority.

Mythopoeic speculation in *Enuma elish* is used to undergird many other areas beyond the political. One of the most interesting to me is the blatant manner in which the author reshaped traditional motifs such as those found in *Atrahasis*. Indeed, one can make a good case for saying that the author intended *Enuma elish* as at least a partial replacement for *Atrahasis*, which by his day had probably become the classic statement (or myth) of origins in Mesopotamia. The opening line of the poem, *enūma eliš* . . . ("When on high the heaven had not (yet even) been named . . .") sounds like a not too subtle polemic against *Atrahasis*, which had opened with the words *inūma ilū awīlum* . . . ("When gods were human / Bore the labor, carried the corvee-basket . . ."). In other words,

Atrahasis had begun with heaven already in existence and each god established in his or her proper hierarchical rank. *Enuma elish* claims to go back behind this time, before the heaven had been created and even before the gods had come into existence. The author of *Enuma elish*, therefore, is claiming theological precedence for his work over all earlier religious statements.

Other examples of similar thematic replacement could be given. I will mention just one more. In *Atrahasis* it was wise Enki who conceived the idea and together with the mother-goddess created humankind out of clay mixed with the blood of We-ila, the god who led the revolt against the high gods. But in *Enuma elish* Marduk is credited with the creation of human-kind. When the gods gathered seeking a solution to the problem of who will do the work of the gods (V.131–142), Marduk their king came up with the solution of creating the primeval humans (*lullû-amēlu*) so the gods might have their rightful leisure as befitting gods (V.143–VI.10). The plan and its execution are recognizably lifted straight out of *Atrahasis*. Humankind is fashioned from clay mixed with the blood of the "ringleader," in this case Qingu, the husband-king of Ti'amat and leader of the "evil" forces who threatened to annihilate the "good" high gods. Enki's role in all this is reduced to being Marduk's counselor and the craftsman who carries out Marduk's instructions (VI.11–38).[50] Earlier in the epic Marduk had been made equal to the god of wisdom when Marduk was made Enki's son; now Marduk supplants Enki entirely by taking over his most prized roles. Indeed, at the conclusion of the epic Enki (Ea) is portrayed as happily acknowledging that Marduk has now supplanted him, by conferring upon Marduk his very own name: "He is indeed even as I; his name shall be Ea" (VII.140).[51]

Throughout I have stressed the deliberateness by which the Babylonian authors composed their new mythic syntheses. This point can be made very tellingly again by noting that when *Enuma elish* reached Assyria, Assyrian editors replaced the name of Marduk with that of their own national god, Ashur. With but a few strokes of the stylus, these Assyrian editors radically altered the original function of the epic. Instead of under-girding Babylonian hegemony, the revised *Enuma elish* now supported Assyrian hegemony over Babylon!

CONCLUSION

In each case, the authors of the three Babylonian epic myths, *Gilgamesh, Atrahasis*, and *Enuma elish*, were shown to have been highly creative thinkers who transformed their societies' religio-politico-literary traditions into universal statements about reality, such that they became paradigmatic for all succeeding generations of that society. The story and intention may have been different in each case, yet all three employed a similar method. Each of these authors consciously and deliberately adapted prior mythic stories and motifs, and created new ones as well, as they crafted their own new literary compositions. Such conscious and deliberate extension of older mythic symbols to new political realities and changing intellectual conceptions is precisely what I mean by mythopoeic speculation. This was more involved than just the creative mind of a poet at work in composing a literary masterpiece, a kind of literary inspiration from the muses, so to speak. Rather, these Babylonian poets—and later, Assyrian editors—were involved in rethinking the basic values of humankind as understood from their societies' perspectives, what we would call philosophizing or theologizing. However, they did their reflective thinking not through syllogistic reasoning or philosophical categories but through the medium of mythic narrative. The result may be less satisfying to us post-Enlightenment thinkers; it may be even less precise than philosophical theologizing. But it is certainly not less appealing to the human spirit. Even today, reading in translation, one can still experience something of the universal appeal of these ancient compositions as a quest after the most profound human questions. No doubt these ancient writers, as poets, intended to entertain. But as theologians they meant their myths to instruct as well. Their success may be judged by the canonical status that subsequent generations afforded to their works.

Chapter 2

◆

THE YAHWIST'S PRIMEVAL MYTH

◆

It is appropriate to begin consideration of mythopoeic speculation in biblical tradition with a study of the Yahwist's Primeval
Myth. "The Yahwist" is, of course, part of the so-called Documentary Hypothesis, which is currently under attack from a
number of quarters. Nonetheless, this theory remains in its
broad outline the best and most widely accepted explanation of
the development of the Pentateuch, the first five books of the
Bible. To be sure, numerous aspects of the theory as originally
formulated in the classical statement by Julius Wellhausen toward the end of the nineteenth century must be revised in light
of more recent research. But as an explanation for the many
doublets and apparently contradictory narratives in the Pentateuch, the Documentary Hypothesis remains unsurpassed. Even
many of the theory's critics either continue to hold to many of
its tenets or else invent substitutes that end up looking very
much like the hypothesis they purport to replace. Accordingly,
in this chapter I will assume the validity of the Documentary
Hypothesis, mindful of the fact that it is a heuristic device for
understanding the complex process by which the Pentateuch as
we now know it came into existence.

Nevertheless, the Documentary Hypothesis fails to account
fully for the literary unity of the Pentateuch. In its classical
formulation the Documentary Hypothesis posits that the Pentateuch is composed of four originally disparate sources—or,
more accurately, literary strands—identified as the Yahwist, the
Elohist, the Deuteronomist, and the Priestly Writer (abbreviated

41

as J, E, D, and P, respectively).[1] These literary strands are thought to vary widely in date, from perhaps the tenth century to approximately the fifth century B.C.E., and to have been assembled only gradually by a succession of redactors, or editors, during the course of some five or six centuries to form a single "Torah." Recent studies, however, have emphasized that the Pentateuch exhibits a greater thematic and literary coherence than previously allowed. This is evident from the presence of such literary conventions as chiasmus, parallel episodes aligned in matching sequence, repetition of themes, linkage of units together through catchwords and phrases, and a host of others besides, which cut across the boundaries of the individual sources as set forth by the Documentary Hypothesis.[2]

Rather than scrap the whole Documentary Hypothesis as some have suggested, it seems more in keeping with the literary data of the Pentateuch to modify the Documentary Hypothesis along the lines suggested by Frank Cross.[3] Cross maintains the basic four pentateuchal traditions, but posits that the early epic traditions (J and E) were subsequently reworked by P, who added his own editorial structure and priestly materials to form a Tetrateuch (viz., Genesis through Numbers[4]). (Following Martin Noth, Cross separates out Deuteronomy, which originally was linked to the books of Joshua through 2 Kings, forming a Deuteronomistic History.) P never existed as a separate source, even though individual portions may have existed in an earlier form. Rather, P's method was to incorporate his[5] own priestly views and materials into an already existing epic tradition, in such a way as to preserve as much of older "Israelite epic" as possible.

My approach will be primarily diachronic. This is not to deny the validity of a synchronic approach. But for my purposes it is necessary to chronicle the various stages of development that a text has undergone. A demonstration of *the process* of mythopoeic speculation in the Bible depends upon being able to glimpse how biblical texts changed shape during their complex history of composition. Accordingly, in this chapter I will consider the earliest (J) form of the Israelite primeval myth. In the next chapter I will discuss how the myth was radically transformed by a later (P) redaction of the Torah.

The earliest of the four pentateuchal traditions, according to most scholars,[6] is that of the so-called Yahwist (J). The high degree of unity and consistency within this literary tradition makes it likely that J is the composition of a single person. The Yahwist is so named because of his characteristic manner of referring to the Israelite deity by the proper name Yahweh. (The other sources or writers in the book of Genesis normally refer to the deity as *Elohim*, a common noun usually translated as "God.") Because his work seems to exhibit a bias in favor of the Southern Kingdom, Judah, it may be assumed that the Yahwist lived and wrote in Judah sometime prior to the fall of its rival kingdom of Israel in 722 B.C.E. Since World War II many scholars, following the lead of Gerhard von Rad, place the Yahwist within the court of Solomon, claiming that he was a propagandist, first, for the legitimacy of the Davidic dynasty over the house of Saul and, second, for the right of Solomon to succeed his father, David, to the throne over the claims of his older brothers.[7] A recent study of J posits that this work was composed even earlier, in the time of David, as legitimation of that ruler's rejection of the Egyptian model of domineering state rule over subject peoples in favor of "bedouin" values of economic independence and autonomy.[8] Such attempts at locating the author within a precise sociohistorical context, however, seem to exceed the meager evidence that may be gleaned legitimately from the biblical data. In any case, my interest here is not so much in the identity of the Yahwist as in his composition.

The actual delineation of the Yahwist's epic within the Pentateuch is at times difficult to discern, particularly as regards its ending. It is a moot question whether this work originally extended beyond the confines of the present Pentateuch into the book of Joshua and beyond, or whether it ended with the book of Numbers. Fortunately for my purpose, the beginning of the epic is not so problematic. The Yahwist's hand is relatively easy to detect within the first twelve chapters of Genesis. Without worrying overly much about precision at this point, it may be said that by scholarly consensus the following passages at minimum in Genesis 1–12 are to be attributed to the Yahwist: the stories of Eden, Cain and Abel, and Lamech (2:4–4:26), the flood (6:1–8:22 [here J and P traditions are intertwined]), the drunkenness of Noah (9:18–27), the tower of Babel (11:1–9), and the call of Abraham (12:1–20). One may assume some elements of the original J epic have been omitted or altered in the process of transmission and subsequent redacting of the Pentateuch. Nevertheless, if we separate these passages out and read them together, they form a fairly coherent story; therefore it is likely that we still possess in all its essentials the opening portion of the Yahwist's epic, which may appropriately be termed the Yahwist's primeval myth.

Beginning with George Smith's discovery in the nineteenth century of a Mesopotamian flood story that was very similar to the Genesis account, scholars have increasingly recognized that the stories in Genesis 1–11 are at least partially derived from earlier Mesopotamian mythic traditions. Especially prominent in such discussions are comparisons of *Enuma elish* with the P creation account in Genesis 1, and *Gilgamesh* and *Adapa* with the J accounts of Eden and the flood in Genesis 2:4–8:25. The recovery of *Atrahasis* is of too recent vintage to have had its influence on Genesis fully recognized.

But it is precisely the recovery of the *Atrahasis* myth[9] that above all necessitates a radical revision of our assessments of both the dependency and the originality of the biblical authors of Genesis.[10] This is especially true in the case of the Yahwist. What I argue in this chapter is that the Yahwist was a highly creative genius who reshaped prior mythic traditions, especially those of the *Atrahasis* tradition, into a new and original literary myth of origins.[11] Because Yahwism—that is, belief in Yahweh as the supreme deity, together with the cultus and value system flowing from that belief—was a relatively new religion, many theoretical issues remained to be worked out. The Yahwist took upon himself the task of integrating Yahwism with contemporary conceptions of the origins of the universe and of humankind in particular. He did this through a kind of mythopoeic speculation. The result was a new primeval myth in which Yahweh was affirmed as the creator and divine sovereign of the universe and the place of humankind assured before the creator for all times.

It may be helpful to contrast the thesis being developed here with a common reconstruction of the Yahwist's method and message. It is commonly assumed that the Yahwist's story is a story of a gracious and loving God who created a perfect world that was corrupted by human sin, which in turn necessitated divine intervention by this gracious deity to salvage a creation gone astray. The story ended with the election of a people whose destiny was somehow to bring hope and salvation to a wounded humankind. In a more theological idiom, this is a story of sin and redemption. According to this interpretation, the Yahwist prefaced his "history of salvation" with a story of "the Fall" and its disastrous aftermath. In Yahweh God's original design, as related in Genesis 2:4–25, the world was created as an idyllic garden in which there was neither illness nor death nor any form of enmity whatever. This paradise was created explicitly for the enjoyment of humankind, itself the apex of God's creation. Genesis 3 tells how this originally perfect creation was subsequently "lost" to humans through their own fault of disobeying the divine command and eating the forbidden fruit. This "Fall," or "original sin," resulted in alienation of humankind from their God, from their world, and even from one another. Once introduced, sin continued to grow like a cancer, corrupting God's perfect work. Such are the stories in Genesis 4 of Cain and Abel, which relate how brother turned against brother, and of Lamech, wherein murder and vengeance became the rule. Even the flood (Genesis 6–8), which was supposed to wash this cancer from the face of the earth, failed to achieve its desired result, as evidenced in the disrespect Ham exhibits toward his father Noah (Gen. 9:20–27) and the presumptuous pride of humankind in building the tower of Babel (Gen. 11:1–9). Stymied at every turn by a recalcitrant humankind "whose every imagination of the thoughts of his heart was only evil continually" (Gen. 6:5; cf. 8:21), the gracious Creator finally embarked upon another plan by which he elected one man and his family to bring about blessing for the others (Gen. 12:1ff.).

As attractive as this common interpretation of the Yahwist may be from a theological point of view, it must finally be given up. As new evidence from *Atrahasis* in particular makes evident, the Yahwist's story is not a story of a "fall" from original perfection at all. Quite the contrary, it is a story about *continu-*

ously improved creation. Similar to the Mesopotamian myths of origins considered in the previous chapter, the Yahwist's story is an Israelite myth of origins. Indeed, the Yahwist seems to have consciously modeled his "creation myth" upon these Mesopotamian myths. Although it is unclear at present whether the Yahwist knew these myths in a written form or learned of them only through oral transmission, it is obvious from the frequent and extensive borrowing of motifs that the Yahwist was intimately acquainted with at least the myths of *Gilgamesh* and *Atrahasis*, and perhaps others (e.g., *Adapa*) as well.

The channel by which the Yahwist came to know these Babylonian traditions is moot. Genesis itself records a tradition that the Israelite patriarchs had Mesopotamian origins (Gen. 11:27–12:5) and later endogamous connections (Genesis 24; 27:43–28:5; 29–31). Undoubtedly the scribal profession also played a role—perhaps the major role. In the second millennium B.C.E. cuneiform scribal schools on the Mesopotamian model ringed the periphery of Mesopotamia, from Susa in the southeast to Hattusha in the northwest and Egyptian Amarna in the far southwest. Excavated tablets reveal that Ugarit had such a school, as apparently did Megiddo and other Canaanite cities. In these schools the standard Mesopotamian curriculum was taught, sometimes with the aid of bilingual cribs. During the Amarna period (fourteenth century B.C.E.) in particular Akkadian was the language of international diplomacy and widely utilized in the area that would later be known as "the land of Israel." Apprentice scribes in these schools read and copied cuneiform literary texts as part of their training.[12] Among the Amarna tablets was a fragment of *Adapa* (El-Amarna 356). At Megiddo was discovered a scribal practice tablet on which was copied the scene about Enkidu's death from *Gilgamesh* (Tablet VII), dating to the same period.

But if such scribal schools played an important role in the dissemination of Mesopotamian literary tradition to the West, they also fostered a tradition of local adaptation of that same literary tradition. Scribes at Amarna, Ugarit, and Emar[13] felt free to adapt the Sumero/Akkadian texts as they saw fit. The activity of these scribes from the Western periphery provides an empirical model which accounts for both the route by which Mesopotamian myths reached the Yahwist and the literary license that allowed the Yahwist to adapt these texts for his own requirements, albeit at a later period.

Like *Atrahasis*, the Yahwist's myth purports to explain the proper place of humankind within the cosmos by showing that "our world" is the result of a series of inchoate attempts on the part of an inexperienced creator to achieve a workable creation; in the process the proper roles of deity and humankind are likewise worked out. Like *Gilgamesh*, the Yahwist's myth sets forth immortality as a divine prerogative that is denied to humankind. But the genius of the Yahwist is that he brought together these disparate mythic themes into a highly original composition that placed the Israelite religious and national traditions at the center of the cosmic story. A complete analysis of the Yahwist's composition would require a lengthy book in its own right. Since the goal of this volume is a more global presentation of myth and the practice of mythopoeic speculation in the Bible, I can do little more in this chapter than sketch with broad brush the general contours of the Yahwist's method and message.[14]

INCHOATE CREATION

The Yahwist began his myth of origins, like *Atrahasis* and its derivative *Enuma elish*, with temporal clauses explaining the situation prior to actual creation. Before Yahweh God began, there was only noncreation—or chaos, as the Greeks called it. In the ancient Near East there were two primary, equally powerful symbols of chaos. One was the primeval flood or ocean, frequently portrayed as a dragonlike monster; the other was the barren desert, sometimes portrayed as a dreadful land beast.[15] Life—at least human life—was impossible under either of these conditions; hence the utility of the sea and the desert as symbols of nonexistence, or chaos.

The author of Job understood and utilized these symbols well. As part of his literary ploy to emphasize the Creator's awesome transcendence vis-à-vis a mere human, the author of Job 40:15–41:34 has Yahweh challenge Job to play the role of creator, if he can, by subduing Behemoth and Leviathan, the traditional twin chaos monsters representing the dry wasteland

and the unformed ocean, respectively. Since Job obviously cannot subdue the chaos monsters, Job has no right to challenge the Creator about the way he runs this world.

As we shall see in the next chapter, the author of Genesis 1 portrayed chaos as primeval flood because he was following the typology of *Enuma elish*. The Yahwist, however, some centuries prior settled upon the barren desert as his symbol for noncreation because he was following the typology of *Atrahasis*.[16] The latter myth is thoroughly Babylonian in assuming that, without the vivifying action of irrigation, the earth is naturally dry and barren like the steppes that surround Mesopotamia. The Yahwist assumes a similar setting for creation.

> At the time when Yahweh God made earth and heaven—there being as yet no field plants on the earth, nor had vegetation of any kind begun to grow, for Yahweh God had not yet made rain; nor was there as yet any human to work the ground—primeval waters were rising out of the underworld[17] and watering the whole surface of the ground. Yahweh God formed the [first] human (*bā-'ādām*), dust from the ground (*bā-'ādāmâ*), and breathed into his nostrils the breath of life and the human became a living being. Yahweh God planted a garden in Eden, in the east, and put there the human which he had formed. Then Yahweh God caused to sprout from the ground all kinds of trees which were delightful to behold and delectable to eat; included in the midst of the garden were the tree of life and the tree of knowledge of good and evil.
>
> A river arises out of Eden, watering the whole garden, and from there it branches out to become four headwaters.[18] The name of the first is the Pishon; it encircles the whole Havilite country, where there is gold. The gold of that country is excellent. There, too, are bdellium and lapis lazuli. The name of the second river is the Gihon; it encircles the whole country of Cush. The name of the third river is the Tigris; it flows east of Assyria. The fourth river is the Euphrates.
>
> Yahweh God took the human and placed him in the garden of Eden to work it and to care for it. (Gen. 2:4b–15)

The Mesopotamian roots of the Yahwist's primeval myth are clear from the first. Some of the place names are perhaps deliberately obscure in an attempt to situate Eden somewhere beyond the historical world yet on its fringes. Those geographical names that are identifiable as historical places are all associated with Mesopotamia and its environs: the Tigris and the Euphrates rivers and the country Assyria. Cush, which elsewhere in the Bible usually refers to Ethiopia, most likely here is a reference to the territory of the Kassites, as in Genesis 10:8.[19] It has been suggested that even the name Eden is derived from Sumerian **e d i n** meaning "steppe," "plain." However, the name Eden was more likely derived from the Semitic root *'dn*, which has a base meaning of "abundance," "luxury," or the like.[20] The garden of Eden, then, would literally have been, as tradition has maintained, a place of abundance, a "paradise"—but for the deity, not for humans.[21]

The root *'dn*, previously known in Hebrew (Neh. 9:25) and Syriac, has most recently turned up in the Aramaic version of a ninth-century B.C.E. bilingual inscription from the site of Tell Fakhariyeh in northeastern Syria.[22] This inscription, which is most illuminating for our discussion on Eden, is part of a statue dedicated to the storm god Hadad. Hadad is praised as

> the irrigation master of heaven and earth, who rains down abundance and provides pastures and water for the whole country; who supplies drink and food for all the gods, his brothers; the irrigation master of all the rivers, who makes luxuriant (*m'dn*) the whole land. (Aramaic version, 11.2–5)

Most of this paean of praise is drawn from stock Akkadian hymnic literature. Nevertheless, the last phrase is noteworthy in that the Aramaic translator chose the rare root *'dn* to express the concept of a well-watered, luxuriant place. One wonders if the name Eden has a longer tradition behind it than we know. This inscription is heuristic for the interpretation of Genesis 2 in other ways as well. Both texts speak of rivers that water the land of, presumably, Mesopotamia. Perhaps one should understand Genesis 2 as implying that Yahweh God, like Hadad, is directly responsible for the vivifying action of the river(s), that is, that Yahweh God is the "irrigation master" who by his control of the cosmic watercourses transforms the dry wasteland into a paradisiacal oasis.[23] Given the many other Mesopotamian vestiges present in the Yahwist's primeval myth, such an interpretation is likely.

As stated earlier, the Yahwist did not conceive of the deity's initial creative impulse as being a complete success, a work of perfection right from its inception. Like the author of *Atrahasis*, the Yahwist conceived of creation as a gradual affair in which the Creator had to work out the kinks through a process of trial and error.

Reminiscent of *Atrahasis*, the Yahwist assumed that creation has to do with organizing an agricultural world. Noncreation is synonymous with there being "no human to till the ground" (2:5). On the positive side, creation began to happen when the creator molded clay of the ground (*hā-ʾădāmâ*) and "formed" humankind (*hā-ʾādām*). There is here, of course, the well-known pun linking humankind to the soil of the earth; the pun can be rendered into English approximately as "the human" (*hā-ʾādām*) is taken from "the humus" (*hā-ʾădāmâ*). But the Yahwist intended more than a mere word play. In his view humankind was indeed intimately linked with the soil, at least in its inception. Humans were created to cultivate "the ground/humus." At the same time that the Creator formed humankind, he also "planted a garden in Eden . . . and put there the human whom he had molded" (2:8). The human cultivator and the cultivated humus are correlative terms. Even after the humans are subsequently expelled from the garden, their function as cultivators of the soil remains (3:17–19, 23).

It is important to notice that Yahweh was the original gardener. It was he who "planted" the garden in Eden and made to grow there all kinds of beautiful shrubbery and delicious fruit trees, including the two mythic, divine trees, "the tree of life" and "the tree of knowledge of good and evil" (2:8–9). It is no wonder that the deity liked to stroll in this marvelous garden in the refreshing afternoon breeze (3:8). Humankind, it seems, was created to work this garden for the deity: "Yahweh God took the human and placed him in the garden of Eden to cultivate it and to care for it" (2:15). Surely we are here picking up an echo of *Atrahasis*. In that myth humans were created as substitute agricultural laborers for lesser gods, who had revolted from performing this arduous chore for the benefit of the high gods. There is, of course, no revolt of lesser gods here. Such a possibility was precluded for the Yahwist, with his emphasis on Yahweh God as the king of heaven and earth. Although the Yahwist did not a priori rule out the existence of other gods,[24] no other deity is allowed in the picture at this point, lest the absolute sovereignty of Yahweh be compromised. Nevertheless, the assumption that humankind was originally created to relieve the deity of the burden of cultivating his own plantation or "garden" is left intact.[25] As in *Atrahasis*, the function of humankind was divine service, a service that included providing provisions for the deity.[26]

inchoate = being partly but not fully in existence or operation

INCHOATE CREATION IN *ATRAHASIS* AND IN THE YAHWIST

imperfectly formed or formulated

Atrahasis	*J's Primeval Myth (Genesis 2–8)*
	to cause to begin
Irrigation agriculture assumes steppe setting of Mesopotamia	Eden (located in Mesopotamia): dry wasteland becomes garden by irrigation
Igigi gods = original laborers	Yahweh = original laborer: planted a garden Yahweh = irrigator of steppe?
Annunaki gods enjoy privileges of divine rank	Eden = Yahweh's private garden with magic trees 1. tree of life 2. wisdom tree (knowledge of good and evil)
Lullû (proto-humans) created as substitute laborers for gods ·modeled from clay + rebel god's blood ·implicitly immortal (no natural death)	Primeval human (*hā-ʾādām*) created to work and care for Yahweh's garden ·modeled from clay + divine breath ·implicit immortality (tree of life)

51

Institution of Marriage	Institution of Marriage
Lullû revolt against the divine sovereign •their "din" and "cries" = rebellion •inherit "spirit" and "plot" of rebel god	*Hā-ʾādām* aspires to divine status by eating from wisdom tree reserved for deity •wisdom makes one "like gods"
Successive outbreaks of "din"/rebellion	Cain, Lamech, "sons of the gods" increase sin
Punishment: life diminished by 1. plague 2. drought 3. famine	Punishment: life diminished by expulsion from garden and tree of life
Flood	Flood (with obvious similarities to *Atrahasis*)
Atrahasis = pious wise king •sacrifice = provisioning of gods	Noah = righteous (and wise?, cf. Ezek. 14:14) •sacrifice = provisioning of deity
Gods smell sacrifice and bless survivors •Enlil reconciled and accepts situation	Yahweh smells sacrifice and swears oath •Yahweh reconciled to flawed humankind (evil from youth onward)
"Regulations for people": limitations on life •provisions for natural death •*lullû* become (normal) humans	Limitation of 120 years placed on each human life •*hā-ʾādām* become (normal) humans
Sign: Nintu's fly necklace	Sign: duration of the earth and its seasons
[End of myth]	[Primeval period ends at Gen. 8:22]

The thesis I am expounding here stands, of course, in direct opposition to the opinion commonly encountered in commentaries on this passage, namely, that the garden was a place of sublime happiness for "our first parents" prior to their "fall."

In that interpretation the garden is assumed to be a symbol of the deity's utter unselfishness and "grace." That is, God created humankind to share his own condition of eternal bliss and immortality, which by definition excluded any form of pain and suffering. If my thesis is correct, this was not the Yahwist's intention at all.

As I said, in the Yahwist's account the original intention of the Creator in fashioning humankind is the cultivation of the ground and improvement of the deity's garden. Very shortly, however, the author will introduce the seeds of premonition that humankind will not live up to its vocation. Rather than furthering creation, humankind will bring a curse upon the ground (3:17). Ultimately, the ground will even cry out in protest from the human violence to which it will be subjected, as when it is forced to drink Abel's spilled blood (4:10–14). Not until the time of Noah and the flood would the ground derive any real benefit from human activity (5:29; 9:20).[27]

A second indication of the tentativeness of the inceptive phases of creation is in the formation of humankind. The original divine blueprint for humankind proved less than adequate. The original human (*hā-ʾādām*) was a solitary being, undistinguished as to gender. Realizing that "it is not good for the human to be alone" (2:18), Yahweh molded additional creatures—the various animals—from clay.[28] Yahweh reasoned that, since these animals were made of the same substance, the human would naturally consort with them. However, the error soon became obvious. Humankind, although similar to animals in many ways, was clearly distinct. But just what constituted humankind's essential character remained yet to be defined.

The dependency of the Yahwist upon stock ancient Near Eastern creation motifs is once again evident.[29] The *Gilgamesh* epic describes the creation of Enkidu similarly. At first Enkidu was not fully human. Indeed, he is not called a human but rather a *lullû-amēlu*, which should be translated as "primeval human," or even "prototype human."[30] At this stage Enkidu is only incipiently human; he is portrayed as having more in common with animals than with humans. He wears no clothes but is instead covered with hair like an animal. He consorts with the beasts, roaming over the steppe as one of them. He eats and drinks as they do. In order to realize his human potential, he must abandon animal companionship for human companionship. His sexual intercourse with the harlot Shamhat is a metaphor for his humanization (*awēliš iwē*) "he become human" (Old Babylonian *Gilg.* II.iii.25, cf. 27). Through Shamhat Enkidu learns of his need for a female companion of his own kind. The harlot is more than a sexual partner, however; she is also a kind of midwife or mother who gives birth to Enkidu the human and educates him. "Holding on to his hand, she leads him like a child" (II.ii.31–32) to civilization and into full humanity. Previously Enkidu had sucked the milk of the wild beasts. Now through the harlot's coaxing, he learns to eat and drink in a human manner (II.iii.1–25). Finally, she clothes him like herself and his transformation is complete.

The human in Genesis 2–3 is portrayed similarly. When Yahweh discovers that the animals are not suitable companions for the human, he redoes his creation of humankind by dividing it into a male and a female: "man" and "woman." The usual translation of *ṣelāʿ* as "rib" obscures the Yahwist's meaning here. The semantic range of the Hebrew vocable includes "side" as well as "rib."[31] The image here is that of reworking "one of his sides," that is, of reshaping the whole into two complementary halves.[32] With this redefinition of humankind, creation has been advanced tremendously, according to the Yahwist. The tiller of the garden now has a "helpmate [*ʿēzer*] corresponding to himself." The complementarity of the sexes is immediately confirmed in the institution of marriage, which is presented as the natural conclusion of the creation of man and woman.[33] With these advances the distinction between humans and animals is clear; humankind is a species unto itself and subject to an entirely different order.

But what of the relationship of humankind to the deity? If humankind shared with the animals a common origin from clay, it also shared divine life with the Creator. Yahweh had breathed his own breath of life into the original humanoid clay figure to make it into a living being. How much of the divine prerogatives could the humans exercise without threatening Yahweh's sovereignty as Creator?

At the end of Genesis 2 the humans are described as being

naked (*'ărûmmîm*, 2:25). This is normally interpreted as a symbol of innocence and sinlessness. Clothes were superfluous until concupiscence perverted the relationship between the male and the female of the species so as to require refuge one from the other, and until sin introduced an imbalance in nature so as to necessitate protection against a hostile environment. In the Yahwist's mind, however, the transition from nakedness to clothed seems to function as another metaphor for humankind assuming its proper place above the animals but below the divine.

In Mesopotamia the ancient bards had long since used the nakedness of the first humans to symbolize that these primitives, without benefit of the divinely bestowed gifts of civilization, were little better than animals. I have already mentioned how in the *Gilgamesh* epic the *lullû* Enkidu originally roamed naked among the animals. Still earlier the Sumerian myth "Ewe and Wheat" (or Lahar and Ashnan) described the original, uncivilized condition of primitive humankind in these words:

> Shakan (god of flocks) had not (yet) come out on dry land;
> Humankind of those distant days
> Knew not about dressing in cloth
> Ate grass with their mouth like sheep,
> Drank water from the water-hole (like animals).[34]

Another Sumerian text (*Ur Excavation texts*, 6.61.i.7'–10'), perhaps a variant of the Sumerian flood story, contains a very similar description of humankind before they learned how to cultivate the earth (i.e., became civilized):

> Humankind of those distant days,
> Since Shakan had not (yet) come out on dry land,
> Did not know how to dress in cloth;
> Humankind walked about naked.[35]

In Mesopotamian tradition the humans' donning of clothes was accomplished with the good graces of the gods. Clothes were one of the gifts of civilization, along with knowledge of irrigation agriculture and the building of cities, which the gods bestowed upon humankind for their advancement. Whereas it was the nature of animals to go about without clothes, gods wore clothing. Along with the horned cap, the flounced garment was the principal symbol of divinity in Mesopotamian iconography. Accordingly, clothes were an effective metaphor of the dignity of humanity, beings closer in nature to the gods than to animals.[36]

Once again the genius of the Yahwist is apparent in the way he manipulated this motif to his own purposes in Genesis 2–3. Traditionally the notice in Genesis 2:25, that the primeval humans were originally naked but felt no shame, has been linked with the verses that precede and regarded as a comment on male-female relationships. Thematically, however, this verse is linked to the succeeding verses and should thus be regarded as the introduction to the human couple's relationship with the deity. As in Mesopotamian tradition, in the Yahwist's story the original nudity of primeval humankind symbolizes the lack of a clear demarcation between humans and animals at this stage in creation. The motif is thus of a piece with the Creator's assumptions earlier in thinking that "the human" could find a suitable companion among the animals.

Although these humans at first were not ashamed of their original condition (Gen. 2:25), the serpent's words stirred their imagination to aspire for a higher dignity, "to become like gods" (3:5). Their eating of the wisdom tree opened their eyes to their nakedness. That is, they recognized that they were closer to animalhood than to the divinity to which they aspired. The act of making clothes for themselves must be seen, therefore, as an act of defiance of their creator and a grasping at divinity.

The crudity of their attempt at clothing—making garments of leaves—reveals the futility in their ambition. Ashamed of their nakedness but unable to make proper clothes for themselves, they hide from the deity whose status they aspired to. For his part the deity, in recognition that these humans had indeed proven to be more godlike than animallike, eventually clothes them, apparently like himself (3:21, cf. 3:22). But the author implies that this investiture is of a compromise. The garments are made of skin rather than cloth, apparently as a reminder that humankind shares the attributes of both deity and animals.

The "problem" of this dual nature of humankind is woven into the very fabric of the Yahwist's primeval myth. On the one hand, the human body is said to have been molded from the same substance (clay) as the animals; on the other hand, humans are animated by the Creator's own divine life principle (2:7). Once again the Yahwist appears to have been guided by the themes borrowed from prior myths, *Atrahasis* especially. In that story also, as I have shown in the preceding chapter, the relationship of humankind to the gods was ambivalent and needed further definition. Created out of clay moistened with the divine blood of the slain rebel god, humankind contained an earthly substance animated by a divine life principle.[37] The task of *Atrahasis* was the working out of the proper role of humankind as subordinate to the gods but yet having their own proper function within the order of being. But considerable patience was required as the gods only gradually through a process of trial and error arrived at a workable "solution." The Yahwist adopted this basic cultural model but consciously modified it to accommodate the requirements of his Yahwistic beliefs.

The ambivalent status of the original human prototypes—at home with neither the animals nor the gods—is suggested also by their presence in the deity's garden.[38] Despite the common assertion that Yahweh created the garden for the benefit of the humans, the narrative suggests otherwise. The garden is presented as the deity's personal preserve where he grew the two divine trees, the tree of life and the tree of knowledge of good and evil.[39] The latter tree is unknown from elsewhere. But the tree of life is a traditional motif in ancient Near Eastern literature and iconography.[40] In iconographic depictions, as in Genesis 3:24, the tree is guarded by protective genii called cherubim. Access to the tree of life was limited to the gods. In traditional exegesis, the fact that "Adam and Eve" had access to the tree means that they were destined to have eternal life, until their sin subverted God's plan. The Yahwist very likely intended another meaning, however. That the protohuman couple had access to the source of immortality suggests that humankind's status was not as yet entirely defined, that the human experiment was still in the developmental stage.

Parallels can be found in both the *Adapa* myth[41] and the *Gilgamesh* myth; in both stories a human progenitor failed to gain immortality. In the one case, Adapa failed to eat "the bread of life" and drink "the water of life" offered him by the king of the gods. Adapa refused at the advice of Ea, the god of wisdom, who claimed that the food and drink were "the bread of death" and "the water of death." Since Adapa is depicted as a special creation of Ea, and since it is unlikely that the god of wisdom would not have known the true nature of the food and drink, one may conclude that Ea deliberately steered Adapa away from immortality, lest humans acquire a prerogative that belongs rightly only to the gods. In the other case, Gilgamesh strove valiantly to gain immortality, with near success. In the end, however, Gilgamesh lost "the plant of life" when the serpent smelled its goodness and stole it away while Gilgamesh was relaxing. In both stories, as in the Yahwist's tale, immortality is found to be inappropriate to humankind and is forever "lost."

The Yahwist posited a second divine tree in the garden, namely, the tree of knowledge of good and evil, whose fruit is highly desirable for its power to make one wise (3:6). The motif of a wisdom tree is not elsewhere attested; it seems to have germinated in and grown from the fertile imagination of the Yahwist. But it was inspired by thematic precedents.

Wisdom, according to ancient Near Eastern psychology, was a trait the progenitors of the human race were supposed to possess. Atrahasis's own name proclaimed that he was the "exceedingly wise" one. Adapa is called "the sage from Eridu." The hero Gilgamesh was also said to have possessed godlike wisdom: "of him Shamash is fond; Anu, Enlil, and Ea have broadened his wisdom" (*Gilg*. I.v.21–22). Indeed, the opening lines of the epic are nothing short of an encomium of Gilgamesh who "was granted all wisdom" (I.i.4). Perhaps most suggestive of all in this context is the transformation of the *lullû* Enkidu that followed his intercourse with the harlot Shamhat. Although he lost something of his closeness with the animals, he is said to have gained wisdom through a broadening of his understanding (I.iv.29), even to have become "like a god."[42]

Wisdom, though shared in by humans, was apparently considered first and foremost a divine characteristic. In Mesopotamia wisdom was especially associated with the god Ea (Enki), who was credited with creating humankind. So it is particularly noteworthy that Adapa and Atrahasis, archetypal humans, are both devotees of Ea and both noted for their wisdom. The imparting of wisdom by the creator to the first humans therefore must have been something of a standard motif. And as noted in the preceding chapter, when the flood story was added to *Gilgamesh*, making it also a quasi-primeval myth like *Atrahasis*, the editor found it appropriate to transform the hero Gilgamesh into a primeval, antediluvian sage as well.[43]

The genius of the Yahwist was that he thought to turn inside out the motif of primeval human wisdom so as to emphasize a distinction between deity and humankind. In his primeval story humankind was forbidden to eat any fruit of the tree of knowledge of good and evil. The exact meaning of the phrase "knowledge of good and evil" is disputed. But the context favors a meaning of universal knowledge or wisdom.[44] The phrase "good and evil" is thus a merism expressing both poles of possible knowledge, and includes everything in between. An equivalent English expression would be, she knows everything from A to Z. Now obviously, omniscience is a divine prerogative; it is particularly characteristic of the Creator. The forbidden fruit of the tree of knowledge of good and evil, then, is the author's symbol for an initial but unsuccessful attempt by the deity to establish a clear demarcation between Creator and creature by declaring wisdom off limits to humankind.[45]

The serpent, the wiliest of the creatures, sized up the situation very quickly. The serpent recognized the prohibition for what it was, a ploy on the part of the Creator to preserve his own turf. In Christian tradition the serpent has been maligned as a figure of Satan, who duped an innocent couple through a blatant lie. But that is hardly the figure the Yahwist intended. In his telling, the serpent spoke the truth. The woman and her husband did not die, as Yahweh God had said, "on the day you eat of it" (2:17). Rather, as the serpent correctly surmised, wisdom is highly to be desired, since its possession makes one "like gods, knowing good and evil" (3:5).

The serpent was said to be "shrewder than all the beasts of the field" (3:1). As has long been recognized, there is a pun intended between the shrewdness (*'ārûm*) of the serpent and the nakedness (*'ărûmmîm*) of the human couple in the preceding verse. But the pun extends beyond mere assonance. I have already noted that nakedness is a symbol of the lack of demarcation between the animals and humankind. Neither the primeval human couple nor this serpent is content to be mere animal. It is likely that the Yahwist derived the character of the serpent in part from *Gilgamesh*, as J's serpent bears some semblance to the serpent that had a part in depriving the semidivine Gilgamesh of the plant of life. In any case, the serpent of Genesis 3 is more a mythic character than an ordinary animal, as is evident from its ability to talk and to walk upright. (The serpent began to "walk on its belly" only after it was cursed in 3:14.) Indeed, given the later presence of cherubim to guard the divine tree of life (3:24), one wonders whether the serpent here is not to be connected with the awesome seraphim who stand in the presence of Yahweh (Isa. 6:1–7), which in turn are to be identified with the divine winged uraeus or cobra well known in Egyptian art as the protector of the deity, and thus a semidivine figure in its own right.[46] The serpent's principal distinction, however, was its possession of wisdom. Notice the intentional blurring of a demarcation between creator and creature in this scene. The perceptiveness of the serpent came from the fact that it, too, possessed divine wisdom. Just so, it perceived an affinity between itself as *'ārûm* and primeval humankind as *'ărûmmîm*. This would account for its urging of humankind to eat from the wisdom tree, as a kind of "divine right." (Put in psychological terms, the serpent is a projection of humankind's own illegitimate aspiration to be divine.) In any case, *'ārûm* and *'ărûmmîm* turn out to be connected. By the end of this story both will have to undergo further delimitation so that the divine prerogatives of the Creator and the limitations of creaturehood are properly defined. But I am getting ahead of myself.

On one level Yahweh God's statement, that eating of the tree of knowledge of good and evil would result in death, can be understood as the truth. The humans did die after eating, though not immediately nor as a direct result of their action of eating. On a more literal level, however, Yahweh God's statement is false. The question arises whether the deity was lying or was mistaken about the outcome. Earlier in the discussion of *Adapa* I suggested, on the assumption that this god was desirous of preserving immortality for the gods alone, that the god Ea deliberately led Adapa astray in advising him not to eat or drink anything offered him in heaven, saying these would be "the bread of death" and "the water of death." Certainly mythology contains ample evidence of gods lying. But in the case of Genesis 3, I am inclined to think that the Yahwist intended to portray Yahweh as innocently mistaken. This would certainly fit the Yahwist's portrait of the Creator thus far, as naive about the outcome of his creation. It also fits the typology of *Atrahasis*, after which the Yahwist broadly patterned his story. And *Atrahasis* portrays the gods as being naive about how their experiment with humans would turn out.

The protohuman couple violated the prohibition and ate the fruit of the tree of knowledge. As the serpent had predicted, they did acquire wisdom and actually became "like gods." Even the deity had to acknowledge this as fact: "Indeed, humankind has become like one of us[47] in knowing good and evil" (3:22). As a story of origins this scene is highly suggestive. It underscores the fact that in the area of intelligence and understanding, and perhaps even in moral decision, humans are more godlike than animallike. What it means to be human has become clearer. But the demarcation between humankind and deity is still blurred at this point.

The Yahwist's dependence upon *Atrahasis* is further evident in the scenes about human sin and its consequences. In *Atrahasis* the gods had not anticipated that humankind would carry on in the spirit of the rebel god from whose flesh and blood primitive human beings were created. In the Yahwist's version the deity had not anticipated the extent to which humankind, animated with his own spirit, would rebel and overreach its limits. In both stories the divine king attempted to deal with the new problems by measures that prove to be less than adequate. In *Atrahasis* Enlil attempted to decimate the rebels by sending various killers such as plague, drought, and famine. In Genesis Yahweh drove the humans forth from Eden so that they lost access to the tree of life and ultimately died. In both stories the rebellion (sin) continues to spread nonetheless, and eventually the divine king attempts to find a definitive solution in the sending of a flood.

The genius of the Yahwist is once again apparent in the manner in which he departs from his model. In *Atrahasis* the human rebellion is hardly more than stated through symbol; the cries of rebellion kept the divine king from sleeping.[48] In contrast, the Yahwist develops with great psychological insight what is involved in rebellion against the divine sovereign. In rejecting the sovereignty of the Creator, humankind also rejected the implicit order in creation ordained by its Creator. Harmony is totally disrupted: harmony between Creator and creatures, harmony between humans and their environment, even harmony among the humans themselves. This disruption of the Creator's ordained order is signaled in the series of curses that follow. Not only the serpent but all animals fall under the curse: "Cursed are you *more than* all beasts and *more than* all living things of the field" (3:14). The full extent of the rupture in the order of creation is manifest in the curse that falls upon "the ground," that prime matter out of which both animals and humankind are taken and out of which plant life grows (3:17–19). The ground will henceforth be more resistant to cultivation for food. In a sense, the creative power of the deity has been negated; the ground slipped back closer to its precreation state as desert, where life cannot be sustained. The image of reversal of creation continued into the final clause of the cursing of the ground. Humans must revert to the dust, that dry primeval matter from which they were molded. The final scene effectively sealed this image. Humankind was driven from the garden and cherubim posted to guard against reentry.

The initial phase of creation had not ended in total failure, however. The definition of humankind had been clarified to some extent. They were a species unto themselves, neither animals nor gods, but with affinities to both. Henceforth they must go their separate ways.

TOWARD A SOLUTION

Now on their own, outside the divine garden, the first of their acts was directed toward propagation of the species. In

Atrahasis the mother-goddess, wise Mami, had been credited with being the creator of humankind (I.193–194). As she, with Ea's help, finished the task of giving birth to the seven original pairs of humans Mami exclaimed with joy, "*I* have created, my hands have made it" (I.289). Since his Yahwistic faith excluded the possibility of the creator having a consort, the Yahwist transformed the mother-goddess role into the first task for Eve, "the mother of all that lives" (3:20). If one recalls that Mami needed the help of the god Ea in performing her task, then Mami's exclamation of joy is paralleled exactly in Eve's exaltation over the first ever birth of a human: "I have created man with Yahweh's help" (4:1).[49]

As was the Yahwist's wont, he continued to flesh out his story with scenes that are not found in his Mesopotamian sources. Whether the Cain and Abel story (4:1–16) and the Lamech story (4:17–24) were original with the Yahwist or derived from some other source is uncertain. Whatever their origin, these stories follow the general theme of *Atrahasis* in that the first humans continued steadfast in their open rebellion against their divine sovereign and against their ordained role as servants of the gods. Abel, the faithful servant whose offering was acceptable to Yahweh, is murdered by his brother Cain, who did not make an appropriate offering to the deity.[50] Creation is undone just a bit more as "the ground" is further "cursed" in being forced to drink the blood—that is, the life—of the pious. The image of a widening gulf between creator and humankind is exquisitely imaged in Cain's punishment. Cain is forced to wander further still away from "the ground" of Eden and, consequently, from Yahweh as well (4:14, 16). With Lamech the revolt against the Creator's ordained order has reached epidemic proportions. Whereas Cain was to have been avenged sevenfold should anyone kill him, Lamech boasts of avenging a mere bruise with a seventy-sevenfold indiscriminate bloodbath of adults and children alike.

In *Atrahasis* the "sin" of humankind was portrayed, apparently, as cyclic, though endemic to the species. The text of the myth is ill preserved precisely at this point in the narrative. But it would appear that there was a periodic recrudescence of the same basic revolt against the divine sovereign, and that at each recrudescence the divine sovereign attempted to suppress the revolt by reducing the human population through a new tactic such as plague, drought, and famine. Each destruction was followed by temporary relief, until the earth was again repopulated and the rebellion broke out anew. The decision to send the flood was an act of desperation, to end the rebellion once and for all.

The Yahwist painted the picture somewhat differently. He portrayed the divine sovereign as more forbearing, on the one hand, and the sin of humankind as continually snowballing and its consequences becoming more grave with each new generation, on the other hand. Consequently, the Creator is finally forced to do something about the problem when the sin of humankind reaches such a magnitude that order in the divine realm itself is threatened.

The momentous event that finally triggered the catastrophe of the flood in the Yahwist's version is told in Genesis 6:1–4.[51] It is described in terms that are most unusual for the biblical tradition:

> Now it happened, when humankind began to be numerous on the face of the ground and daughters were born to them, that the sons of the gods saw how beautiful the human daughters were and they took the choicest ones as wives for themselves. Thereupon Yahweh said, "My spirit shall not reside in humankind forever. Surely he is flesh and his lifetime shall be (limited to) a hundred and twenty years." It was at that time, and afterward, that the Nephilim appeared on earth—when the sons of the gods went into the human daughters and they bore offspring for them. These were the fabled warriors of ancient time.

The origin and function of this strange passage have long puzzled scholars. But once again, new light is cast on these problems by the similarities to be found in *Atrahasis*.[52] In this Babylonian myth the onset of the antediluvian human revolt against the divine sovereign is described thus: "Twelve hundred years had not yet transpired, when the country expanded and the peoples became many" (I.352–353). The Yahwist's statement here that the climactic incident occurred "when humankind began to be numerous" is too similar to be mere coincidence. He must be consciously patterning his story on the Babylonian forerunner.

There are other indications, as well, that the Yahwist has reworked the Babylonian story to fit his own composition and audience. Yahweh's decision to decrease the life span of humankind was an attempt to squelch a "sin" that involved both human and divine participation. Moreover, the author intimates that the problem was compounded by the divine spirit abiding in humankind, hence Yahweh's decision to restrict the residence of "my spirit" in them to 120 years maximum. This was a drastic reduction of "life" since, even without access to the tree of life, the antediluvian humans were accustomed to live unhumanly long lives.[53] The limiting of an individual's lifespan at a maximum of 120 years is not found in *Atrahasis*. However, a recently published bilingual (Sumerian and Akkadian) text from Emar also gives 120 years as the upper limit for human beings:

> The days of the human-being are approaching;
> Day to day they verily decrease,
> Month after month they verily decrease,
> Year and year they verily decrease!
> One hundred twenty years (are) the years of humankind
>   —verily it is their *bane*(?);
> (This is so) from the day that humanity exists until
>   today![54]

It would appear that at this point the Yahwist has imported a traditional West Semitic literary topos into his story.

In *Atrahasis* the human rebellion was rooted in the fact that humankind, fashioned from the flesh and blood of the slain rebel god, had inherited his divine "spirit":

> From (the god's) flesh and blood
> Let Nintu[55] mix clay.
> Let god and human
> Be thoroughly mixed together in the clay,
> That we may hear the drum for the rest of time.
> In the flesh of the god (his) spirit shall remain.

> Let (Nintu) instruct him while alive about his sign.
> So that it not be forgotten the spirit shall remain.
>
> (I.210–217)

The rebellious divine spirit beating within the human breast was the source of the problem. It would appear that at first Enlil merely sought to limit the numbers of humankind. Plague, drought, and famine—unlike the flood—are not tactics designed to annihilate humankind completely. Accordingly, whether Enlil in *Atrahasis* or Yahweh in Genesis, the deity's initial reaction was to limit the rebellion on earth by diminishing the divine spirit within humankind.

If this line of reasoning is correct, then there is no need to search further for the Yahwist's source for this odd passage in Genesis 6:1–4. The Yahwist himself created it by rewording Babylonian precedents into an Israelite garb. Moreover, the explanation for the birth of the Nephilim is now obvious. The Nephilim, mentioned here and in Numbers 23:33, apparently were legendary antediluvian[56] giants reputed in Canaanite lore to be ferocious warriors.[57] They were, to the Yahwist's mind, a perfect translation for the antediluvian generations of *Atrahasis*. In this Mesopotamian myth the original generation created by Ea and Mami were not ordinary humans but rather *lullû* (I.195). The term *lullû* is used only in mythic texts and only in reference to the first created humans—what I have been calling protohumans—and to Enkidu in his original condition before he "became human."[58] No physical description of these protohumans is given either in *Atrahasis* or in the derivative passage in *Enuma elish*. But presumably they were conceived to be much like the *lullû* Enkidu described in *Gilgamesh*. In his original prehuman condition Enkidu was characterized as an awesome sight indeed. He was created specially by the gods to be a worthy foe for the mighty Gilgamesh, himself two-thirds divine and only one-third human, the hero of many superhuman feats. The hunter who first glimpsed Enkidu was so awed by the sight that he nearly died of fright (*Gilg*. I.45–50). Later the hunter described what he had witnessed as being "the mightiest in the land," with strength like that of the great high god Anu himself (I.iii.34).

Now an interesting detail about the origin of these *lullû* is that in both *Atrahasis* (I.249–305 and parallels) and *Gilgamesh* (I.i.30–35) they are depicted as a special creation of the god Ea through the agency of the mother-goddess. She not only molds them from clay but also in some way conceives them and even goes through a process of ritual gestation and birthing so as to bring the *lullû* into being. This detail from the Babylonian myth very likely inspired the Yahwist's description of the birth of the Nephilim. Just as the Yahwist earlier had turned the mother-goddess's role as the creator of humankind over to a human woman (Eve), so here also the Yahwist remodels the mother-goddess's role into one of human agency, namely "the daughters of humankind" (*hā-ʾādām*). But the Nephilim, although now born of human mothers, still bear resemblance to their Babylonian prototypes in that they retain their divine paternal origins.

In *Atrahasis* it was the continuing revolt of the offspring of this primeval "union" that brought on the flood. In the Yahwist's version the offspring of this "union" were themselves the symbol of that intolerable human propensity to sin that triggered the flood: "And Yahweh saw that the wickedness of humankind was great in the land and that every impulse of the reckoning of his mind was evil only, always!" (Gen. 6:5). The Yahwist's deity reluctantly concluded that he had made a mistake and so determined to "exterminate humankind which I created from the face of the ground" (Gen. 6:7).

Ever since George Smith's discovery in the nineteenth century of a Mesopotamian version of the flood story, biblical scholars have recognized that the biblical flood story was in some way dependent upon its Mesopotamian counterpart. Details such as the seven-day grace period in which to build the ark, the flood hero taking aboard his family and representative animals, the multiple sending out of birds toward the end of the ordeal, and finally the offering of a fragrant sacrifice to the deity or deities immediately upon disembarking from the ark-boat, all point to literary dependency. However, as long as our knowledge of the Babylonian flood story was limited to *Gilgamesh* Tablet XI and older Sumerian prototypes, it was easy for biblical scholars to assert that the biblical version bore only superficial resemblance to Mesopotamian versions. But since the publication in 1965 of major new portions of the *Atrahasis* myth it has been necessary to reevaluate the relationship of the biblical stories to their Mesopotamian counterparts. Nonetheless, early studies of *Atrahasis* missed the point of the flood, claiming that the flood was due to the capriciousness of the king god, who decreed the flood for the frivolous reason that he was unable to sleep because of excessive noise generated by an overpopulated earth. But as pointed out in chapter 1, that interpretation cannot be correct. Rather, *Atrahasis*, like Genesis after it, posits that the flood was caused by human "sin." Indeed, nowhere did the Yahwist follow his Babylonian model more closely than at this juncture in his story.

Like the pious flood hero Atrahasis, Noah is depicted as a "just" man, that is, in biblical idiom, one who displays the correct human posture vis-à-vis God. Although neither tradition says so explicitly, the creator in each case (Ea and Yahweh, respectively) apparently saved a pious remnant in the hopes of starting over on a better foundation the second time around.

But this time the deity was much the wiser because of his first, naive attempt at creating a dutiful humanity. *Atrahasis* had concluded with the gods decreeing additional "human regulations" (*uṣurāt niši*), which greatly restricted the vitality of postdiluvian humankind so that it might never again overreach its legitimate limits and aspire to divine status. Yahweh imposed similar limitations.[59] The postdiluvian world was to be populated with a vastly different breed of humans. Not only were they much shorter lived, but also their semidivine autonomy had been curbed. Never again would humankind be allowed to challenge the Creator's sovereignty.

And with this point the goal of the Yahwist's primeval "history" has been reached. At long last the definition of humankind is complete. An effective demarcation between the divine and the human realms has been established. There can no longer be any doubt that humankind is subordinate to the divine sovereign. This point is tellingly made in the final scene—also borrowed from *Atrahasis*—of Noah, the "just" hero of the flood story from whom the earth will be repopulated, dutifully offering sacrifice to the deity.

> Noah built an altar to Yahweh. He took some of every
> clean beast and some of every clean bird and he offered
> them up on the altar. Yahweh inhaled the sweet aroma;
> Yahweh said to himself, "I will not continue cursing any-
> more the ground because of humankind, for the impulse
> of humankind, from youth on, is evil. I will not continue
> smiting every living thing as I have done. For the duration
> of the earth sowing and harvesting and frost and heat and
> summer and winter and day and night shall not cease."
> (Gen. 8:20–22)

Noah, like Atrahasis, fulfills the role originally ordained for
humans, that is, of provisioning the deity. Only now he does it
from outside rather than from inside the divine garden, as befitting his newly defined human status. Noah's offering, then, is
symbolic of a humankind that has at last accepted its proper
posture vis-à-vis the deity, namely, as servant of the god(s).

At the same time the Creator has grown a long way from his
initial naïveté. Of necessity Yahweh has learned to "fine tune"
his creation. Moreover, he has experienced firsthand the human
capacity both for good and bad. And that experience has taught
him that even under the best of circumstances, humankind will
never be completely subservient to the deity nor completely
obedient to its vocation, that the human impulse, from its very
inception, tends to evil. But on the balance, as in *Atrahasis*, the
deity decided to reconcile himself to a flawed creation.[60] He
bound himself under oath never again to curse the soil because
of humankind. Like the bow in the P account (Gen. 9:12–16)
and the mother-goddess's fly necklace in the Mesopotamian
flood story (*Atra.* III.v.46–vi.4; *Gilg.* XI.163–165), the permanency of the earth with its seasonal cycles serves as the symbol
that the Creator henceforth remains committed to his creation,
flawed though it may be.[61]

With this conclusion, the Yahwist brought his primeval "history" to an end. It is commonplace to think of the primeval
history as extending through Genesis 11. But this is incorrect.
The Yahwist, like *Atrahasis*, concludes the primeval period
with the story of the flood.[62] To bridge the gap between the
primeval period and the Israelite patriarchs, the Yahwist created another period, "the World History."[63] However, that is

another subject and so we may conveniently conclude our investigation of the Yahwist at this point as well.

CONCLUSION

It is surely no accident that the Yahwistic creation narratives in Genesis share many motifs in common with other ancient Near Eastern creation stories, on the one hand, and are uniquely Israelite in their religious perspective, on the other hand. The obvious explanation for this situation is that the author was truly a literary genius who brought together disparate mythic themes and worked them into an original composition that reflected so authentically the basic Yahwistic religious values that the Israelite Yahwistic community adopted this new composition as an authentic statement of their religion. That is to say, the Yahwist's "epic" became Israel's myth of origins.

The Yahwist consciously drew together elements from both *Atrahasis* and *Gilgamesh* and other mythic traditions for his new epic. As far as we know, these motifs were not previously put together in this fashion. Those who argue for two originally distinct traditions behind the Eden story miss the point that the Yahwist's story was unique and original. Granted that the Yahwist used earlier materials. But his was a new, deliberate creation designed to meet the needs of his Yahwistic faith. As is entirely to be expected, the Yahwist shared a common cultural world with his ancient Near Eastern neighbors. But it is the uniqueness of his vision over against that of his neighbors that the biblical tradition affirms.

If the cultural traditions of the time suggested a deity who was so like one of us—so immanent—as to be almost human, the Yahwist elevated this anthropomorphism to a virtue. His portrait of the deity revealed a god so authentically "human" that he grew in stature and character through adversity. Yahweh God not only learned from his mistakes as Creator but actually grew to love his creatures through his dealings with them. This last feature of Yahweh's character, adumbrated in the primeval period, will emerge fully only later in the Yahwist's epic. The humankind of the postprimeval period will exhibit the same proclivity to rebellion against the divine will as before. The impiety of Ham (9:20–27) and the hubris of the builders of the tower of Babel (11:1–9) are indicative of this fact. But the Israelites themselves, the covenanted elect to whom this epic was directed, are no better. In the Yahwist's portrayal Abram/Abraham, despite being specially chosen by Yahweh, failed to trust his god in a famine-stricken land (Genesis 12). Abram preferred to trust in his own devices and leave the land of promise. When Abram's own lying machinations failed him in Egypt, he was rescued by a caring deity. True, Abraham did go on to become a great model of faith (Gen. 15:1–6; 22:1–14), but his descendants failed to heed his example. Like the younger Abram, Jacob lacked faith in Yahweh and attempted to secure the blessing through deception (Gen. 27:1–45). Like Cain, the patriarchs out of jealousy were willing to kill their own brother (Genesis 37).[64] The pattern extended to the generation of the exodus as well.

Despite the great display of power with which Yahweh forced the Egyptians to let the Israelites go, the Israelites never fully committed themselves to Yahweh. The point is made time and again in the book of Exodus. One of the Yahwist's more poignant examples comes at the conclusion to the deliverance at the Red Sea. He tells how the Israelites watched as Yahweh rescued them by drowning their Egyptian pursuers in the sea. Duly impressed, "the people feared Yahweh and they trusted in Yahweh and in his servant Moses" (Ex. 14:31). But the shallowness of their faith was revealed three days later when they came to a camping place in the wilderness where the water was too "bitter" to drink and they complained against Yahweh and his servant Moses (Ex. 15:22b–25). One would have expected more from a people who had previously witnessed both the changing of the Nile to blood and the routing of the Egyptians in the sea. (The supreme irony of the Israelites' lack of faith in their god who both subdues the sea and rules the waters will be even more obvious after reading the next chapters.) The way to Sinai is literally a story of rebellion after rebellion by the Israelites against Yahweh. Nonetheless, Yahweh entered into covenant with the Israelites at Sinai (Exodus 19–24) and even reestablished that covenant when the Israelites broke it through their apostasy in worshiping the golden calf (Exodus 32–34).[65]

And lest anyone think that the pattern will ever change, the Yahwist relates how even after the Israelites left Sinai and made their way to the Promised Land, they continued to repeat the very same rebellion against Yahweh and Moses as before Sinai. (Cf. esp. Numbers 11 with Exodus 16 and Num. 20:2–13 with Ex. 17:1–7.)

In the Yahwist's telling, then, the primeval story established the essential relationship between creator and creature, between deity and humankind, which was to become the paradigm for subsequent generations of believers. The Creator may have experienced initial disappointment with the work of his hands. But having overcome that initial disappointment, the Creator learned to accept his handiwork with all its flaws. Or to use the language of parenting, Yahweh is portrayed as a parent who has bonded thoroughly with his child; he overlooks obvious defects in the child and accepts it as it is, as his own. To a faith community deeply conscious of its own defects—its rebellions against its Maker and its frequent lapses of faith with its covenanted deity—the story of Yahweh God who never gives up on his creation, including his elected people, is indeed a story worthy of celebration. It is a myth of the highest order.

Of course, the Yahwist "created" his own myth by a process of mythopoeic speculation similar to that we observed in the previous chapter at work among the Babylonian theologian-poets. That such a process was also operative in ancient Israel should occasion no surprise, since Israel shared the same general cultural milieu as its neighbors. What may be surprising is that the Yahwist's myth should have been adopted as the basic myth of Israel. But then again, why should this surprise us? Part of the Yahwist's genius was in capturing both Israel's own self-image and the image of an "engaged" deity proclaimed frequently elsewhere in Israel's sacred literature.

Chapter 3

◆

THE PRIESTLY REVISION
OF THE CREATION MYTH

◆

The primeval story now contained in Genesis is quite changed from the Yahwist's primeval myth discussed in chapter 2. Here, as elsewhere in the first four books of the Pentateuch, another stratum of tradition, namely the so-called Priestly source (P), has been spliced into and around the Yahwist's tradition.[1] Although it is customary to speak of the whole of Genesis 1–11 as "primeval history," P (like J) concluded his[2] primeval period with the flood and the making of the Noachite covenant (9:1–17), as will be evident later. In this chapter, then, I shall be concerned principally with the priestly materials within Genesis 1–9.

How the J and P literary strands came to be bound together in Genesis is a moot question. Defenders of the traditional Documentary Hypothesis generally hold that P once existed as a separate tradition and was, originally, intended as a polemic against J. A redactor (or a series of redactors) is credited with having joined these sources together—and in a somewhat clumsy fashion at that, since the seams are so clearly visible. This approach does not adequately account for the presence of themes and literary devices that cut across the boundaries of the respective traditions. Moreover, it tends to slight the shape of the canonical text. Partially in reaction to the inadequacies of the Documentary Hypothesis approach, it has become fashionable within the past decade to ignore such source critical questions as either unsolvable or inconsequential. Instead, scholars increasingly read Genesis synchronically, that is, as a single meaningful and coherent text. While this approach has the advantage of giving greater attention to the shape of the received (canonical) text, it fails to account adequately for definite seams and contradictory passages within the text.[3]

In chapter 2 I expressed my preference for a diachronic approach that posits that the Priestly Writer was the author-editor who revised the J epic and at the same time added new materials of his own. This revision was so sweeping and substantive that the priestly edition deserves to be considered a new work, and the Priestly Writer may be regarded as "the author" of the Tetrateuch. Such a theory both takes seriously the differences between the J and the P strata and at the same time accounts for the thematic and literary coherence within the received text, which numerous recent commentators have noted. In this chapter I will examine how the priestly additions within Genesis 1–11 changed both the storyline and the meaning of the primeval myth first penned by the Yahwist in order to meet the new existential faith needs of his community. Numerous clues in the text reveal that P wrote out of the experience of the Babylonian exile and that his purpose was to restate "Yahwistic" beliefs in such a way as to bolster the sagging faith of a disillusioned exilic community in the face of an apparently superior Babylonian claim about the universal sovereignty of Marduk, patron deity of Babylon.[4]

I proceed on the assumption, first, that the Priestly Writer accepted the storyline established by the Yahwist as the basis of his own composition.[5] That P deliberately set out to revise and supplement the Yahwist's epic tradition is clear. His motivation is not completely transparent. Perhaps he agreed with the basic thrust of the Yahwistic tradition. Or perhaps this older epic tradition was so well established that P found it impossible to set it aside altogether. In any case, P judged it not entirely satisfactory for his audience and so thoroughly revised it as to make it an entirely different story. This is nowhere more evident than in the primeval cycle within Genesis 1–9.

The first and most obvious change is the placement of a new creation account at the head of the work (Gen 1:1–2:3). The perspective of this account is radically different from that of J. P posits creation as transpiring within a seven-day structure, with God working during the first six days and resting on the seventh. At the conclusion of each activity the Creator—always referred to as Elohim—surveys his work and finds it "good." The precreation condition was not that of a dry wasteland but that of a lightless and lifeless watery abyss. The Creator's activity consisted not of producing a verdant garden from a waterless wasteland but of drawing dry ground out of that lightless and lifeless watery abyss. And he does not bring about vegetation by "planting trees" or make animals and humankind by "shaping clay"; rather he "creates" all things merely by the command of his word. Finally, the creation of woman is not an afterthought but an integral part of the Creator's design. Humankind was intended to be "male and female" right from the start—and this "in the image of Elohim [God]" no less!

With such pronounced differences, it is difficult to believe other than that the Priestly Writer intended his creation account as a corrective to the Yahwist's version. Commentators are fond of noting that the P account dispenses with some of J's more blatant anthropomorphisms, such as the Yahweh God creating by modeling clay or walking in the garden or accidentally discovering the humans' sin. Granted that P's Creator is more transcendent, still P does not really seem to be scandalized by anthropomorphisms per se. His own account contains numerous instances: "God said," "God saw," humankind created in God's "image," "God rested," and so forth. Indeed, it is difficult to conceive how one can speak about the deity without using anthropomorphic metaphors.[6] The issue is not anthropomorphisms, but the adequacy of conception of the God being conveyed by the metaphors. P was obviously unhappy with some aspects of the J account and set out to reform it according to his own theological conception. By placing a new frame around the J stories, P gave them an entirely new look. But like his Yahwistic predecessor who had borrowed heavily from *Atrahasis* and other Babylonian myths, P manufactured his new frame in part from prior mythic tradition, in this case the Babylonian creation myth *Enuma elish*.[7]

CREATION AS A BATTLE AGAINST CHAOS

In a pioneering work written at the end of the nineteenth century, Herman Gunkel pointed out that the P creation account had close similarities to the Babylonian myth *Enuma elish*.[8] Gunkel used the term *Chaoskampf*, or "battle against chaos," to describe this mythic typology now generally referred to as the Combat Myth. "Chaos" is of course a term borrowed from Greek mythology, but it fits well the Semitic conception of the precreation state of being. As Gunkel reconstructed the basic outline of the *Chaoskampf*-type creation myth, the creator deity had to defeat in battle his archfoe, usually depicted as a watery monster or dragon, and from its carcass construct the various parts of the cosmos. Allusions to this Combat Myth are to be found in many parts of the Bible, from Genesis to Revelation. But in Gunkel's day the best—indeed, virtually the only—complete exemplar of this myth was *Enuma elish*. Consequently, Gunkel concluded that the Priestly Writer knew *Enuma elish* and had borrowed much of his cosmology from this Babylonian work. One of the bits of evidence to which Gunkel pointed was the fact that in Genesis 1:2 the precreation condition of "the earth" was described as a dark chaotic water mass called *těhôm*, usually translated as "the deep" but which might more accurately be translated as "the Abyss." The Hebrew word *těhôm* is cognate to Akkadian *ti'āmat*. "Ti'amat," which literally means "ocean, sea," is the name of Marduk's archfoe in *Enuma elish*. Thus both Genesis and *Enuma elish* opened with an unorganized primeval ocean enveloped in darkness. Creation came about through a division of this primeval ocean and organizing the watery mass so that dry land might appear.

Approximately a half century later Alexander Heidel restudied the question and found definite similarities in outline between Genesis 1:1–2:3 and *Enuma elish*, which he expressed in the following diagram.[9]

ENUMA ELISH	GENESIS
Divine spirit and cosmic matter are coexistent and co-eternal	Divine spirit creates cosmic matter and exists independently of it
Primeval chaos; Ti'amat enveloped in darkness	The earth a desolate waste, with darkness covering the deep (*těhôm*)

Light emanating from the gods	Light created
The creation of the firmament	The creation of the firmament
The creation of dry land	The creation of dry land
The creation of [humankind]	The creation of [humankind]
The gods rest and celebrate	God rests and sanctifies the seventh day

Nonetheless, Heidel concluded that the parallels were so inexact that the question of actual literary dependency must remain inconclusive. Others, however, have been less hesitant to affirm that P did know the Babylonian work. Ephraim Speiser, for example, claimed that Heidel had understated the evidence. Speiser maintained that the precreation situation in Genesis was the same as in *Enuma elish*; in both the divine spirit and cosmic matter were coexistent and coeternal.[10] Still other scholars have resisted a conclusion of direct literary dependency of Genesis upon *Enuma elish*. They note that the Semitic Combat Myth was widespread in the ancient world and is attested in different versions among the Canaanites, the Egyptians, and the Hittites.[11] In particular, the Ugaritic Baal myth, wherein the Canaanite storm god Baal defeats Yam (literally "Sea"), has close affinities with numerous passages elsewhere in the Hebrew Bible that speak of Yahweh's battle against the sea.[12]

Nevertheless, the case for the priestly dependency specifically upon *Enuma elish* rather than some other version of the Combat Myth is not easily dismissed. Unlike the situation elsewhere in the Bible (e.g., the Psalms and Job) where allusions to God's battle with the sea/dragon seem to depend upon the Canaanite (Ugaritic) version of the Combat Myth, the peculiar combination of creation motifs and vocabulary found in Genesis 1:1–2:3 is actually closer to that of *Enuma elish* than to the Ugaritic Baal myth.[13] In addition to the similar outlines noted by Heidel and Speiser, one finds in both texts a stress upon the *power of the word* of the (chief) deity: Marduk controls the destinies, making entities appear or disappear by his word alone; in Genesis 1 God makes creation appear by his mere word. Also, both texts stress the unique creation of humankind (admittedly, though, for different reasons).[14] The Baal myth does not speak of creation of the world or of humankind. In Canaanite mythology El rather than Baal was considered the creator.[15] Moreover, in the Baal myth humankind is assumed to be previously created.[16] Also not to be ignored is the similar function in P and *Enuma elish* of the sign of the bow placed in the sky, which will be discussed shortly.

But most important is the linking of divine rest (Gen. 2:1–3) with creation. As I have shown elsewhere,[17] common to all versions of the Semitic Combat Myth is a motif of divine rest. After his victory over his archfoe, the chaos monster, the creator deity builds a palace (or temple) from which he rules the cosmos. (In the ancient Near East a temple was not so much a place of public worship as the palace of the deity; the word for "temple" was frequently the same as the word for "palace.") As the deity's home, this palace was also a place of leisure and rest. Indeed, the portrayal of the creator as resting after his victory over his foe is an ancient Near Eastern metaphor for that deity's status as the supreme ruler of heaven and earth. The deity can afford to lay down his weapons and relax because the enemy has been subdued and the deity's status as the divine sovereign is unchallenged. In the Canaanite Baal myth the motif of rest is barely discernible, overshadowed by the building of Baal's palace. In *Enuma elish*, however, rest is a prominent theme. Marduk himself rested after his victory over Ti'amat. Moreover, he created humankind so the other gods might have the leisure appropriate to their divine status and have freedom from the labor of providing their own food. In gratitude the gods built the temple-palace Esagila in Babylon for Marduk, from which he should rule over them and the cosmos. Marduk thereupon literally hung up his weapons. He placed his warbow in the sky where, as the bow star (probably Sirius), it would shine forever as a sign of Marduk's victory and divine kingship. In a further gesture of kingship, Marduk declared his palace to be a place of rest not only for himself but for the other gods as well. The prominence of rest in the conclusion of the priestly account of creation thus finds its closest parallel in *Enuma elish*.[18] (P reserved the sign of the bow until after the flood, however, for reasons to be discussed later.)

Some scholars have tried to downplay the presence of mythic themes in Genesis 1:1–2:3, saying that any hint of a battle between the creator and primeval sea has been thoroughly suppressed in this biblical passage.[19] It is true that the more blatant polytheistic notions have been suppressed, in keeping with the norms of Israelite religion and its emphasis upon the exclusive worship of Yahweh. But the image of creation as victory over an unruly primeval sea is still clearly visible. Confirmation may be found in Psalm 8, which is generally acknowledged to have close affinities with the P creation account. Psalm 8:2 says of the Creator, "You built a fortress for your habitation, having silenced your adversaries, the foe and the avenger."[20] The "fortress" is the temple-palace of Yahweh from which he rules. Behind Genesis 1:1–2:3 lies the same conception of the victorious divine warrior who retires to his palace to a leisurely kingship after subduing the foe.

Yahweh's "resting-place" was his temple on Mount Zion. But as was the case with Marduk's temple in Babylon and Baal's temple on Mount Zaphon, Yahweh's earthly temple was conceived as the physical manifestation of the deity's mythic-heavenly temple-palace. So despite an awareness of the theological problems inherent in claiming that God dwells in a house built by human hands (e.g., 1 Kings 8:27), royal Davidic theology did not hesitate to claim that the temple in Jerusalem was authentically Yahweh's chosen residence, his eternal "resting place":

> For Yahweh has chosen Zion,
>   he desired it for his residence
> "This is my resting place for ever;
>   here I will reside because I have desired it."
>   (Ps. 132:13–14; see also v. 8)

In Exodus 15:17 also the theme of Yahweh's victory over his foes is linked with the designation of Zion as Yahweh's resting place.

Finally, there is the evidence of Jeremiah 31:35–37. This Jeremian oracle is a twofold assurance to a disheartened exilic community that Yahweh has not abandoned the covenant with his people Israel. This twofold assurance is said to be grounded in the irrevocable word of the Creator.

> Thus has spoken Yahweh,
> Who established the sun a light by day,
> The ordering of moon and stars as light by night,
> Who stills the sea when its waves rage[21]—
> Yahweh of the (heavenly) Armies is his name:
> "If this order could ever fail in my presence
>   —Oracle of Yahweh—
> Then Israel's seed would also cease
> From being a people in my presence for all time."
>
> Thus has spoken Yahweh:
> "If the heavens above could be measured
> Or the underworld's foundations below be fathomed,
> Then I, too, would reject the whole of Israel's seed
> Because of all that they have done
>   —Oracle of Yahweh."

This twofold assurance likely is literarily dependent upon the received version of Genesis in that the first assurance seems to be derived from Genesis 1:14–17 (P) and the second from Genesis 8:22 (J).[22] Because Jeremiah 31:35 links creation with the implicit Combat Myth language about the subduing of the chaotic sea, it is clear that the author understood such motifs to be present or implied in his source. Clearly, then, the ancient readers understood Combat Myth motifs to be part and parcel of the Priestly Writer's creation account in Genesis 1:1–2:3. But it is another matter to determine from where P borrowed these motifs.

Without denying the influence of Canaanite mythic traditions upon P, mediated through Israel's common heritage with Canaan, the preceding considerations strongly suggest that the Priestly Writer also knew and utilized the Babylonian myth *Enuma elish* in writing his own composition. Indeed, the conclusion that the Priestly Writer wrote out of the experience of the Babylonian exile seems unavoidable. As is evident in much literature of the Hebrew Bible, the catastrophe of the Babylonian exile forced the Judahite exiles to reexamine their religious presuppositions and to rewrite, sometimes radically, their sacred literature.

It may also be, as often suggested, that the Priestly Writer's creation account is an implicit polemic against the Babylonian myth. As suggested by 2 Kings 18:28–19:37 [= Isa. 36:13–37:38], such polemics and counterpolemics were a common psychological strategem of the day in fighting against a national enemy. Certainly, the polemical attacks upon Babylon and her gods were common enough in other exilic compositions.[23] In this view P was attempting to bolster the shaken faith of his coreligionists. In the religious psychology of the ancient Near East, religion and politics were integrally linked. The defeat of Judah and the destruction of the temple in Jerusalem implied to many that the Babylonian god was more powerful than Yahweh. To others it implied that Yahweh had abandoned his chosen people to the enemy because they somehow had angered him. If the first group were right, then they had backed the wrong deity. If the second group were right, then the covenant whereby Yahweh was their God and they were his chosen people was now null and void. In either case the past religious traditions upon which Israel had relied were no longer of any use. The Priestly Writer not only had to convince his audience that their covenant with God remained intact but also that Yahweh truly was the creator and divine sovereign of the whole world.

But rather than a conscious polemic against *Enuma elish*, it is more likely that the Priestly Writer found the Combat Myth imagery better suited than the Eden story to convey his theological agenda. Certainly other exilic biblical writers used Combat Myth motifs to great effect. Nowhere is this more evident than in Isaiah 51:9–11, the so-called ode to Yahweh's arm. Here an exilic poet—known to the scholarly academy as "Deutero-Isaiah"—calls upon Yahweh to rouse himself from his rest and as in primeval times to slay the chaos monster anew.

Awake! Awake! Robe yourself in Power,
  O arm of Yahweh.
Awake as in primordial days,
  (the) primeval generations.
Is it not you who cleaves Rahab in pieces,
  who pierces the Sea-dragon?
Is it not you who dries up the Sea,
  the waters of the great Abyss (*tĕhôm*)
The one who makes the depths of the Sea a road
  for the redeemed to pass over?

In context this poem is part of a dialogue between the exiles and God. The exiles lament that God has no thought for his people. God answers with a series of divine assurances (51:12–16; 51:17–23; 52:1–2) that he has not forgotten his people but is even now in the process of returning them to their homeland.

The appeal in this passage to a tradition of God's saving events in the past as a motive for how God should act in the present crisis is instructive. God's salvific power is presented as most evident in two events: in his victory over the chaos monster at the creation of the world, and in the splitting of the (Red) Sea when he freed his people from Egypt. This is not a case of myth in one instance and history in the other (as I will show in the next chapter). Rather, the two are understood as essentially one and the same act of salvation. Just as Egypt and other foreign enemies could be viewed as historical manifestations of the power of chaos (see chapter 6), so also the exodus was seen as an extension of God's creative power. Just as God split the primeval sea to create dry land, so he split the sea again during the exodus from Egypt to create a special people for himself. But given the depths of the present crisis, the exiles might be forgiven for doubting whether all that ancient display of divine power was really relevant to their own existential situation. In calling upon Yahweh to "wake up," the exiles imply that Yahweh had retired prematurely to his "resting place." Far from being over, the battle against the chaos monster continues right into their own time in the person of the Babylonian marauders. With the temple razed and Jerusalem in ashes, it was obvious that the chaos monster was far from vanquished. But far from being a cry of despair, Isaiah 51:9–11 is actually an expression of Judah's continuing confidence in Yahweh as "her maker, who stretches out the heavens, who lays the foundations of the earth" (Isa. 51:13). Stung by the taunts of his captors, who claimed it was their god Marduk who slew the chaos monster and created the world, Deutero-Isaiah did not flinch at attributing these very powers to Yahweh. The recrudescence of chaos in the form of their Babylonian captors, therefore, need not be feared. The divine sovereign Yahweh is still very much in control, "stilling the sea when its waves rage" (Isa. 51:15).[24]

A similar picture emerges from Psalm 74, which also was composed during the Babylonian exile. With the images of the infidel Babylonian army razing Jerusalem and desecrating Yahweh's temple-palace on Mount Zion still fresh in his mind (vs. 2–8) the psalmist challenges Yahweh to act. Is not Babylonian havoc as much a defiance of divine sovereignty and a subversion of creation as the primordial battle with the seven-headed chaos monster?

> How long, O God, shall the enemy blaspheme?
>   Is the adversary to revile your name forever?
> Why do you restrain your hand?
>   your right hand remain idle inside your cloak?
> O God, my king from primeval times,
>   who works salvation in the middle of the earth,[25]
> It was you who broke apart[26] the sea by your might,
>   who smashed the heads of the dragon on the water.
> It was you who crushed the heads of Leviathan,
>   who gave him to the desert folk[27] as food.
> It was you who opened springs and brooks;
>   you who turned primordial rivers into dry land.
> To you belongs the day and the night as well;
>   it was you who established the moon and the sun.
> It was you who fixed the boundaries of the earth;
>   summer and winter, you created them.
>
>   (Ps. 74:10–17)

It would appear that the Combat Myth had particular appeal to the exiles. It allowed them to acknowledge that their world had been shattered without losing their faith in Yahweh as the supreme ruler of heaven and earth. Their own suffering was part of the cosmic struggle between creation and noncreation, between Yahweh God and the monster of chaos, between good and evil. Even though it may not have been apparent from the historical circumstances of their time, they could be confident of being on the side of the victor.

The Priestly Writer was right at home in this exilic mode of theologizing, and probably for the same reasons. Part of P's agenda was to assure his coreligionists that they had a future, however difficult to believe that might be in the present dark hour.

Whatever the specific source of his Combat Myth imagery, the Priestly Writer was thoroughly in control of his materials and shaped the myth to his own theological understanding. He downplayed the motif of an actual battle, probably for the same reason that he refused to call the sun and the moon and the stars by name. His audience was still so close to the polytheism of their ancient Near Eastern neighbors that the mere naming of things many considered to be gods might lend credence to a belief in their divinity. In 2 Kings 23:5, for example, we read of idolatrous priests who made offerings to the sun and moon (see also Deut. 4:19 and Ezek. 8:16). Consequently P reduced the "Abyss" (Gen. 1:2) to the raw material of creation; and "the great sea-dragon" (v. 21), like "the two great lights" that rule the day and the night, to a mere creature. The motif of the creator resting, however, he made the climax of his creation account. Stripped of its blatant polytheism, the motif of the creator resting evoked precisely the right theological message. With its ancient Near Eastern connotations of all things firmly under the control of the divine sovereign, the motif served as a guarantee that nothing happens apart from the divine will. The deity who in primordial time transforms the unruly waters of chaos into an ordered universe by the power of his word is the same deity who has sworn everlasting covenants with Noah (Gen. 9:8–17), with Abraham (Genesis 17), and last of all, with the Israelites at Sinai (Ex. 31:16–18). As the remnant of Israel, therefore, the Judahite exiles need not doubt that they have a future, since by divine calling Israel has a continuing mission to accomplish in this world.

THE FLOOD AS AN EXTENSION OF THE BATTLE AGAINST CHAOS

The ancients understood well that the myth was a statement about enduring realities. Human experience taught them that the ideals of a divinely ordered world were easily shattered by nihilistic, evil forces that daily threatened to snuff out meaningful life and existence.[28] The battle against the chaos was an eternal struggle. The Egyptian text known as "the Repulsing of the Dragon" tells how each day the sun god Re arises out of the primeval ocean Nun to repulse anew the dragon Apophis, thus daily dispelling darkness and chaos from the world.[29] The Babylonians celebrated an annual New Year Festival in honor of Marduk's kingship. At least during Neo-Babylonian times, *Enuma elish* was ritually recited during the course of the festival, intended perhaps to be as much a periodic renewal as a celebration of Marduk's primeval victory over Ti'amat. A prayer toward the end of *Enuma elish* suggests that Marduk's battle with Ti'amat was understood to be a perpetual conflict:

> May he vanquish Ti'amat, constrict and shorten her life.
> Until the last days of humankind, when even days have
> grown old,
> May she depart, not be detained, and ever stay away.
>
> (VII.132–134)

The Priestly Writer manipulated his primeval story to express the same basic concept. The flood story formed no part of the common Semitic Combat Myth. Even the Babylonian author of *Enuma elish* did not think to incorporate a flood scene into his myth, despite the fact that he appropriated other scenes from "the Babylonian flood story" of *Atrahasis* into his composition. However, under the Priestly Writer's skillful hands both the flood story and the battle against chaos are masterfully recomposed into an integrated new primeval myth. P reworked the older Yahwist's version of the flood to attribute the flood to a recrudescence of the power of chaos. Whereas in J the waters of the flood came from a forty-day deluge of rain (Gen. 7:4, 12; cf. 8:2b), in P the waters flooded the earth when the barriers placed by God to hold back the primeval ocean (1:6–7) broke:

"In Noah's six hundredth year, on the seventeenth day of the second month, on that very day all the sources of the great Abyss (*tĕhôm rabbâ*) split open and the windows of the heavens opened" (7:11). The use of nifal grammatical forms for the verbs "split" and "opened" suggests a "middle voice" rather than a passive. Thus the onslaught of the water resulted from a rupture in the firmament, rather than being directly caused by God.[30] The force of chaos was too great to be contained by the "firmament" and chaos once again overwhelmed dry land. In short, the good order imposed by the Creator was undone and the world reverted to chaos.

The point is tellingly made in Genesis 6:11–12: "Now the earth became corrupt (*wattiššāḥēt*) before God, and the earth was filled with violence (*ḥāmās*). And God observed the earth, and behold it was corrupt (*nišḥātâ*), because all flesh had corrupted (*hišḥît*) its behavior on the earth." The Priestly Writer attributes the flood to the fact that the face of the earth had become thoroughly polluted through the violence of its inhabitants. The P literary strand contains no intervening stories of sin. The reference must therefore be to the Yahwistic stories sandwiched between the P creation account and the flood, that is, to the stories of humankind's revolt against God in Eden, Cain's murder of his brother Abel, and Lamech's wanton slaughter of a youth merely for bruising him. P intended these stories to be read as evidence of a steadily increasing "violence" (*ḥāmās*) upon the face of the earth. The power of chaos gradually reinfiltrated the earth through human violence until eventually it overwhelmed creation. Once the good order ordained by the Creator was subverted, life itself was impossible. Thus chaos— or translated theologically, evil—was responsible for snuffing out life. God only confirmed what humans had brought upon themselves through their own violence.[31]

God proved himself to be the divine sovereign still, however, by once again subduing the primeval ocean. Reminiscent of the storm gods Baal and Marduk in their respective battles with Sea and Ti'amat, "God forced a wind across the earth so that the waters subsided and allowed the sources of the Abyss and the windows of the heavens to close up" (8:1b–2a). The victory over primeval ocean signaled first in Genesis 1:1–2:3 was once more confirmed. Echoes of the earlier scene are here heard again. The wind that subdues the water in 8:1 is apparently the same as "God's wind" that "hovered over the surface of the water" in 1:2 while God worked his creative transformation upon the Abyss. The Abyss itself is again contained and inhabitable land allowed once more to reappear. Creation of new life is unnecessary, of course, as all life forms were saved in the ark. But the command to populate the earth is issued again (9:1–7).

By now the author's method is transparent. He has recomposed both the Combat Myth and the Yahwist's primeval myth into another, completely original story. He used the battle against chaos as the skeleton of his story, but fleshed it out with the stories of the Yahwist's myth. In imitation of the storyline of his basic source, he split in two the story of the battle against primeval ocean, and in the process created a new story. By splitting the battle into two scenes he was able to reveal the two sides of chaos. The one is a metahistorical force of evil that stands outside of history but exerts a powerful negative influence upon human existence. The other is very much a historical reality, the proclivity of humankind to do violence to each other and so eliminate the divinely ordained order—even life itself—from the face of creation. The genius of the Priestly Writer was to reveal the interconnection of the two manifestations of chaos and then show the divine sovereign victorious over both. In the priestly perspective, the waters of the primeval ocean (Genesis 1) merge with the waters of the great flood (Genesis 6–8). If the battle had to be told in two scenes, so did creation. Only with the reestablishment of order and life after the flood was victory over the chaos-dragon assured and creation complete.

Once the literary method of the Priestly Writer is understood, one can discern why he detached the bow scene from its traditional setting and placed it as the final episode in the flood scene (9:8–17). In *Enuma elish* Marduk hung his warbow in the sky at the completion of his palace, following the slaying of Ti'amat. On this pattern one should have expected to find a similar scene within the context of Genesis 2:1–3. Instead, P held it in reserve until chapter 9. In P's retelling of the story, only at this point has it become clear that the myth of God's sovereignty also provides assurance against the threat of humans undoing their own world. (It is difficult to avoid reading this as an exilic composition, written to encourage a community tempted to give up hope that their world, shattered by the Babylonians, could ever be put back together.) As with the similar bow star in the Babylonian myth, the rainbow was conceived to be the warbow that the deity had used in his battle against the chaos monster. That the deity can now lay it aside—evident in its visibility just hanging there in the sky—was a comforting symbol of God's firm control over creation.[32]

For the Priestly Writer the hanging up of the bow signaled both the end of the primeval period and the beginning of the "historical" period. In this matter he was following the pattern of both of his sources. *Enuma elish* concluded—apart from the singing of Marduk's praises in his fifty titles—with the storm god hanging his bow in the sky. Also, the Yahwist had ended his primeval period with the flood story, as noted in the previous chapter. The Priestly Writer followed suit. By this point in the storyline the essential character of human existence has been established. What remained was to tell how humankind developed from the sons of Noah into the families of nations that populate the earth, and what is their relationship with God and to the chosen people.

Commentators usually posit a break between chapters 11 and 12, and describe Genesis 1–11 as "the Primeval History" and Genesis 12–Numbers 36 as "the Israelite History." But this was not P's design. He organized the "historical" period according to three covenants: (1) the Noachite covenant with all flesh (Gen. 9:8–17), (2) the Abrahamic covenant (Genesis 17), and (3) the Mosaic covenant (see Ex. 31:17). Each of these covenants is said to be an "everlasting covenant." The constituency of each successive covenant may be more restrictive than that of the preceding one, but all three were understood as enduring into the "present." The Noachite covenant belongs just as much to the "historical period" as the Abrahamic or the Mosaic covenants. Thus, P understood the demarcation between the primeval period and the present to occur at the advent of the first of these three concurrent, ongoing covenants.

A PERFECT CREATION

Another key to understanding the Priestly Writer's literary intentions is to be found in the concept of the goodness of God's creation, which runs like a leitmotif throughout Genesis 1. There is certainly a deliberateness in the author's method. Six times the phrase "How good!" (*kî ṭôb*) is repeated. Upon completion of each major work, the author has God survey what he has wrought and marvel at its perfection: "and God saw, how good (it was)!" The account is so structured that the theme of the goodness of God's creation builds in a two-part crescendo to the grand finale on day six with the Creator's evaluation of the whole: "And God saw everything that he had made, and behold, it was *exceedingly* good!" (*hinnēh ṭôb mĕ'ōd*, 1:31).

	DAY	WORK	EVALU-ATION	
Part A	1	light	*kî ṭôb*	
	2	firma-ment (heaven)	. . . . . .	3x
	3	dry land	*kî ṭôb*	
		vegeta-tion	*kî ṭôb*	
Part B	4	heavenly lights	*kî ṭôb*	
	5	sea crea-tures and birds	*kî ṭôb*	3x
	6	beasts	*kî ṭôb*	
		humans	. . . . . .	
Summary:		every-thing God made	*hinnēh ṭôb mĕ'ōd*	

The two-part structure of this schema has been noted before.[33] The first three days consists of three works of separation, light from darkness, waters above the firmament from those under, and dry land from the seas, with the whole culminating in the appearance of vegetation. Each work of Part B has its counterpart in Part A; in Part B appropriate denizens are created to fill up each of the spaces created in Part A. The heavenly lights (sun, moon, and stars) of day 4 give definition to the light created on day 1. The double creation of beasts and humankind of day 6 appropriately fulfill the double creation of day 3 in that both groups live on the dry land and both depend upon its vegetation for food. (Permission to become carnivores was not given until 9:3–4.) Only the middle member in each part presents a problem. The birds of day 5 appropriately fill the heavens created on day 2. But one might have expected that the sea creatures would have been created on day 6 since the seas were produced on day 3, when God collected the waters under the firmament in one place so as to produce dry land. It appears, however, that the author thought of the principal work of day 3 as the creation of dry land; the seas seemingly were considered a continuity with the ordering of the waters on either side of the firmament of day 2. The deliberateness of this structure can hardly be questioned.

By the same token, the theme of the goodness of creation is obviously part of the author's schema. The formula "How good!" (*kî ṭôb*) is repeated three times in each part, for a total of six times, corresponding to the six days of creation. At the conclusion the whole is summed up and culminates in the exclamation that everything was "exceedingly good" (*wĕ-hinnēh ṭôb mĕʾōd*), similar to the manner in which the six days culminate with God at rest on the seventh day. The goodness of God's creation is demonstrably a theme that the author wished to highlight.

Seen in this perspective, it becomes rather easy to discern why the Priestly Writer felt it necessary to preface the Yahwist's primeval myth with his own account of creation. As we have seen, the Yahwist had drawn a picture of the Creator as originally naive and his initial creation as less than perfect. The Priestly Writer was clearly disturbed by such a picture and set out to redraw it. In P's conception the Creator acted with full understanding of his purpose and with complete control over his raw materials. Every stage of the process was "good," not flawed, so that the end product was a perfect creation. Or was it?

In P's schema the formula *kî ṭôb* is omitted for two works:

the firmament on day 2 and humankind on day 6. If, as suggested above, the author imposed a sixfold *kî ṭôb* in imitation of the six days of creation, then he was required to omit the formula for two of the eight works. The omission in the case of the firmament may be due to the conception of the author, discussed previously, that the work of day 2 was completed only on day 3 with the definition of the seas. But a comparable suggestion is not forthcoming in the case of humankind. A simpler explanation is at hand. These two works did not merit the judgment that they were perfect. The firmament would later prove defective when it allowed the waters of the Great Abyss (*tĕhôm rabbâ*) to come cascading through at the time of the flood (7:11). Humankind, too, would prove defective, indeed beginning with the very next episode (Genesis 2–3) and culminating in the violence that brought on the deluge (6:11–12).

This implies, of course, that the Priestly Writer intended to integrate the Yahwist's primeval myth into his composition and planned ahead for it. The specifically P sections of Genesis 1–11 contain no account of humans sinning; the accounts of human sin are to be found only in the J sections. If the omission of the *kî ṭôb* formula for humans is to be explained as anticipation of a story about human sin, then it seems unavoidable to conclude that the Priestly Writer is responsible for juxtaposing P and J materials in Genesis.

The omission of the *kî ṭôb* formula is not meant to imply that the work of the Creator was imperfect, however. The final evaluation stresses that "everything which [God] had made was exceedingly good." Rather, the flaw soon to be manifested arose from within the humans themselves; it was not a defect to be credited to the Creator.

By placing this new creation account as the introduction to the J story, the Priestly Writer radically altered the shape and message of the primeval myth. More accurately, he turned the story inside out. With the juxtaposition of these two passages the primeval myth now, for the first time, became a story of a "Fall"—to use traditional Christian terminology. The Yahwist's story of an originally imperfect humankind gradually being perfected was now inverted and transformed by P into a story of an originally perfect humankind become quite imperfect.

The author drew the contrast between the two conditions as starkly as possible. If the Yahwist's original human was animated by the divine breath, the priestly portrait of original humankind is even more godlike. In P's telling, during the primeval deliberations in divine council concerning the creation of humankind, the decision was taken to make humans in the divine model:

> And God said, "Let us make humankind in our image, after our own likeness. They shall rule the fish of the sea, the birds of the sky, the beasts, and the whole earth, including all the creepy things which crawl on the earth." So God created humankind in his own image. In the divine image he created him; male and female he created them. Then God blessed them and he, God, said to them, "Be fruitful and become many. Fill the earth and subdue it. Rule the fish of the sea, the birds of the sky, and all living things that crawl on the earth." (1:26–28)

The use of the grammatical plural in verse 26 reflects the originally polytheistic setting of this episode in the mythic divine council, when the high gods decided to create the first humans.[34] It has been claimed that this originally polytheistic setting, in a once independent cycle, accounts for the different pattern used here in the creation of humankind, as compared with the other works of creation (i.e., by word alone).[35] However, this alone would be insufficient to account for the difference; the Priestly Writer was too much in control of his materials, as we have observed, to let stand something that violated his purpose. Here the difference in pattern helped underscore the author's message that the creation of humankind was of vastly greater significance than the other works of creation. For the others the Creator might act on his own. But the creation of humankind carried such importance, it would seem, that a consultation of the whole heavenly council was required. One is reminded of the similar setting in many ancient Near Eastern creation myths. In particular in *Enuma elish* Marduk acted alone in creating the physical world out of the carcass of Ti'amat. But when it came to creating humankind, he acted in consort with his father and counselor, Ea. As with Marduk, the Creator alone holds center stage throughout, but other gods are still to be found on the periphery in the shadows.[36]

Over the centuries there has been much controversy concerning the meaning of the phrase "in the image and likeness of God."[37] Unquestionably, the precise meaning is slippery. But as C. Westermann has observed, the vast majority of commentators have gone astray by failing to note the importance of context. They have assumed that we have here a universal statement about human nature. However, the Priestly Writer is speaking of a primeval event only, more specifically, of the creation of primeval humankind.[38] As such, "created in the image and likeness of God" is a datum that need not apply to the descendants of the original humans. Indeed, if it be true that the Priestly Writer has fully integrated the Yahwist's myth into his own composition, then it seems that something of the divine likeness was lost when the human and his wife lost Eden. "The image of God" sounds awfully close to J's statement, "Humankind indeed has become like one of us" (3:22). So that they might not enjoy fully the divine prerogatives in the future, the human couple were driven from Eden and the way back barred to them.

This is not to say that the Priestly Writer thought of the divine likeness as completely lost in Eden, however. It would be more accurate to speak of the divine likeness as tarnished or diminished, rather than lost. In his "book of the generations of (primeval) humankind (*'ādām*)[39]" the Priestly Writer spoke of "(Primeval) Humankind" generating offspring "in its likeness, after its own image" (5:1–3), rather than "in (God's) image, after (God's) likeness" as in 1:26. The reversal in positions of the words "likeness" and "image" seems deliberate. This would seem to be the author's way of calling attention to the notice that the likeness being passed along was *'ādām*'s, which is now twice removed from the deity's own being.[40]

The systematic reduction in length of the life spans may be a related concept. To the antediluvian generations in Genesis 5 P assigns life spans of 900 years or more. However, the life spans of postdiluvian generations fall off rapidly. According to Genesis 11:10–32 Shem lived 600 years; Arpachshad, Shelah, and Eber each approximately 450 years; Peleg, Reu, and Serug each approximately 240 years; Nahor 148 years; and Terah 205 years. The Israelite patriarchs live even fewer years: Abraham 175 years (25:7); Isaac 180 years (35:28); Jacob 147 years (47:28); and Joseph 110 years (50:26). Presumably P accepted from J the idea that in God's original design humankind was to be immortal but was later limited to 120 years (6:3); however, P understood this reduction not to have been introduced all at once, but phased in gradually during the "genesis" period. Although the pattern for gradually diminishing life spans may derive from ancient Near Eastern precedent,[41] it is probable that the Priestly Writer understood it as a symbol of the gradual reduction of the "image and likeness" of God in humankind.

Such tarnishing of the divine image in humankind corresponds also to a major theme to be found throughout the whole of the priestly work, namely the sinfulness of humankind. Central to the priestly agenda is the revelation by God of a cultic system that will overcome the inherent sinfulness of humankind. The P system of covenants culminates in the Mosaic covenant, of which the prime benefit was the "tabernacling" presence of God among his people. As Frank Cross has noted, "The entire cultic paraphernalia and cultus was designed to express and overcome the problem of the holy, transcendent God visiting his pervasively sinful people."[42] The primeval story was designed to explain how humankind, created perfect, became so corrupted as to make God's further revelation necessary.

Confirmation of the thesis here proposed, namely, that the Priestly Writer portrayed primeval humankind as perfect and that this portrait depended upon seeing the Eden story in a new frame, is vividly confirmed by the Oracle against Tyre in Ezekiel 28. Using language and mythic themes drawn in large part from Genesis 1–3, the prophet roundly condemns the hubris of Tyre, whose geographic location as an island city at once situated her as an ideal international trading center and made her seemingly secure from foreign assault.

> Because your heart is arrogant,
>   and you claim, "I am god;[43]
> I dwell in the divine abode
>   in the heart of the Sea!"[44]

> You are human (*'ādām*), and not god,
>   despite your pretensions to divinity.
> You are wiser indeed than Dan'el;[45]
>   no mystery is too deep for you![46]
> Through your wisdom and your intelligence
>   you have made yourself mighty.
> You have made gold and silver
>   within your own storehouses.
>
> (Ezek. 28:2–5)

Behind this satirical tirade lies a twofold image. The first is that of the creator deity, who according to common Semitic Combat Myth ruled the world from a palace built over the subdued primeval sea. The image is applied to Yahweh in Psalm 29:10, where Yahweh sits "enthroned over the Flood" as the eternal sovereign of heaven and earth. This image is present in Genesis 1:1–2:3 as well. The rest of God, which follows upon his subduing and ordering of the unruly primeval waters, was intimately linked in the priestly mind with Yahweh having chosen Zion as his "resting place forever" (Ps. 132:13–14). As Jon D. Levenson has demonstrated so well, the Jerusalem temple was understood as a microcosm of creation itself.[47] The point of Ezekiel's satire is thus clear. Through her prowess in trading, Tyre has amassed great wealth and power, which the prophet sardonically likens to a creator gone mad in using his creative powers to fill his own treasuries.[48] Some creator!

The second image is derivative from the first. Instead of creator, perhaps Tyre is only creature, or more precisely, the primeval human (*'ādām*) who aspired to divinity by usurping divine wisdom. The image is strengthened in the lamentation raised over Tyre later in this chapter. Here the real Creator speaks—and condemns the usurper:

> You, O Serpent of perfection,[49]
>   full of wisdom and perfect in beauty.
> You were in Eden, the garden of God,
>   every precious stone your clothing . . .
> You are a wing-spread Cherub,
>   I appointed you as the guardian.
> On the holy mountain of God you were;

in the midst of the stones of fire you walked.
You were perfect in your ways
    from the day of your creation
    —until iniquity was found in you! . . .
Your heart became proud because of your beauty;
    you spoiled your wisdom for the sake of your splendor.[50]

                       (Ezek. 28:12–17)

Ezekiel here plays freely upon the Yahwist's creation myth of Genesis 2–3. In that story the serpent embodied the illegitimate human aspiration to divine wisdom. Likewise, the cherubs symbolized the nearness to divinity that in the end was impossible to maintain because of human hubris. Then, too, precious stones were to be found in Eden, though not in the embellished forms here nor as items of clothing. In Genesis 2–3 there was no mention of "the stones of fire" nor of "the holy mountain of God," much less any "divine abode in the heart of the Sea." Accordingly, most commentators have posited that Ezekiel must have relied upon a variant of the primeval myth, other than the Yahwist's, now lost to us. The likelihood of another as yet unattested version of the Eden myth is extremely remote. Rather, as I argue in a later chapter with regard to the similar case of the Oracles against Egypt,[51] Ezekiel has freely adapted the older mythic traditions in original mythopoeic speculations of his own, at times by spelling out more fully the mythic imagery adumbrated in his sources. If our understanding of verse 12 is correct, Ezekiel has combined the topoi of the wise (saraph-) serpent (Gen. 3:1–5, 13–15)[52] and the guardian cherub (Gen. 3:24) and linked these with the topos of the semidivine primeval human to further strengthen the motif of reprobate human hubris in the face of divine goodness.

Of course, Ezekiel was not limited to mythic imagery and data obtainable from Genesis. Both the biblical and extrabiblical texts show an acquaintance with mythic lore in numerous forms and permutations. The prophet was no less acquainted with a host of these. But there is no attestation outside Ezekiel 28 of this combination of Combat Myth themes and Eden themes in the same text—unless one admits the combined J and P accounts (hereafter called J-P) in the opening chapters of

Genesis *as a single text*. It seems that one must conclude that either Ezekiel 28 was the model for the completed text of Genesis, or that the completed P work was the model for Ezekiel 28. I argue for the priority of P over Ezekiel, though the difference for my thesis is not terribly significant. The Priestly Writer and Ezekiel reveal many affinities and are generally grouped together as descendants of a common priestly heritage. I see no compelling reason to question the opinion that both the Priestly Writer and Ezekiel were writing at about the same period, at the time of the Babylonian exile. On the question of priority, it seems easier to me to derive Ezekiel from the J-P creation accounts, rather than vice versa.

Ezekiel demonstrably understood the primeval human associated with the garden of Eden to have been originally perfect. P, writing about the same time and under similar circumstances, surely did also.

CONCLUSION

Quite possibly we have failed to reckon seriously with the sophistication of the ancient Israelite authors. At least until very recently it has been commonplace for biblical scholars to accuse the "editors" of the Pentateuch of clumsily splicing together diverse materials, apparently oblivious in numerous instances to their contradictory storylines and messages. Such a judgment is grossly inaccurate of the priestly author-editor of Genesis 1–9. P was very deliberate in his method and very much in control of his material. (The limited analysis I have done in this chapter is far from exhausting either the literary or the theological depth of P.)

Seemingly prodded by the need to provide reassurance to a community disheartened by the Babylonian devastation of its "world," P consciously set out to rework Israel's primeval myth. His goal was to assure his exilic audience that at core their traditional Yahwistic faith was as relevant as ever, while at the same time suggesting alternative ways in which to reimagine that faith so that it answered their existential questions about a world seemingly without a stable foundation. He kept the now well-established J primeval myth but placed it in a new framework of Combat Myth imagery, apparently drawn in part from the Babylonian *Enuma elish* myth. The Yahwist's conception of a naive Yahweh God who only gradually learned how to make his creation work was unacceptable. P found in the Semitic myth of the battle against chaos the theological emphasis he was looking for. That myth affirmed that the world was ruled by an intelligent and all-powerful creator who would never permit it to disintegrate into meaninglessness or succumb to the nihilistic force of evil at work in the world. This was a message that needed to be broadcast loudly and often among the exilic community, still reeling from the Babylonian blow that had shattered their Zion-centered world and scattered their families across the face of the earth. Despite appearances, despite the boasts of the victorious Babylonians about the supremacy of their patron god, Yahweh God is Divine Sovereign still. The Babylonian challenge is not unexpected. As the Combat Myth acknowledges, the chaos dragon is always lurking somewhere just over the horizon—or perhaps even within one's own house.

If on the one hand the Combat Myth affirmed the perfection of the Creator's design of the world, on the other hand it also acknowledged the awesome presence of evil, which threatened to undo the divinely ordained good order. The chaos monster perpetually took on historical incarnation in the form of humans doing violence to one another and to their world. P reused the storyline of the older J myth for this purpose. J had presented humankind as manifesting a definite proclivity toward evil. Placed within P's new interpretative framework, these stories served to show how God's perfect work of creation became corrupted through humankind's own hubris, which was the cause of "all flesh" turning upon one another in destructive violence.

It would be a mistake, however, to compare the Priestly Writer's method to a Wagner composing new operas out of old Germanic legends or to a Shakespeare reworking the character of "Julius Caesar" into a new literary masterpiece. For P the older J myth was more than a traditional *fabula* or "story" begging to be reworked into an original work of art. Nor were the "human" (ʾādām) and the woman (Eve), Yahweh, and the serpent merely literary *characters* placed on a set (the fabulous garden with its magic trees) to play out the drama.[53] Rather, P recognized in the older J primeval myth a tradition-honored statement of his community that deserved to be preserved for its authentic insights into human nature and humankind's relationship to the deity. But he recognized also that the God of Israel had to be more in control of the universe than allowed by the Yahwist's crudely anthropomorphic portrait of Yahweh as a "trial and error" creator. Like the Christian philosopher Aquinas learning from the pagan philosopher Aristotle, the Priestly Writer found in the Semitic Combat Myth a way to portray the deity that more adequately expressed his community's belief that the God of Israel was the universal divine sovereign and the creator of all—a fundamental truth that needed to be restated with fresh vigor during the dark days of Babylonian exile. To this purpose P added the "remythologizing" frame of Genesis 1:1–2:4a within which to hear the story of creation. He did not consider having two different stories of the same "event" to be contradictory or problematic. Instead, he likely regarded them as complementary, much as the average Christian regards the two irreconcilable infancy narratives about Jesus in the Gospels of Matthew and Luke as complementary rather than contradictory.

P would also have difficulty understanding our modern concern over whether there literally existed a paradisiacal divine garden or whether God actually created humankind by modeling a clay anthropoid figure into whose nostrils God blew the breath of life, or similar questions. His ability to pose other, even new, ways of looking at creation shows that he understood that one is dealing here with something other than historical literalism. But that did not make such stories less true. The notion that something is true only if it is historically accurate is a prejudice we moderns inherited from our Enlightenment mentors. For P these primeval stories were vehicles that enabled one better to approach the *mysterium tremendum* of the divine.

P reminds his exilic audience that God created humankind to be a reflection of the divine being. Everything that tarnishes the divine image in humankind, including gender subordination, disharmony, and violence, is "sin," a revolt of humankind against the original goodness ordained by the Creator. Such rebellion may be either exterior or interior.

As P the theologian well understood, human rebellion against the will of the deity is but a historical manifestation of that power which myth names as the chaos monster. P the mythmaker made this explicit in his recomposition of the flood story. He turned the waters of the flood into a resurgence of the primeval ocean, which gained new strength from the sin of humankind. The myth of God's sovereignty required that God crush every incarnation of evil, even when it appears within God's own creation. The sign of the (war-/rain-)bow functions as an effective metaphor of divine sovereignty. On the one hand, it provides assurance to beleaguered believers that a benevolent creator watches out to preserve an essentially good world. Hence the "Babylonian" dragon, the external devil working its evil in the world, need not be feared. On the other hand, it serves as a warning to a humanity prone to rejecting the divinely ordained order that such behavior is self-destructive and will not be tolerated by God. Hence, the "human" dragon also, the internal devil lurking within each human breast, must in the end be subdued so that the reign of God might become manifest. At this point P the theologian and P the mythmaker have become one—or were they ever distinguishable?

The Priestly Writer was a child of his age. Like other ancient Near Eastern authors, his motives were more sociopolitical and religious than artistic. He conveyed his message through narrative and mythic imagery. Indeed, for Genesis 1–9, the care that he exercised in extending older mythic motifs to express new theological content seems to assure that he intended to compose a new primeval myth. For P mythmaking and mythopoeic speculation are virtually synonymous with theological method. Allowing for the differences between the Yahwism of the Priestly Writer and the polytheism of the Babylonian poet-theologians, the method and purpose of the Priestly Genesis 1–9 are very analogous to the three Babylonian myths analyzed in the first chapter.

It must be emphasized, however, that in both instances we are dealing with *literary* myth. The writers are not mere stenographers for oral tradition. Rather, as true authors they selected and arranged older, traditional materials for their own new purposes. They composed—or recomposed—freely, often with great originality. They were not stifled by the traditions of the past, but used these to obtain continuity with the heritage of their respective communities. In the case of the Priestly Writer, the resulting product resonated so well with the community's self-identity that it became the canonical statement on the subject.

Chapter 4

◆

THE EXODUS AS MYTH

◆

It is one thing to find myth within the primeval stories of Genesis 1–11; for many people it is quite another to suggest that the story of the exodus may be myth as well. After all, the primeval stories by their literary genre are not history. Lacking true science or actual knowledge of how their world began, the ancient Israelites naturally utilized the cultural conventions of the day to explain the origins of the universe and humankind. At that level, Israel had nothing but her faith in Yahweh as the lord of heaven and earth to guide her in revamping culturally conditioned notions of how the world came into being. But once we reach the specifically Israelite story (the patriarchs, the exodus from Egypt, the covenant at Sinai, and beyond), we attain a different plateau where myth is replaced by historical consciousness, it is claimed. Biblical religion is at core historical. To suggest otherwise is to deny the essential characteristic of biblical religion that distinguishes it from other, "natural" religions. This view may be aptly summed up in the maxim, "History is the chief medium of revelation."[1]

Fortunately, this view is increasingly out of vogue among contemporary biblical scholarship, particularly for the early books of the Bible. A more recent assessment recognizes that the biblical narrative in the books of Genesis through Joshua owes more to the folkloric tradition of the ancient Near East than to the historical genre[2] and cannot be used to reconstruct an authentic history of ancient Israel.[3] Nevertheless, the notion that the Bible is largely a historical work remains firmly entrenched in many minds. Likewise, its corollary that history is an appropriate medium of revelation while myth is not, is unfortunately still the prevailing view.

Without denying that biblical revelation frequently has revolved around historical events, it is important to recognize that myth, no less—perhaps even more so—than history, has also served as a medium of biblical revelation. In this chapter we examine the exodus narrative and conclude that, whatever the historicity of the events that lie behind the biblical narrative, the exodus *as story* has been elevated to mythic proportions in such a manner as to emphasize its paradigmatic character for all subsequent generations.

The choice of the exodus is deliberate because of its acknowledged centrality within Israelite religion. The issue in question, however, is whether biblical tradition conceived of the exodus as a *historical* event or whether biblical tradition attempted to present the exodus as a *timeless* story. Was the intention of biblical writers to present the exodus as a past event, something that happened to their forefathers and foremothers at a particular geographical place at a particular moment in the past? Or was it the biblical writers' intention to explode the exodus into an "event" that transcends the particularities of space and time, making it the story of every Israelite in every generation? In short, is the exodus narrative primarily historical memory or is it myth?

The centrality of the exodus within the Hebrew Bible is not in question. B. W. Anderson has called the exodus the "crucial historical experience that made her (Israel) a self-conscious historical community—an event so decisive that earlier happenings and subsequent experiences were seen in its light."[4] Martin Noth was equally emphatic about the fundamental character of the exodus theme in the Old Testament: "In the case of the 'guidance out of Egypt' we are dealing with a *primary confession (Urbekenntnis) of Israel*, one that is expressed rather strictly in hymnic form and at the same time with the kernel of the whole subsequent Pentateuchal tradition."[5] But the exodus that we are dealing with in this case is not the historical event, whatever that may have been, but rather the exodus of tradition. The latter has been thoroughly mythologized and reinterpreted as an "event" of suprahistorical character through various mythopoeic processes.

THE DELIVERANCE AT THE SEA

From the point of view of structural divisions within the Pentateuch, the exodus may be defined as the "events" narrated in Exodus 1–15. In a narrower sense the exodus narrative extends from Exodus 7:8–15:21, from the time when Moses and Aaron present themselves before Pharaoh with the request to leave Egypt to their celebration of victory over Pharaoh at the Red Sea. Here, however, I am concerned only with the deliverance at the Sea (Ex. 13:17–15:21).

Within this narrative, critical scholars posit the usual three pentateuchal literary strands: the Yahwist (J), the Elohist (E), and the Priestly Writer (P). In addition, the Song of the Sea (Ex. 15:1–18) may be considered another, independent tradition antedating J, E, and P.[6] A study of the deliverance at the Sea in each of these four traditions reveals just how shallow is the historical core, on the one hand, and how deep is the mythological reinterpretation, on the other hand.

For convenience I have arranged the three literary stands (J, E, and P) here in a synoptic format so that their relative shapes may be more easily seen. The divisions are approximate, of course, since source critical scholars are not unanimous in their assignments to the different literary strands.

THE EXODUS NARRATIVE*

ELOHISTIC NARRATIVE	YAHWISTIC NARRATIVE	PRIESTLY NARRATIVE
13 [17]When Pharaoh let the people go, God did not lead them by way of the land of the Philistines, although that	**13** [21]And Yahweh went before them by day in a pillar of cloud to lead them along the way, and by night in a pillar	**13** [20]And they moved on from Succoth, and encamped at Etham, on the edge of the wilderness. . . .

was near; for God said, "Lest the people repent when they see war, and return to Egypt." ¹⁸But God led the people round by the way of the wilderness toward the Red Sea. And the people of Israel went up out of the land of Egypt equipped for battle. ¹⁹And Moses took the bones of Joseph with him; for Joseph had solemnly sworn the people of Israel, saying, "God will visit you; then you must carry my bones with you from here." . . .

of fire to give them light, that they might travel by day and by night; ²²the pillar of cloud by day and the pillar of fire by night did not depart from before the people. . . .

14 ¹Then Yahweh said to Moses, ²"Tell the people of Israel to turn back and encamp in front of Pi-ha-hiroth, between Migdol and the sea, in front of Baal-zephon; you shall encamp over against it, by the sea. ³For Pharaoh will say of the people of Israel, 'They are entangled in the land; the wilderness has shut them in.' ⁴And I will harden Pharaoh's heart, and he will pursue them and I will get glory over Pharaoh and all his host; and the Egyptians shall know that I am Yahweh." And they did so. . . .

14 ⁵ᵃWhen the King of Egypt was told that the people had fled . . .

14 ⁵ᵇthe mind of Pharaoh and his servants was changed toward the people, and they said, "What is this we have done, that we have let Israel go from serving us?" ⁶So he made ready his chariot and took his army with him . . .

⁷[he] took six hundred picked chariots and all the other chariots of Egypt with officers over all of them. . . .

⁸And Yahweh hardened the heart of Pharaoh king of Egypt and he pursued the people of Israel as they went forth defiantly. . . .

9a The Egyptians pursued them . . .

10b the people of Israel lifted up their eyes, and behold, the Egyptians were marching after them. And they were in great fear. . . .

11 And they said to Moses, "Is it because there are no graves in Egypt that you have taken us away to die in the wilderness? What have you done to us, in bringing us out of Egypt? 12 Is not this what we said to you in Egypt, 'Let us alone and let us serve the Egyptians'? For it would have been better for us to serve the Egyptians than to die in the wilderness." 13 And Moses said to the people, "Fear not, stand firm, and see the salvation of Yahweh, which he will work for you today; for the Egyptians whom you see today, you shall never see again. 14 Yahweh will fight for you, and you have only to be still! . . .

9b [and they—] all Pharaoh's horses and chariots and his horsemen and his army[—]overtook them encamped at the sea, by Pi-ha-hiroth, in front of Baal-zephon. 10 When Pharaoh drew near . . .

10c And the people of Israel cried out to Yahweh . . .

15 Yahweh said to Moses, "Why do you cry to me? Tell the people of Israel to go forward. 16 Lift up your rod, and stretch out your hand over the sea and divide it, that the people of Israel may go on dry ground through the sea. 17 And I will harden the hearts of the Egyptians so that they shall go in after them, and I will get glory over Pharaoh and all his host, his chariots, and his horsemen. 18 And the Egyptians shall know that I am Yahweh, when I have gotten glory

106

¹⁹ᵃThen the angel of God who went before the host of Israel moved and went behind them . . .

¹⁹ᵇand the pillar of cloud moved from before them and stood behind them, ²⁰coming between the host of Egypt and the host of Israel. And there was the cloud and the darkness; and the night passed without one coming near the other all night. . . . ²¹ᵇand Yahweh drove the sea back by a strong east wind all night, and made the sea dry land. . . .

²⁴And in the morning watch Yahweh in the pillar of fire and of cloud looked down upon the host of the Egyptians, and discomfited the host of the Egyptians . . .

²⁵ᵃ[He clogged] their chariot wheels so that they drove heavily . . .

²⁵ᵇand the Egyptians said, "Let us flee from before Israel; for Yahweh fights for them against the Egyptians." . . . ²⁷ᵇAnd the sea returned to its wonted flow when the morning appeared; and the

over Pharaoh, his chariots, and his horsemen." . . .

²¹ᵃThen Moses stretched out his hand over the sea . . .

²¹ᶜand the waters were divided. ²²And the people of Israel went into the midst of the sea on dry ground, the waters being a wall to them on their right hand and on their left. ²³The Egyptians pursued, and went in after them into the midst of the sea, all Pharaoh's horses, his chariots, and his horsemen. . . .

²⁶Then Yahweh said to Moses, "Stretch out your hand over the sea, that the water may come back upon the Egyptians, upon their chariots, and upon their horsemen." ²⁷ᵃSo Moses stretched forth his hand over the sea. . . .

²⁸[And] the waters returned and covered the chariots and the horsemen and all the host of

Egyptians fled into it, and Yahweh routed the Egyptians in the midst of the sea. . . .

[30]Thus Yahweh saved Israel that day from the hand of the Egyptians; and Israel saw the Egyptians dead upon the seashore. [31]And Israel saw the great work which Yahweh did against the Egyptians, and the people feared Yahweh; and they believed in Yahweh and in his servant Moses.

Pharaoh that had followed them into the sea; not so much as one of them remained. [29]But the people of Israel walked on dry ground through the sea, the waters being a wall to them on their right hand and on their left. . . .

---

*Translation after RSV.

The Yahwist account, presumably the oldest of the prose narrative accounts, presents a relatively "naturalistic" depiction of an escape at the Sea.[7] The fleeing Israelites, caught between a pursuing Egyptian army and an impassable sea, cry out against God and his servant Moses. Moses challenges them to have faith in their God, commanding them simply to stand still and watch Yahweh single-handedly defeat the enemy. During the night Yahweh temporarily dries the sea bed with a strong east wind. Toward morning he somehow panics the Egyptians and causes them to flee headlong into the dried sea bed, whereupon the waters return to their channel and the Egyptians are drowned. The Israelites praise their God and continue on their way. Remarkable in this version is the absence of the familiar motif about the Israelites crossing the sea dry shod. Only the Egyptians enter the sea; the Israelites never move. They are but passive observers of the combat between God and the Egyptians. In other words, this version predates the priestly rewriting of the narrative as an extension of the Combat Myth. J's emphasis is on how thoroughly the Creator has bonded with his flawed but nonetheless elected people, such that Yahweh continually watches out to promote the Israelites' welfare despite their shallow faith and devotion.

The Elohist is ill represented in this section.[8] There is a notice that God did not lead his people by way of the main coastal road but rather in a circuitous route by way of the Red Sea. Of the rest, little more can be attributed with certainty to E beyond a statement that Pharaoh, upon learning that the Israelites "had fled," mustered his chariot army and pursued them. Due to the truncated form in which E was transmitted, no certain references to any miracle at the Sea have been preserved.[9]

The P version is the most familiar.[10] When the Israelites, trapped between the Red Sea and the pursuing Egyptians, cry out to Yahweh for help, Yahweh commands Moses to stretch his staff over the sea. Moses does so and the sea is split in twain. The Israelites dramatically march dry shod through the middle of the sea, a wall of water to the right and to the left, with the Egyptians in hot pursuit. Upon reaching the other side, Moses at God's command once more stretches forth his staff. The walls of water collapse, drowning the Egyptians in the midst of the sea.

The Song of the Sea, although now situated in the narrative as a victory song celebrating Yahweh's defeat of the Egyptians, originally had a quite different setting. This ancient composition may date to the tenth century B.C.E.[11] The hymn praises Yahweh not only for his victory over Pharaoh but also for bringing the Israelites into the Promised Land and planting them firmly around Yahweh's mountain sanctuary. This combination of exodus and conquest motifs suggests an origin in the Gilgal cult.[12] As regards what transpired at the Sea, if one strips away the mythopoeic language, the Song says little beyond that the Egyptians perished in the sea.

The function of the sea in each of these four traditions serves as a good indicator of the degree to which "history" has been mythologized in the exodus narrative. In J the sea functions somewhat ambiguously. It appears to be completely passive. It is temporarily pushed back by a strong east wind and later returns to its channel, apparently because the wind died down. The sea does engulf the Egyptians, but in the circumstances this could be interpreted as a wholly natural phenomenon. One would scarcely advert to mythological overtones, were they not so prominent in other levels of the tradition and were the idea of sea itself not so heavily freighted with mythological connotations in the whole of the ancient Near East.

The truncated condition of E precludes judgment concerning the role and function of the sea in that tradition.

With P, however, the situation is completely different. There can be no doubt that the sea is heavily laden with mythological overtones. The clearest indication of this is in the concept of the "splitting" (*bqʿ*) of the sea, a motif clearly drawn from the West Semitic Combat Myth about the smiting of the sea-dragon.[13] In this myth the creator God overcomes his foe, the watery dragon of chaos, by splitting it in two. In the Babylonian version of *Enuma elish* Marduk defeated Tiʾamat by blasting his storm winds into her mouth and distending her belly. Marduk then cleaved Tiʾamat's carcass in twain, fashioning one half into the earth and the other half into the heavens. In other words, P is using the wind here as he did at Genesis 1:2 and 8:1–2 as the divine sovereign's instrument in the battle against chaos in all its manifestations.[14]

As noted already in the previous chapter, mythopoeic speculation based upon this Combat Myth flourished within the Israelite community around the time of the Babylonian exile.[15] Deutero-Isaiah used its imagery to great effect in prophesying that Yahweh would free the exiles from their captivity. The dominant motif of Deutero-Isaiah is appropriately a new "exodus" by which Yahweh will once again free his people from captivity in a foreign land. But inseparably intertwined with this exodus motif are creation motifs. Yahweh, alone, and no other god is affirmed as the authentic creator and sole lord of the world (Isa. 40:12–31; 45:18–22; 48:12–19).[16] For Deutero-Isaiah the most important creative activity of Yahweh was not primeval creation, however, but Yahweh's creation of a people for himself through the exodus out of Egypt. Nevertheless, as important as that first "historical" exodus out of Egypt was for Israel, it will pale into insignificance before the coming new exodus with which Yahweh will inaugurate the eschatological Israel, this exilic prophet assures his audience.[17]

Even more important than the fact that Deutero-Isaiah interpreted the exodus as an act of divine creation is the manner in which he made that interpretation. For him the exodus as an accomplished "historical" event had little value. Rather the exodus was significant as an ongoing reality; Yahweh is perpetually redeeming his people through a never-ending exodus:

> But now thus speaks Yahweh,
>   The one who creates you, O Jacob,
>   and the one who forms you, O Israel.
> Do not fear, because I redeem you,
>   I call [you] by name. You are mine.
> When you pass through the waters, I am with you,
>   and through the rivers, they will not overwhelm you.
> When you walk through fire, you will not be burned,
>   and the flame will not consume you.
> Because I, Yahweh, am your God,
>   the Holy One of Israel, the one who saves you.
>
> (Isa. 43:1–3)

It is difficult to capture in translation the polyvalent usage of tenses in Deutero-Isaiah. The peculiar combination of imperfect, perfect, and participial forms suggests a conscious attempt by the poet to transcend categories of past, present, and future tense.[18] It is not exact to speak of the new exodus as an eschatological event. For Deutero-Isaiah the exodus is an eternal actualization of God's redemptive activity; past, present, and future merge as a single divine action that irrupts into the human realm at provident points in "history." Perhaps a novel translation of Isaiah 43:18 will help to elucidate the prophet's meaning:

> Remember not the primeval events;
>   and the primordial acts do not consider.
> Lo! I do it anew;
>   even now it is bursting forth,
>   can you not perceive it?

It is not that Deutero-Isaiah places no store in the myths of

111

primeval creation. Indeed he does. But these are not past events. They are the very foundation of present reality, of the continuation of God's creative will.

In the so-called Ode to Yahweh's Arm Deutero-Isaiah reapplies the Combat Myth to Yahweh. But Deutero-Isaiah is not content to retell the myth, simply substituting the name of Yahweh for that of Marduk or Baal. Through a process of mythopoeic speculation the poet reinterprets the combat with the sea-dragon as applying first and foremost to the exodus.

> Awake! Awake! Robe yourself in Power,
>   O arm of Yahweh.
> Awake as in Primordial days,
>   (those) Primeval generations.
> Is it not you who cleaves Rahab[19] in pieces?
>   who pierces the Sea-dragon (*tannîn*)?
> Is it not you who dries up the Sea?
>   the waters of the great Abyss (*tĕhôm*)?
> The one who makes the depths of the Sea a road
>   for the redeemed to pass over?
>
> (Isa. 51:9–10)

Invariably modern translators miss the import of Deutero-Isaiah's mythic language here by rendering the mythic motifs in the past tense, "Was it not thou that *didst* cut Rahab in pieces," "that *didst* make the depths of the sea a way," and so on (RSV translation). As post-Enlightenment readers, we all too readily project onto the biblical author our own understanding, namely, that the slaying of the sea-dragon is a symbol only, a vestige of a now defunct primitive mentality. But for Deutero-Isaiah these were no vestigial symbols. For that reason he uses participial constructions here, as so often throughout his composition.[20] Participles connote recurrent realities, "events" that are not bounded by time. The writer affirms that the battle against the nihilistic forces of chaos, far from being a thing of the past, still rages. Save for the perpetual creative presence of the divine sovereign, Israel would long since have perished in the chaos of the sea that daily threatens to engulf us.

The Priestly Writer was right at home in this mythic climate.

We have already witnessed his restructuring of the creation story in Genesis along the lines of the Combat Myth. He has also reshaped the exodus narrative along similar lines. The same mythopoeic impulse that allowed Deutero-Isaiah to see release from Babylonian captivity as a recrudescence of the myth of divine creation is likewise operative in P's retelling of the exodus from Egypt. P portrays Egypt as an extension of the chaos dragon. In Egyptian belief Pharaoh was the incarnation of their chief god. Israel's theologians inverted this Egyptian "theology" by turning Pharaoh not into the creator god but the Creator's arch foe, the chaos dragon who opposed the Creator's benevolent design.[21] In the priestly version the book of Exodus opens with Israel trapped inside the anti-god, Pharaoh-Egypt. That is, Israel at this point is a "nonpeople"; it is "uncreated" because the anticreator refuses to allow Israel to exist. In a series of spectacular battles Yahweh overwhelms and finally kills Pharaoh-Egypt in the midst of the sea. Through this same battle Israel emerges from out of the midst of the defeated enemy as God's newly fashioned people, the final "work" of the Creator who brings forth life out of the midst of the unruly sea.

That this interpretation of the exodus as a new creation is correct is confirmed by the placement of the Song of the Sea at this juncture in the exodus narrative. Whether the Song was first inserted into the narrative by P or had already been attached by earlier tradition, P certainly found the new creation themes in it appropriate to his purposes.

Contrary to those who claim that the Song of the Sea describes a historical battle,[22] whatever historical core the exodus may have had, it is already thoroughly transformed into mythic proportions even in this early poetic composition. The Song exhibits the same basic structure as *Enuma elish* and the Ugaritic Baal cycle.[23] The Divine Warrior overcomes his watery foe of chaos, creating a new order in the process. Although the creation motifs in the Song extend beyond any individual word or verse, Israel is explicitly called "the people whom you [Yahweh] created" (*'am zû qānîtā*) in verse 16.[24] As in the Combat Myths, the Divine Warrior then retires to his (newly constructed) mountain sanctuary, from where he eternally rules his newly ordered cosmos (vs. 17–18):

You bring [your people] in and plant them
  on your very own mountain,
  the foundation of your throne
    which you have made, O Yahweh,
  the sanctuary, O Lord,
    which your own hands have established.
Yahweh is king
  for ages without end and for ever!

Yahweh's mountain sanctuary here is of course the temple on Mount Zion—Yahweh's eternal "resting place" as described in the preceding chapter. Thus here as in Genesis 1 the themes of creation and the creator's temple-palace are intertwined.

The creation myth structure of the Song alone should be confirmation enough that Pharaoh and his hosts are viewed in larger-than-life proportions, that Pharaoh-Egypt has been metamorphosed into the primeval foe of the Creator. For this reason the poet has Pharaoh and his army cast into the sea and sunk to its abyssal depths. Pharaoh and the sea merge as a single entity. This explains why in verses 6–8 Yahweh's ire seems to shift from Pharaoh to the sea itself:

Your right hand, Yahweh,
  is awesome in strength;
Your right hand, Yahweh,
  shatters the foe.
With the greatness of your majesty
  you crush your adversaries;
You send forth your fury,
  it consumes them like stubble.
At the blast of your nostrils
  the waters piled up;
  the currents stood up like a hill;
  The Abyss (*tĕhōmōt*) congealed(?) in the heart of the Sea.

As an aside, one may speculate that the much commented upon alternation between the perfect and the imperfect forms of the verbs in this Song may be the poet's way of contemporizing the scene, suggesting that the "event" extends into the present.[25]

The mythological imagery in the Song of the Sea is even more pervasive, however, than just a structural similarity to the Combat Myth. Behind the reference to *yam sûp* (15:4) lies another major, largely unrecognized mythic allusion. Exodus 15:4–5 reads:

> Pharaoh's chariots and his army he cast into the Sea (*yām*)
> His picked officers are sunk in *yam sûp*.
> The Abyss (*tĕhōmōt*) covers them;
> They went down into the depths (*mĕṣôlōt*) like a stone.

It has been fashionable to translate *yam sûp* as "Reed Sea" and to suggest that we have preserved here an authentic historical memory that Israel escaped from Egypt by wading across a shallow papyrus marsh—hence the name "Reed Sea/Marsh"—which their Egyptian pursuers were unable to negotiate in their heavy horse-drawn chariots. Elsewhere[26] I have argued that the presence of *yam sûp* here cannot be due to authentic historical memory that the battle occurred at some "Reed Sea." The whole Reed Sea hypothesis is nothing more than a figment of scholarly imagination. Biblical *yam sûp* always and everywhere refers to that body of water which we today identify as the Red Sea or one of its extensions, whether to the north into the Gulfs of Suez and Aqaba, or to the south into the Indian Ocean and connecting waters.[27] Even so, it is not likely that the placement of Israel's deliverance from Pharaoh in or near the Red Sea in the Song of the Sea derives from authentic historical memory.

Rather the presence of *yam sûp* here is explained by the mythological connotations inherent in the name itself. *Yam sûp* literally means "the Sea of End/Extinction" (from the Hebrew root *sûp*, "to come to an end," "to cease"). To these ancient Israelites *yam sûp* really was the sea at the end of the world. As such it was heavily freighted with all the mythological connotations associated with primeval sea. Located at the extremity of the created world, most remote from the sacred palace of the Creator in Mount Zion and the center of the cosmos where meaningful existence was possible, "the Sea of End" implied a condition of noncreation or nonexistence. But because the ancients conceived of the created world as floating in the primeval sea, *yam sûp* was also under the cosmos. Accordingly, the images of the great Abyss (*tĕhôm/tĕhōmōt*) and the depths (*mĕṣôlōt*) were equally present (v. 5), as well as all other images of primeval chaos (Sheol, the Pit, the Underworld, Death, etc.). Note that in verse 12 the action of the sea is paralleled by the action of the "underworld" (*'ereṣ*) in swallowing up the Egyptian foe. Thus, *yam sûp* in Exodus 15:4 stands simply as the second member in the poetic pair *yām* / *yam sûp*; as such it had no more historical or geographical referent than does *yām*. Both terms are used for their mythological connotations as primeval ocean. The battle against Pharaoh was viewed as an extension of the cosmic battle of the deity against chaos. Through this traditional mythical language the poet expressed the belief that the emergence of Israel as a people during the exodus was due to a creative act by Yahweh equal to that of the original creation of the cosmos itself. The Egyptians, the evil force that threatens the existence of this new creation, are appropriately cast into the sea to perish. A more powerful symbol for Egypt-Pharaoh as the chaos dragon could scarcely be found than submergence into "the Sea of End/Annihilation."

But if in Israel's earliest written traditions *yam sûp* functioned purely as a mythological symbol, the situation was quite different by the time of the latest traditions. By the time of P the exodus has been definitely historicized and localized at, or in, the geographical body of water we know as the Red Sea. The Priestly Writer makes the Israelites pass quite literally through the Red Sea, as a comparison with Numbers 33 shows. P has utilized an old list of camping stations preserved in Numbers 33 as the framework around which he organized the wilderness itinerary:

Station	Numbers 33 (verse)	The Book of Exodus
Start:	Rameses (5)	Raamses and Pithom (1:11)
1.	Succoth (5)	Succoth (13:20)
2.	Etham "on edge of the wilderness" (6)	Etham "on the edge of the wilderness" (13:20)

3.	Pi-hahiroth "before Baal-zephon . . . before Migdol" (7)	Pi-ha-hiroth "between Migdol and the sea before Baal-zephon" (14:2)
4.	"passed through . . . the *sea*" (*yām*) (8)	Passage through the *Red Sea* (*yam sûp*) (14:22–23, 29; 15:22)
5.	"three days' journey in the wildness of Etham" (8)	"three days in the wilderness of Shur" (15:22)
5a.	Marah (8)	Marah (15:23)
6.	Elim: twelve springs and seventy palms (9)	Elim: twelve springs and seventy palms (15:27)
7.	*Red Sea* (*yam sûp*) (10)	. . . .
8.	wilderness of Sin (11)	wilderness of Sin (16:1)

In making the exodus itinerary conform to the list of camping stations of Numbers 33, the Priestly Writer has made one very important alteration. In Numbers 33 the station at the sea of the crossing (no. 4, v. 8) is quite distinct from the station at *yam sûp* (no. 7, vs. 10–11), since the Israelites arrive at the latter only some three camping stations later. In the Exodus narrative, however, P has deliberately suppressed the latter station at *yam sûp* and changed the setting of the miraculous crossing from an unnamed sea to *yam sûp*. By thus telescoping the stations at "the sea" and at *yam sûp* into one, P deliberately historicized the "event" as a crossing of the vast and deep Red Sea!

The mythic elements have not been lessened any, however. On the contrary, P has *yam sûp* split and the Israelites, freed from the slavery of Pharaoh, emerge out of its midst as Yahweh's new creation (even as Marduk cleaved Ti'amat in twain and out of her carcass created the cosmos). The continuation of the Combat Myth motif from the primeval myth in Genesis is clear.

The implied message is also clear—especially, if as seems likely, P's audience is in exile in Babylon. The Creator who manifested sovereignty over the power of chaos "in the beginning" is the selfsame Yahweh who has chosen Israel as his own. Israel can have no greater foundation for trusting that it has a purpose and a future, however bleak they may appear at the moment.

The distinction between myth and history so important to post-Enlightenment readers seems completely lacking in this exodus narrative. Indeed, the Priestly Writer appears to have deliberately blurred the boundaries between the two as myth merges with history and history with myth.

THE EXODUS AS PRIMEVAL EVENT

The Priestly Restructuring of the Torah

I have traced the history of development of the sea tradition at some length because of what it reveals about the mythological method and understanding of the ancient Israelites toward their sacred traditions. The same mythic character may be said to apply to the whole of the exodus narrative, and beyond that to the whole of the priestly Tetrateuch (Genesis–Numbers). I accept Frank Cross's thesis that the books of Genesis through Numbers plus Deuteronomy 34 are the work of a single tradent, the Priestly Writer, and that these books come to us substantially as they were redacted by the Priestly Writer, except that the concluding chapter, the death of Moses, was subsequently moved to its location in the Received Text at the conclusion of Deuteronomy.[28] Likewise, I accept the view that the storyline of the earliest Israelite literary tradition of J and E once extended beyond the limits of the present Pentateuch, likely concluding with a story of how the promise to the patriarchs was fulfilled with the Israelites gaining possession of the land of Canaan— hence originally a Hexateuch?—or in the case of J extending even to the establishment of David's kingship.[29] The decision to eliminate the conquest of the Promised Land and the history of its settlement was deliberate on the part of the Priestly Writer, even though it meant doing violence to the shape and the themes of the older (J-E) "Israelite epic." The Priestly Writer deliberately ended the story of Israel's foundations with the death of Moses. He thus drew a sharp distinction between the Age of the Torah and all succeeding periods.

In the priestly retelling the whole of the Age of the Torah has become primeval time, the mythic age of origins. The deeds and activities of that period are paradigmatic and normative for the "historical" period, the here-and-now world in which the biblical writer and his audience live and move. The historical Israel owes its existence and special character to what happened *in illo tempore*, "in that time" of paradigmatic origins.[30]

The Priestly Writer's intention is clear from his recasting of the exodus story to parallel his revision of the primeval creation story (Gen. 1:1–9:17). The genius of the Priestly Writer was thus to posit two creations. Or more correctly, he rewrote the creation story to contain two acts. The first secured the foundation of the cosmos and humankind in general; the second, the foundation of God's people. The first he inherited from the cultural matrix of the ancient Near East, the second from the Yahwistic faith of Israel. Both were transformed under his pen into a new myth of origins.

In the first act of creation Yahweh founded the heavens and the earth and all the denizens thereof. Like his ancient Near Eastern contemporaries, the Priestly Writer was enculturated into a mythological worldview that assumed the cosmos is maintained in existence by the vigilant rule of the divine sovereign who keeps at bay the nihilistic forces of chaos, whether these be the chaos monster itself, or one of the many historical incarnations of evil.[31] Analogous to the manner of other ancient Near Eastern national myths that served to undergird national origins and destiny (e.g., *Enuma elish* in Babylon and later in Assyria), the Priestly Writer rewrote the Combat Myth to conform to his faith in the god of Israel as the Lord of heaven and earth. But in the Priestly Writer's genius the creation story did not end with the securing of the cosmos.

In the second act of creation Yahweh went on to found his people Israel as his covenanted people and establish his "resting place"—the place from which he rules the cosmos—in their midst. Act two is told in the book of Exodus. From P's perspective the exodus, no less than the creation in Genesis, is an "event" of cosmic proportions, a story of origins through which the cosmic order is established and actualized. Israel can never be just one of the nations. It was specially created to be the dwelling place on earth of the very Lord of heaven and earth. Israel's existence is thus unique among the nations. Its story is bound up in some essential way with the myth of creation.

The primeval character of the Mosaic period can be seen in the manner in which the Priestly Writer treated the Mosaic revelation. At the conclusion of the covenant ceremony in Exodus 24, P has Moses return to the mountaintop where the deity was (24:15–31:18). The glory of Yahweh in the cloud covered the mountain for six days. On the seventh day Yahweh called Moses into the midst of the cloud. For forty days and forty nights Moses remained in the presence of Yahweh, during which time he was shown the heavenly "model" (*tabnît*) for the tabernacle and its furnishing (25:9, 40; 26:30; 27:8; see also Num. 8:4). There can be no doubt that the Priestly Writer intends this scene to parallel the opening scene in Genesis with six days of active creation and a seventh day in which God ceased his activity and "rested." By implication the Creator completed a new work during the six days when the glory of Yahweh shrouded the mountaintop. This new work is the "model" that the Creator revealed to Moses during the next forty days. Upon returning to "earth" Moses executed an exact replica of the heavenly exemplar (Exodus 35–40). One could scarcely ask for clearer evidence that P believed Israel's cult to be an imitation of mythic archetypes.[32] The same is true of the whole of the Mosaic Torah revealed to Moses on the mountaintop. Thus, even though Moses himself was fully human and lived in time, through priestly mythopoeic speculation the institutions of the Mosaic period acquired a definitive primordial status. The divine archetypes revealed "in that time" formed the basis by which the historical Israel lived and worshiped in the "here and now." The Mosaic institutions are themselves timeless; they remain paradigmatic for all time, as much as the cosmogonic myth in Genesis.[33]

Exodus as the Gesta Dei

It has been objected that the exodus is not really presented as myth since the story turns on the action of humans (Moses and the Israelites, Pharaoh and the Egyptians, etc.) rather than of the gods. Herman Gunkel stated this viewpoint most clearly: "Myths . . . are stories of the gods, in contradistinction to the legends in which the actors are men."[34] Gunkel's definition of myth is overly simplistic, however. It is true that myth usually deals with gods or divine beings (demons, angels, and others), but polytheism itself cannot be considered a litmus test for the presence of myth. Given the Yahwistic faith of ancient Israel, one should expect that the most blatant aspects of polytheism have been suppressed. A better criterion is whether the *functions of myth* are present, even if dressed in more or less "monotheistic" garb.

Mircea Eliade speaks of myth as the significant "*gesta* [deeds] of Supernatural Beings and the manifestation of their powers" in primeval times; it is these *gesta* that are the origin of "all significant human activities."[35] The exodus narrative can hardly be described as anything other than the story of the *gesta Dei*, the acts of Yahweh God.

The old epic traditions are more explicit in this regard than the later priestly version. In J Moses told the people, "Yahweh will fight for you, you have only to be still" (Ex. 14:14). As discussed above in chapter 2, the Yahwist thought of Yahweh as an engaged deity. Accordingly, here Yahweh is the Divine Warrior who acts on behalf of his elect people. From his station in the pillar of cloud he strikes terror into the hearts of the Egyptians so that they flee headlong into the sea and perish, thus allowing the Israelites to continue unmolested on their way.

This description of Yahweh can hardly be distinguished from similar descriptions of other ancient Near Eastern gods. George Mendenhall has demonstrated that the "pillar of cloud / pillar of fire" of exodus is typologically the same phenomenon that appears in ancient Near Eastern iconography as the winged disk or in the literature as the '*nn* (cloud) of Baal at Ugarit or the *melammū* of Ashur in Mesopotamia, that awesome brilliance which surrounds the deity and strikes terror into the heart of the enemy.[36]

Like J, E saw God as the principal agent in this narrative: "*God led* his people" in their wilderness trek (Ex. 13:17–18), journeying with them as the "messenger of God" and protecting them along the way (Ex. 14:19a, 25a). Similarly, the Song

of the Sea can scarcely be called anything other than an encomium of the *gesta Dei* in the combat against Pharaoh, who, as
we noted above, was also given a quasisupernatural status.

The priestly version is somewhat deceptive at first blush,
since in this tradition it is Moses who wielded the staff that split
the sea. P attempted to emphasize the deity's transcendence by
placing intermediaries between the deity and ordinary mortals.
Thus in P Yahweh characteristically speaks through Moses and
Aaron and accomplishes his will indirectly through human
agency. Nevertheless, even in P Yahweh is still the principal
actor. As elsewhere P presupposes the older epic traditions and
builds upon them. Within the Priestly Writer's own contribu-
tions to the exodus narrative Moses acquired a unique status as
Yahweh's chosen servant, yet he does nothing on his own, only
what he is commanded by God. This is the same pattern we
have observed in P with regard to the founding of the cultic
institutions. Moses merely carries out his instructions according
to the pattern that Yahweh showed him on the mountaintop.

Even in subtle details P emphasizes that it is Yahweh who is in
absolute control. Robert R. Wilson[37] has shown that the hardening of Pharaoh's heart motif, which in the earlier epic traditions
was applied only to the plague narratives, was extended by P to
the account of the crossing of the sea (Ex. 14:4, 8, 17). By the
addition of holy war themes to the hardening motif, P has turned
the whole of the exodus into Yahweh's holy war against Egypt.
Yahweh personally hardened Pharaoh's heart—as opposed to
Pharaoh hardening his own heart in J—so that Pharaoh would
persist in his obstinate actions and provide Yahweh with just
cause for destroying Pharaoh and his cohorts. Thus P also is insis-
tent that Yahweh personally triumphed over the enemy and that
to Yahweh alone belongs the glory (Ex. 14:18). What Wilson
ignores in all this, however, is that Yahweh's war is not against
mere flesh and blood, but against an incarnation of the chaos
dragon itself and that this accounts for the unrelenting manner in
which Yahweh systematically set out to crush Pharaoh.

Undoubtedly some readers would prefer, with Gunkel, to regard the exodus as legend or saga because of its "historylike"
narrative structure. Admittedly there is a great deal of similarity
and overlap between myth, saga, and legend; in the Bible as in

all literatures the narrative easily slips from one form to another. All three make a truth claim and all three have a narrative structure. Sagas are for the most part stories about great heroic figures of the past who have played a significant role in decisive events. Sagas usually are bound to specific locations and a definite time. Legends are similar to sagas except that the protagonists are as a rule great religious figures, models of piety. The purpose of the legend is to edify the listener to imitate the virtue of the model.[38] Although supernatural beings figure more prominently in myths and humans are more prominent in sagas and legends, this is not an essential difference. In *Gilgamesh* and in *Atrahasis* the protagonists are representatives of humankind and not gods, yet both are readily classified as myths. The essential difference, as I see it, is that sagas and legends take place in the past time, in secular time, whereas myths take place outside of secular time. Myth stands outside of time as we know it and serves as the *principle* or source of secular time and order. Myth is paradigmatic for the society in which that myth is operative. Such is the purpose of the book of Exodus.

The Elevation of Moses to Mythic Stature

Let me offer one final line of argument that the priestly author intended to depict the Mosaic Age as unique and the story of that age as a true myth.

Under priestly mythopoeic speculation the figure of Moses himself has acquired mythical status.[39] Deuteronomy 9:9 says that during the forty days and nights Moses spent on the mountaintop (i.e., in heaven) with the Creator, Moses neither ate nor drank, suggesting that through his close association with the deity Moses at least temporarily transcended the human condition. In P's portrayal the metamorphosis has gone much further. Consider the description of Moses' face and the reaction of the people in Exodus 34:29–35:

> When Moses came down from Mount Sinai with the tablets of the covenant in his hand . . . Moses did not know that the skin of his face had grown horns while he had been speaking with him (Yahweh). And when Aaron and all the Israelites saw Moses they feared to approach him. But Mo-

ses called them and they returned to him . . . and he laid upon them the whole commandment which Yahweh had spoken to him on Mount Sinai. And when Moses finished speaking to them, he put a veil over his face. But whenever Moses went before Yahweh to speak with him he would remove the veil until he came out; then he would go out and tell the Israelites whatever Yahweh had commanded him.

To translate *qāran ʿôr pānāyw* (vs. 29, 30, cf. 34) as "the skin of his face shone" (RSV) or "was radiant" (JPSV, similarly NAB), is to obscure the full import of what P intended here. A divine radiance is certainly present, as will be mentioned momentarily. A more literal translation of the phrase *qāran ʿôr pānāyw* would appear to be "the skin of his face horned"; that is, horns sprouted from Moses' forehead.[40] This image points to an alternative metaphor for divinity. In ancient Near Eastern iconography, horns were a symbol of divine status. In Mesopotamia the gods are typically pictured wearing a horned cap. Farther to the West, in Syro-Canaanite conception the horns protrude directly from the forehead of the deity.[41] As would be expected, the priestly portrait of Moses follows the geographically closer Syro-Canaanite tradition. By a graphic mythopoeism of depicting horns growing from Moses' forehead, the author has ascribed to Moses a quasidivine status that all can immediately recognize. The reaction of Aaron and the Israelites is in keeping with Moses' new dignity; they fall back in fear in Moses' presence, just as one does at a theophany. (It is interesting that the author of John 18:6 also uses this device to reveal Jesus' divine status: the soldiers attempting to arrest Jesus in the garden "drew back and fell to the ground when (Jesus) said to them, 'I AM.' ")

The fact that Moses must afterward veil his face whenever he appears before the people points to the same conclusion. Apparently the divine aura, that awesome brilliance that emanates from the deity, now surrounds Moses.[42] The people can no longer look upon Moses' face, any more than they can look upon the face of the deity. Moses, however, is no longer subject to the taboos imposed upon ordinary humans. When he goes into the presence of the deity, Moses removes the veil. In other words, he speaks to Yahweh "face to face" (cf. Deut. 34:10); he no longer has to hide his face from looking upon the deity, as ordinary humans must. This is certainly not the same Moses as before. When that Moses encountered Yahweh for the first time in the burning bush, the text says, "Moses hid his face, for he was afraid to look at God" (Ex. 3:6, J-E; cf. 33:22–23).

Nevertheless, P is careful to preserve a distinction between deity and humankind. No matter how extraordinary, P's heroes always remain mortal. Even Noah is made to die in P (Gen. 9:28), despite the ancient Near Eastern tradition that the legendary hero of the flood was later rewarded with immortality (cf. Utnapishtim in *Gilg.*, Tablet XI). But with Moses, P stretched the limits of mortality as far as humanly possible. Genesis 6:3 may be regarded as the classical text, defining the difference between deity and humankind: "My spirit shall not abide in humankind forever . . . ; he is flesh and his days shall be a hundred and twenty years."[43] P seems to have had this text in mind in describing Moses' death:[44] "Although Moses was a hundred and twenty years old when he died, his eye had not dimmed nor had his vigor gone" (Deut. 34:7).[45] Thus P says Moses did not die of old age like other humans. He was still in the vigor of his manhood when he reached the prescribed limit for a human lifespan. Rather this virtual immortal died because Yahweh decreed it (*'al pî YHWH*, v. 5).[46] Moses is not allowed to rival the deity's dignity; he remains completely subject to divine authority.

Even in death Moses is not an ordinary human, for P says that "[Yahweh] buried him" so that "no one knows even today the place of his burial" (Deut. 34:6). Can this be another mythopoeic speculation by P that somehow Moses escaped the usual separation from the Author of life that death brings, when the Creator's creative power over chaos is partially foiled as the underworld claims another life? Whether the author intended a suggestion of immortality or not, this passage inspired speculation in postbiblical times that Moses in fact did not die.[47] But if the author's intentions are ambiguous regarding the question of Moses' immortality, the author leaves no doubt that he regarded Moses as an absolutely unique figure in the history of humankind. The Priestly Writer concluded his work with the words:

> And there has not arisen a prophet since in Israel like Moses, whom the LORD knew face to face, none like him for all the signs and the wonders which the LORD sent him to do in the land of Egypt, to Pharaoh and to all his servants and to all his land, and for all the mighty power and all the great and terrible deeds which Moses wrought in the sight of all Israel. (Deut. 34:10–12, RSV)

These words may be a polemic against Deuteronomy (18:15, RSV): "The LORD your God will raise up for you a prophet like me [Moses] from among you, from your brethren—him you shall heed." P could not let that text stand, or else his whole schema would collapse. By definition Moses and the Mosaic Age can never be replicated. According to P, what happened in that sacred time of origins remains paradigmatic for God's people forever. It is precisely because Moses acquired exemplary or mythical status that he can serve as the model for the elect community in the historical present. It thus seems clear that P had every intention of making the Mosaic Age into a foundational myth that established the *unchanging reality* of Israel as the people of God.[48] Future generations can confidently rely upon what happened in that foundational age as paradigmatic of the Creator's will for all times.[49]

CONCLUSION

The vast differences in the manner in which the various literary strands of the Pentateuch portray the Israelites' escape from Egypt force us to conclude that we are dealing primarily with a developing literary tradition that owes as much—or more—to myth as to history. In the absence of additional archaeological discoveries, whatever historical core the exodus may have had is now irretrievably lost to us. Indeed, future finds are unlikely to resolve our uncertainty. Ancient Egyptian documents recovered thus far have more often than not increased suspicions about the historicity of the exodus narratives. Thus there does not seem to be any hope of ever arriving at a reliable historical reconstruction of any aspect of the actual "event" itself. At every stage of its transmission the exodus was interpreted and embellished by mythopoeisms, often very deliberately.

126

Perhaps the most obvious example is the way in which the Priestly Writer altered his source, which clearly distinguished the sea of the crossing from the Red Sea (*yam sûp*). It would appear that P deliberately telescoped the two so as to make the Red Sea to be the sea that was crossed. His warrant for this change was apparently derived from the old hymn, the Song of the Sea, in which "sea" and Red Sea (*yam sûp*) were poetically paralleled. In localizing the sea event right in the middle of the Red Sea, P not only "historicized" the event as a miracle of awesome magnitude in crossing the vast, deep Red Sea but he also was able to underscore what to his audience would have been the suprahistorical connotations implied by the Hebrew name of that sea: *yam sûp*, "the Sea of End," that is, the sea that marked at once the end of the creation and the beginning of noncreation or chaos. This in turn allowed for the suggestion that the splitting of the sea and the walking on dry land in the midst of the sea was an extension of the creative action of God. The victory of Yahweh over Pharaoh was identified with his splitting of the sea, which was identified with his primeval victory over the waters of chaos at creation and again at the flood. The placement of the Song of the Sea at this juncture further underscored Yahweh's victory over primeval sea and his enthronement on the mountain of Zion as divine sovereign. Following the pattern he set in revising the primeval myth, P has rewritten the narrative of the deliverance at the sea as a continuation of the deity's battle against chaos. Again, this must have been a reassuring theology for an exilic community that felt itself threatened with extinction.

A similar spirit pervades the rest of the priestly Tetrateuch as well. The whole of the Mosaic revelation has been granted foundational or paradigmatic status. In the priestly retelling of the story, not only were the Mosaic institutions patterned after divine, heavenly models, but also their "author" Moses was by divine will transformed into a quasidivine being. One could scarcely ask for a clearer example of mythopoeism. Contrary to those who claim that mythopoeic speculation was almost entirely foreign to ancient Israel, myth and mythopoeic speculation make up the very fabric of Israel's core tradition.

Chapter 5

◆

CROSSING DRY SHOD:
MYTHOPOEIC SPECULATION IN CULT

◆

Myth is frequently linked to ritual.[1] Without endorsing a theory that makes ritual a necessary complement to myth, I assert that the two often do function in tandem.[2] In this chapter I propose a case study of how ritual cult actually promoted the growth of mythic tradition. More specifically, I will examine the growth of the crossing of the sea motif. The thesis set forth in this chapter is that the crossing dry shod motif originally formed no part of the exodus tradition. The motif of crossing dry shod originally was associated with the conquest traditions about the Israelites crossing over the Jordan River at Gilgal to take possession of the land of Canaan. But gradually over the course of several centuries, through their use in cultic celebration at the sanctuary at Gilgal, the motif of crossing dry shod was transferred to the exodus tradition, until eventually the motif of crossing dry shod came to be associated more closely with the exodus and the Red Sea than with the conquest and the Jordan. A powerful influence in this transformation of the motif was the linking of River and Sea in the Canaanite version of the Combat Myth (the Baal myth).[3]

The importance of cult as a locus of mythopoesis, or myth-making, should not be overlooked.[4] Cult, here, means not only ritual—that is, the worship ceremonies and cultic paraphernalia of a sanctuary—but also that whole system of beliefs and expression (priestly instruction, sacred songs, legends, texts, etc.) that undergirds and makes possible an authentic, meaningful participation in the rituals of a community. Cult serves as a

128

primary carrier of the believing community's traditions by re-peating the ancient sacred stories to each new generation. At the same time it plays an active role in the reformulation of tradition by retelling the ancient stories as meaningful contem-porary statements.

Cult had just such a dual burden in the "traditioning" of ancient Israel. First, through the cult the Israelite story (or to-rah) was preserved and passed on from generation to generation as the principal statement of what Israel believed about its iden-tity and mission. The principal elements of this Israelite story are familiar to us from the narratives of the first books of the Bible. Second, through the cult that primal story was "contem-porized" for each successive generation. The cult not only re-presented—that is, made present again—the foundational event for later generations of Israelites, it also reinterpreted so as to make available that event's full power and significance for participants who lived in circumstances quite different from their forefathers. Through this process of contemporization and adaptation the shape of the primal story changed, often drasti-cally.

The addition of the motif of crossing dry shod to the Red Sea tradition is a case in point. In its earliest forms the deliverance at the sea in the exodus narrative contained no story about crossing dry shod through the midst of the (Red) Sea. An expla-nation of how a crossing dry shod motif came to be an essential ingredient of the exodus narrative must be sought in part in the history of Israel's own cult and in part from the influence of Canaanite myth on Israel's religious traditions. We begin with a look at Canaanite myth.

THE CANAANITE VERSION OF THE COMBAT MYTH

While researchers have always been able to catch glimpses of Canaanite myth from references in the Bible and from else-where, the recovery of the Canaanite myth began in earnest in this century with the unearthing of the ruins of the ancient city of Ugarit (Ras Shamra) on the north Syrian coast. In 1928 a Syrian plowman accidentally uncovered a Late Bronze Age cemetery in his field. The excavations that followed revealed the remains of an ancient town. Among the finds were a temple library that included clay tablets inscribed in a hitherto unknown alphabetic cuneiform script. Decipherment came quickly. The name of this ancient city was found to be Ugarit, so its language was promptly dubbed Ugaritic. The language itself proved to be a branch of West Semitic, cousin to Phoenician and Hebrew. Biblicists were justifiably excited because the new texts provided the context for numerous obscure allusions in the Bible, on the one hand, and lexical and grammatical help for translating difficult Hebrew verses, on the other hand.

None of the new texts created more excitement than a series of six fragmentary tablets belonging to the so-called Baal cycle (or alternatively, the Baal and Anat cycle). This Baal cycle was in fact a new version—the Canaanite version—of the Combat Myth. It is this myth to which we now turn our attention.

The interpretation of the Baal cycle (*CTA* 1–12)[5] is controversial, again as so often with ancient texts, largely because of the ill condition of the tablets. Only tablets 1–6 seem to belong to the cycle about Baal's combats with Yam (primeval sea) and Mot (death). Of these, only tablets 2–6 are complete enough to yield any clear narrative. Moreover, the beginning and ending lines are preserved only in the case of tablets 5–6, so that the proper sequence of the remaining tablets cannot be established. Most researchers have assumed that all six tablets belong to the same tale, and that it is only a matter of establishing their correct order—though no consensus on that order has been reached. However, the problem is deeper than the correct sequencing of the tablets. Richard J. Clifford seems to be on target in arguing that we are dealing here with not one but two (or more) versions of the Baal myth.[6] It is to a brief analysis of the myth with its variant versions that we now turn.[7]

The Baal myth is at core the old Combat Myth in a new guise. Like the Babylonian *Enuma elish*, the Baal myth is a cosmogonic myth. In this Canaanite version, however, the actual process of creation—whether of the gods or of the physical world or of humankind—is not told. Rather the emphasis is on affirming that the cosmos is stable because it is firmly under the control of the divine sovereign. The myth presumes a prior stage in creation when the "most high" El, the ancient and kindly king of the gods, seemed inadequate to the new challenges of chaos afoot in his world. As was the case with Marduk in *Enuma elish*, the challenge is met by a younger deity, the storm god Hadad, more commonly known by his title as Baal. Like Marduk, Baal too appears to have been a newcomer to the inner circle of the traditional high gods, since Baal was known as "the son of Dagon" and not one of the sons of El. In any case, Baal was the patron deity of Ugarit, so it is only natural that Ugaritic tradition should have put Baal at the center of their cosmogonic myth. But unlike his Babylonian counterpart, Baal does not so much supplant the older god, as the older king god El makes the younger and more vigorous storm god Baal his associate in divine rule. Together El and Baal form a united rule, the transcendent father of the gods from his mountain sanctuary in the distant recesses of the cosmos, and the immanent young warrior god from his temple-palace installed on nearby Mount Zaphon.

In one version of the myth Baal battles Yam (primeval sea); in the other version his opponent is Mot (death). Both Yam and Mot are said to be sons of El. So in both versions the issue is which principle will rule the cosmos: Baal as the life-sustaining force of an ordered and stable world, or Yam/Mot as the life-threatening force in an already precarious and chaotic world. In both versions Baal defeats his opponent and then rules from a newly built palace on the cosmic Mount Zaphon—a metaphor for the stability of a world founded on divine order. In his struggles to overcome Yam/Mot, Baal is sometimes aided by his sister and wife, virgin Anat, a veritable warrior herself.

In the Mot version, at the point where the narrative becomes intelligible (tablet 4), Baal's young reign is extremely tenuous. Baal and Anat scurry about trying to get permission from El to build a palace for Baal. They succeed by bribing Asherah, El's wife, to intercede for them with El. The palace itself, magically constructed from silver and gold and adorned in lapis lazuli, is the handiwork of the divine craftsman, Kothar-wa-hasis. At first Baal refused to allow any windows in his palace, seemingly to prevent Mot (death) from gaining entry. Later he relented and a window was cut. From this window Baal thunders majestically across the earth. At this point the tablet breaks off.

When the text picks up again (tablets 5–6), Baal is seated at a banquet with the other gods. They are interrupted by messengers from Mot demanding that Baal, the storm god, be handed over to him. The gods have no choice but to accede to Mot's demands. The storm god, along with his winds and life-giving rain, is forced to descend into the underworld into the jaws of death. Drought of course reigns upon the earth and El himself lapses into mourning. Anat, however, takes matters into her own hands. She confronts Mot and pulverizes him. In a kind of sympathetic magic fertility rite, like so much grain Anat cuts Mot down with her sword and winnows him; part she parches and grinds into flour, part she sows in the field. Her actions have their desired effect. Baal is freed from his deathly imprisonment, the drought broken. Baal returns to vivify the earth with his rains once more. In a final episode Mot arises to challenge Baal once again. In this battle neither is able to get the better of the other until Shapash, the sun god, enters the fight on the side of Baal. Frightened, Mot flees. The tablet ends at this point. But the reader intuits that the story itself has not been concluded— death still lurks in the shadows and must be confronted again.

This Mot version clearly has some connection with the fertility character of Canaanite religion. The contest between the weather god Baal and the underworld god Mot replicated itself in the agricultural economy of ancient Syria, where one's very livelihood depended upon sufficient rainfall. Drought was disastrous—nay, it was deadly. Perhaps this myth was recited in connection with a fertility ritual.

The alternative Yam version (*CTA* 2–3),[8] though less complete, is the more interesting for our investigation, since it parallels more nearly the Babylonian *Enuma elish* and biblical passages having to do with Yahweh's defeat of the chaos dragon, alternatively the sea. Once again major portions of the tablets are lost, making it difficult to establish the context for Baal's battle with Yam (primeval sea). In this version Yam rather than Mot is the one who sends messengers demanding that the gods hand over Baal to him. Although the other gods are cowed, Baal defiantly strides forth to meet Yam.

The combat itself is rich in poetic description, especially in use of parallelism. "Baal the Conqueror" is also the "Rider on

Clouds." Yam is alternatively named first "Prince Sea," then "Judge River." Baal carries with him two awesome clubs fashioned by Kothar-wa-Hasis: "Driver," to drive Prince Sea from his throne, and "Chaser," to chase Judge River from his royal chair. With his powerful weapons the Cloud-rider succeeds in defeating Yam:

> And the club danced in Baal's hands,
>   like a vulture from his fingers.
> It struck Prince Sea on the skull,
>   Judge River between the eyes.
> Sea stumbled;
>   he fell to the ground;
> his joints shook;
>   his frame collapsed.
> Baal captured and drank Sea;
>   he finished off Judge River.
> Astarte shouted Baal's name:
> "Hail, Baal the Conqueror!
>   hail, Rider on the Clouds!
> For Prince Sea is our captive,
>   Judge River is our captive."[9]

This is followed by the proclamation: "Sea indeed is dead, Baal reigns!"

Just what Anat's role in the battle was is unclear. In *CTA* 3, after a long break, we find Anat engaged in a gory battle of her own, but against humans. Baal sends messengers to tell her to cease. Anat mistakes them as bearers of ill news, though she cannot fathom its source because, as she boasts, she has herself defeated all Baal's enemies, including Yam. The messengers assure Anat that Baal's rule is secure and that Baal wishes her to desist from war, that Baal desires peace, and that Anat should put (plant) peace into the earth.[10] Baal then creates lightning as a symbol of this new condition on earth. The tablet breaks off with Baal and Anat in the process of securing permission from El to build a palace for Baal.

Unlike the Mot version, which was clearly linked to the fertility character of Canaanite religion, the Yam version is manifestly more cosmogonic. As with the Babylonian *Enuma elish*, the struggle here is between the primal principles of cosmos and chaos. For the biblically attuned reader, Baal's smashing of Yam's head evokes similar images of Yahweh as he "who smashed the heads of the dragon on the water, who crushed the heads of Leviathan" (Ps. 74:13–14); while Baal's drinking up Yam evokes images of Israel's creator "who dries up of the sea" (Isa. 51:10). Even lacking the ending, it is quite obvious that this myth of Baal's defeat of Yam served to affirm for its baalistic adherents that their god indeed had matters firmly under control and that their world was secure.

All of these texts were found in the temple library and written in the same hand. According to the preserved colophons, the text was "dictated by Attanu-Purlianni, the chief priest, the chief herdsman," and written by the scribe Ilimilku, under the patronage of Niqmaddu, king of Ugarit, who reigned from c. 1375–1345 B.C.E. We do not know the precise manner in which these mythic texts were used, but the likelihood is great that they had some function in temple ceremonies. It has been suggested that these and other texts from the temple library served as the librettos for actual rituals.[11] If so, this is significant for our reconstruction of how cultic legend developed within the cult in ancient Israel.

The variations within the Canaanite Baal cycle provide an empirical model for the hypothesis that Israel developed more than one version of the exodus story, and that they could be operative at the same time and in the same place. Moreover, cult was a significant contributor to this process. The full impact of this Canaanite myth will not become obvious until later in the chapter, however, after we have studied both the changing shape of the exodus tradition and the role the cult at Gilgal played in shaping that tradition.

THE SHAPE OF THE LATE EXODUS TRADITION

It is relatively easy to observe development in the shape of the exodus traditions, even if the precise history of development cannot always be sketched with confidence. As intimated in the preceding chapter, the early traditions are noticeably different from the late ones. The precise shape of the late tradition is established by Nehemiah 9, a text that is unquestionably post-exilic (fifth or fourth century B.C.E.) and one of the latest prose texts of the Hebrew Bible to describe the exodus. In Ezra's prayer to Yahweh, the deliverance at the Red Sea is described thus:

> You saw the oppression of our fathers in Egypt and heard their cry at the Red Sea, and you worked signs and wonders against Pharaoh and all his servants. . . . You split the sea before them, allowing them to cross on dry ground right through the middle of the sea. Their pursuers, however, you hurled into its depths, into the mighty waters, like a stone." (Neh. 9:9–11)

At this late period three motifs predominate in the description: (a) the sea is the Red Sea (*yam sûp*), (b) whose waters are split in two (*bāqāʿ*), (c) allowing the Israelites to cross (*ʿābār*) through its midst on dry ground. (The lateness of Neh. 9:9–11 is also evident in its dependency upon the received text of Exodus 14–15; v. 11b is a free quotation of Ex. 15:5.)

Another postexilic text, Isaiah 63:11–13, although in poetic form, features essentially the same characteristics:

> Then he remembered those ancient times,
>   of Moses his servant.
> Where is he who brought them forth from the sea
>   with the shepherd of his sheep?
> . . . who split the water before them
>   thereby establishing his fame forever;
> Who caused them to walk through the abyss
>   without stumbling like horses in desert sand?

Poetic form has allowed the author to be somewhat free with the tradition, but the characteristic splitting of the sea and the motif of effortlessly crossing dry shod are nonetheless prominent.

These same two motifs are equally characteristic of the priestly literary strand of the exodus narrative in Exodus 13:17–15:21, but not of the J and E strands. As noted in the last chapter, P had specified that the Israelite deliverance took place in the Red Sea, when its waters were split (*bāqāᶜ*) in twain, allowing the Israelites to walk through its midst on dry ground, the waters forming a wall to their right and left. By way of contrast, neither J-E nor the Song of the Sea mentions a crossing of the sea by the Israelites—despite the prominence of the sea and the drowning of the Egyptian pursuers in those traditions. The fact that P is in agreement with other demonstrably late texts, in opposition to the situation in J-E and the Song of the Sea, is prima facie evidence of the validity of the hypothesis that P derives from a much later date than J-E and the Song of the Sea, and likely from the exilic period (as the majority of critical scholars think).

But a question immediately presents itself. If the motif of crossing the Red Sea dry shod formed no part of the early traditions about the exodus, when did the motif arise to become the most prominent feature of the late traditions and how did such a radical transformation come about? A partial answer is provided by ancient Near Eastern myth. It is obvious that the description of the splitting (*bāqāᶜ*) of the sea has been influenced by and adapted to the morphology of the common Semitic Combat Myth wherein the creator god defeated his archenemy, the chaotic Sea, by splitting her in twain and in the process creating the heavens and the earth out of the dead carcass.[12] But a fuller answer would involve factors at work within the Israelite cult, particularly at the sanctuary of Gilgal. From a combination of myth creatively adapted and the contemporization of an ancient cultic legend, the motif of crossing the Red Sea dry shod was born, very likely at the sanctuary of Gilgal.

GILGAL AS THE SOURCE OF THE MOTIF
OF CROSSING DRY SHOD

According to the narrative of Joshua 3–5, Gilgal was the very first sanctuary set up by the Israelites upon entering the Promised Land. However, the origins of Gilgal as a sacred place antedate the Israelite settlement.[13] In its pre-Israelite phase Gilgal was the site of a Canaanite agricultural festival each spring. Very likely these Canaanites knew and utilized in their cult similar, if not the same, mythic traditions as their Canaanite cousins at Ugarit at approximately this same time. It is not unthinkable that these Gilgal Canaanites were accustomed to reciting the Mot version of the Baal myth in thanksgiving for an abundant harvest and another year without serious drought. And if the Mot version and the Yam version of the Baal cycle were paired into some kind of unified myth as many scholars think, then it is not impossible that the drama of Baal overcoming Prince Sea/Judge River was also recited in this sanctuary overlooking the Jordan.

The legend that underlies Joshua 3–5, that the invading Israelites built the sanctuary and used it as a base camp from which to stage further conquests, perhaps reflects primarily the history of the tribe of Benjamin, in whose territory Gilgal is situated, and its immediate neighbors. Very likely the Benjaminites wrested control of the sanctuary from the Canaanites and made it their own. Over a period of several centuries, however, the original Canaanite agricultural festival was gradually wedded to the invaders' conquest traditions. Of course the Israelites would have replaced the Canaanite deity with their own deity. Or more exactly, to judge from indications elsewhere in the Bible, Baal's attributes would have been shifted onto Yahweh in syncretistic fashion. Through some such route as this, the original Gilgal agricultural festival of unleavened bread came over time to be celebrated as Yahweh's giving of the land with its fruits to the Hebrew newcomers. As the Gilgal cultic legend became increasingly "historicized" as the story of Israelite conquest, its original agricultural themes were reduced to the point of mere vestiges (Josh. 5:10–12). The actual stages by which this happened can no longer be reconstructed with certitude.

Gilgal served at times during the Tribal League period as a central sanctuary of the Israelite tribal league.[14] After the destruction of Shiloh by the Philistines in the middle of the eleventh century, Gilgal clearly emerged as the political and religious center of Israel (1 Sam. 4; Jer. 7:12, 14; cf. 26:6, 8). It was here that Samuel brought Saul to anoint him king (1 Sam. 11:14–15). As the ark of the covenant was not present during this period (1 Sam. 7:1 and 2 Sam. 6–7), Gilgal's emergence as the central Israelite sanctuary was based on other factors. It may have been during this period that Gilgal's Benjaminite cultic traditions were expanded to incorporate "all Israel."

This was a two-way process, however. Not only were the other Israelite tribes made to be participants of the Gilgalite conquest, but also the heritage of the other tribes was assimilated into the Gilgalite traditions to form a new tradition that "all Israel" had shared in the mysteries of salvation as celebrated at this sanctuary.[15] "All Israel" would have included not only other Israelite tribal groups but even numerous converts from among the original Canaanite population. At work here was the cultic principle that one who joins the believing community of faith and joins in its rituals as a believing participant is fully incorporated into the community. The community's faith and traditions become one's own. Henceforth one's own identity is inseparable from that of the community of faith.

(For a frequently cited modern-day analogy, we Americans need to look no further than our own backyard. Like other Americans, as a school child I learned—and still personally think of—"the Thanksgiving story" as a story of *our* forefathers and foremothers, even though *my* forebears did not immigrate to this country until more than two centuries *after* that event had transpired.)

But if Gilgal inherited and assimilated the traditions of "all Israel," it also molded them within the form of its own special traditions. This is the case with the traditions about the so-called conquest of the land of Canaan. The Bible contains vestigial accounts of more than one "conquest" by "Israelite" invaders and even recollections that some of the twelve tribes of (later) Israel did not participate in the exodus and conquest.[16] Nevertheless, the version that came to predominate in the biblical tradition is that all Israel had been in Egypt and all had participated in the exodus with Moses and all had entered the land of Canaan with Joshua by crossing the Jordan at Gilgal. It was probably during this period when Gilgal served as the central sanctuary of the Israelite League that the old spring agricultural festival of Gilgal was transformed into a ritual conquest of the whole land of Canaan in which "all Israel" had entered the land by crossing the Jordan dry shod.

Such a ritual can be reconstructed from the cultic legends

preserved in Joshua 3–5.[17] The ritual would have been part of a conquest festival, that is, a celebration of entry into Canaan to take possession of the rich land into which "Yahweh, lord of all the earth" had led them (3:11–13).[18] This conquest ritual began with a reenactment of the desert march "from Shittim to Gilgal" (Josh. 3:1; cf. Micah 6:5). Shittim was the traditional last station in the wilderness itinerary of the exodus; Gilgal was the traditional first site in the Promised Land to be occupied by the Israelites. The high point of the ritual apparently was a ceremonial crossing—whether actual or symbolic—of the Jordan River by the worshipers in a solemn liturgical procession. This portion of the ritual was designed to recall for the participants the belief that their God had literally laid open the land to them, for Yahweh temporarily caused the waters of the Jordan to stop flowing so that his people might cross dry shod into the Promised Land.

A cultic legend or "story" would have accompanied and explained the ritual. It is undoubtedly such a cultic legend that lies behind the narrative of Joshua 3–5, now incorporated into the Deuteronomistic History.[19]

The narrative of Joshua 3–5 is the story of the Israelites' crossing of the Jordan prior to their conquest of the land of Canaan. On the surface the narrative appears to be a unified story in that everything has to do with the crossing of the Jordan dry shod, preliminary to the taking of the city of Jericho. Yet a closer reading of the narrative reveals that the unity is an imposed one. At least two versions of the incident have been joined together to form the present narrative.[20] A couple of illustrations will suffice. In 4:11 the crossing seems to be complete; "all the people" and "the ark of Yahweh together with the priests" (carrying the ark) are said to have completed the crossing. The reader is therefore more than a little surprised to read later at 4:15–18 that the priests are still standing in the river bed! Also the manner of the handling of the twelve stones in chapter 4 suggests at least two parallel recensions of the same incident. On the one hand Joshua instructs twelve men to carry one stone each from the east bank of the Jordan to set them up in the middle of the Jordan as a memorial for future generations (4:4–5, 9). On the other hand the twelve stones were supposed to be taken from the midst of the river bed and carried to the western bank and set up as me-morials at Gilgal (4:1–3, 8, 20). The scholarly debate over the complex history of composition is far from settled.[21] But such duplications within the text make it necessary to posit the pres-ence of at minimum two versions of the crossing, prior to the reworking of the story by the Deuteronomist, who further adapted it to his own historical and theological schema. (Here it may not be inappropriate to recall the analogous situation at Ugarit where two or more versions of the Baal myth at Ugarit functioned side by side.)

The idea of crossing dry shod is completely at home in this cultic legend. The motif is deeply embedded in every level of the narrative and is itself the focal point of the story. Even the later editorial gloss about the crossing taking place during a flood period (3:15b; cf. 4:18) points to the same conclusion. We may conclude, therefore, that from the very beginning the motif of crossing the Jordan dry shod was part and parcel of the Gilgalite conquest tradition. A miraculous crossing of the river was an essential element in this story of entry. Although there are fords in the area (Josh. 2:7), an ordinary fording of the river is nowhere even hinted at and would be contradictory to the spirit of this cultic legend.[22] From beginning to end the narra-tive emphasizes the "cutting" of the waters and the crossing on dry ground as indicative of the manner in which God opened up the land before the Israelites, in fidelity to the divine promise that the land would be given to the descendants of the pa-triarchs.

This situation is in direct contrast with the exodus narra-tive (Ex. 13:17–15:21), where the motif of crossing dry shod through the Red Sea is found only in the latest (P) recension. It is completely absent in the earlier J-E tradition and in the Song of the Sea, as we noticed in the preceding chapter.

Likewise here in Joshua 4–5, a parallel between the crossing of the Jordan and the crossing of the Red Sea is made in 4:23 but is glaring in its omission from the alternative recension at 4:4–7. In Joshua 4:23 we read, "Yahweh your God dried up the waters of the Jordan before you until you passed over, even as Yahweh your God did to the Red Sea which he dried up before us until we passed over." This statement forms part of a catechetical instruction (4:21–24) intended for the benefit of future generations. However, an older version of that same catechesis has been preserved at Joshua 4:4–7. In the older form no connection between the Jordan crossing and the Red Sea deliverance is drawn. *A priori*, this would suggest that a parallel between the Jordan crossing and the sea deliverance was unknown in the early period, undoubtedly because the motif of crossing dry shod formed no part of the earliest exodus tradition at Gilgal, exactly as witnessed by the older (J-E) epic traditions and the Song of the Sea. When and where a connection between the Jordan motif of crossing dry shod and the deliverance at the (Red) Sea was first made is difficult to determine, but there is strong evidence to suggest that the association was inspired by cultic developments at Gilgal.

Certainly the motif of crossing dry shod was already being applied to the exodus tradition by the time of the Deuteronomist, c. 600 B.C.E. In addition to Joshua 4:23, it appears again at Joshua 2:10; both of these texts predate the Deuteronomist.[23] Just how much earlier the motif was introduced is unknown, but some indication is provided by the Elijah-Elisha cycle.

In the legend of Elijah's translation into heaven in the fiery chariot (2 Kings 2:1–18) Elijah and Elisha traveled to Gilgal to the place of translation on the other side of the Jordan. When they arrived at the Jordan, "Elijah took his mantle, rolled it up, and struck the water; and the water was parted to one side and the other, till the two of them could go over on dry ground" (v. 8). After his master's disappearance in the fiery chariot, Elisha took up Elijah's mantle and returned to the Jordan. He repeated his master's action of striking the water with the mantle, whereupon the waters parted once more and Elisha recrossed the Jordan dry shod, thereby demonstrating that he had become heir to Elijah's office.

This legend is patterned after the traditions concerning Moses and his successor-disciple Joshua. Elijah on Mount Carmel (1 Kings 18) is not unlike Moses on Mount Horeb (Sinai) mediating a renewal of covenant between Yahweh and his faithless people (Exodus 32–34). Also like Moses, Elijah miraculously is fed bread and water in the wilderness for a forty-day journey to Horeb, where (again like Moses) he is allowed to see the deity pass by (1 Kings 19) possibly from the very same cave where Moses earlier stood (cf. 1 Kings 19:9, 13 with Ex. 33:21–23). Elijah is taken away in the fiery chariot, with no trace of his body ever found in the mountain or valley region of the trans-Jordan (2 Kings 2:15–18), the very same region as Mount Nebo where Moses died and was buried by Yahweh in a valley, with his body likewise never to be found (Deut. 34:1–6). And as Joshua succeeded to Moses' office, so too was Elisha anointed to succeed his master Elijah (1 Kings 19:16–21; 2 Kings 2:1–15). Clearly the Moses-Joshua pattern is intentional in these Elijah-Elisha legends. Thus it is evident that the portrayal of the disciple Elisha dividing the waters of the Jordan is intended to parallel the disciple Joshua's crossing of the Jordan dry shod. But it is also evident that the master Elijah's dividing of the water implied a similar feat by Moses, namely, the familiar crossing of the Red Sea on dry ground.

Thus the Elijah-Elisha cycle provides the earliest datable attestation of the motif of crossing dry shod being applied to the sea tradition. As some time must be allowed after the death of Elisha (c. 825 B.C.E.) for the cycle to have attained its present embellished legendary form, the motif can hardly predate the middle of the eighth century B.C.E. Nevertheless, by the end of the seventh century B.C.E., when the Deuteronomist incorporated this cycle into his History, the motif of crossing the Red Sea dry shod was firmly entrenched in the Gilgalite cultic legends.

In this context, it is important to note that the Elijah-Elisha cycle was preserved and nurtured within Gilgalite circles. Gilgal functions as the center of the two prophets' activities. Elisha is even portrayed as the leader of the prophetic guild located at this sanctuary (2 Kings 4:38) and the surrounding regions (2 Kings 2:15–22). The story of the prophets' dual crossing of the Jordan dry shod is explicitly attached to the region of the Jordan near Jericho (2 Kings 2:4), that is, at Gilgal. One can only assume, therefore, that this story reflects Gilgalite traditions. Thus the prominence of the crossing dry shod motif in these prophetic legends again points to Gilgalite cult as the source for the application of the crossing dry shod motif to the exodus sea tradition.

This development was, no doubt, encouraged by the expansion of the Gilgalite festival from being a *conquest* festival to being also a *passover* festival, in which were celebrated Yahweh's mighty deeds of salvation wrought during the exodus. Once the festival became also a celebration of the exodus, it was a simple and natural step to regard the memorial ritual of crossing through water as applicable not only to entry through the Jordan but to deliverance at the sea as well. On both occasions a body of water had figured prominently in Yahweh's mighty act of salvation on behalf of his people. Gradually the two events acquired a kind of homogeneity in the minds of the worshipers, so that eventually the elements that properly belonged to the original cultic legend of crossing the Jordan were (perhaps unconsciously) transferred to the sea tradition. Chief among these was the motif of crossing dry shod, which finds its ultimate expression in the catechesis of Joshua 4:23, which presents the "events" at the Red Sea and at the Jordan as essentially identical miracles of divine guidance through mighty waters— replete with much of the mythic underpinning that we noted in the previous chapter.

Mythic influence from the direction of the old Canaanite Combat Myth would also have been at work here. Canaanite traditions and religion did not die out with Israelite ascendance. The Bible reveals that they continued to exert influence until the end of monarchical Israel and even beyond. The parallelism between Prince Sea and Judge River as twin names for the chaos dragon in the Baal myth would have been highly suggestive in this context. Sea was historicized as the Red Sea, and River as the Jordan. With the distinction between myth and history blurred, Yahweh's "splitting" of the Jordan was a datum that applied equally to *yam sûp*, the "End Sea." This is a theme to which we will return in the following section.

Gilgal of course lost its position as the central Israelite sanctuary when the political and religious focus shifted to Jerusalem in the Southern Kingdom and to Shechem, Dan, and Bethel in the Northern Kingdom. Nevertheless, Gilgal maintained its importance as a major religious center. In the ninth century it gained renewed prestige when it became the favored sanctuary of the prophets Elijah and Elisha (2 Kings 2:1; 4:38). Even at the end of the eighth century Gilgal had not lost its appeal as a place of pilgrimage (Hos. 4:15; 9:15; 12:11). It would appear that Gilgal escaped destruction at the hands of the Assyrians in 721 B.C.E. and continued as a center of religious activity into the next century. Certainly its influence survived long after, for its religious traditions appear to have been championed by the deuteronomic school, which is responsible for a major portion of the Hebrew Bible.[24] This is very likely the path through which the story of the crossing of the Jordan (Joshua 3–4) found its way into the Deuteronomistic History.

THE HYMNIC EVIDENCE FOR CULTIC MYTHOPOEIC SPECULATION

In the preceding sections I have attempted to reconstruct the history of the motif crossing dry shod, especially the central role that the cult of Gilgal played in the development of the motif and its eventual transfer to the exodus narrative of deliverance at the Red Sea. In the present section I propose to examine various hymns in the Psalter and elsewhere for additional evidence on how the exodus was being interpreted within ancient Israel. If it is true, as most scholars think, that most psalms originated within the cult,[25] then individual psalms should provide another avenue into the cultic expression of biblical revelation and give confirmation to the thesis just elaborated.

It has been suggested that the Song of the Sea (Ex. 15:1–18) originated in the cult of Gilgal.[26] Certainly this hymn links exodus and conquest themes in a manner similar to the cultic pattern we have observed for Gilgal. The latter part of the Song celebrates Yahweh's providential leading of his people through the wilderness before dumbfounded nations (vs. 13–16a) and the crossing of the Jordan (v. 16b) en route to Yahweh's sanctuary (v. 17). This poem was composed sometime after the Israelites had become entrenched in the land—in the words of the song: planted around Yahweh's holy mountain, the sanctuary that his hands have established (v. 17). In the received version of this hymn the sanctuary referred to here is Zion and not Gilgal. Nevertheless, it is possible that the Song of the Sea may have had a prehistory of origins in the Gilgal cult. Verses 14–16 are reminiscent of Joshua 2:10–11 and 5:1. Rumor of what Yahweh did to Edom and Moab (Sihon and Og) caused the courage of the Canaanites to melt away, while the Israelites crossed ('ābār) the Jordan unmolested. Finally, note should be taken that there is no crossing of the sea but of the Jordan only, precisely as was the case in the original Gilgal tradition.

A second hymn that couples the exodus with the Jordan crossing is Psalm 114. Although one may encounter a few vague allusions elsewhere in the Psalter (e.g., Ps. 66:6), Psalm 114 is unique in seeing a perfect parallel between the two "events."

> When Israel went forth from Egypt,
>   the house of Jacob from a people of strange language,
> Judah became his sanctuary,
>   Israel his dominion.
> The sea looked and fled,
>   Jordan turned back.
> The mountains skipped like rams,
>   the hills like lambs.
> What ails you, O sea, that you flee?
>   O Jordan, that you turn back?
> O mountains, that you skip like rams?
>   O hills, like lambs?
> Tremble, O earth, at the presence of the LORD,
>   at the presence of the God of Jacob,
> Who turns the rock into a pool of water,
>   the flint into a spring of water. (RSV)

There is every reason to think that this psalm originated in the Gilgal cult. The setting is a celebration of the exodus in its larger sense of events that led to Israel's settlement in Canaan as God's "sanctuary," and not just the leaving of Egypt. Also the parallelism between the sea and the Jordan is exact; the waters of the sea retreated exactly as did the Jordan before Israel. It is probable that the poet had in mind for the sea only the tradition of Yahweh blowing back the waters with the wind-breath of his nostrils as in the Song of the Sea (Ex. 15:8) or in the Yahwistic epic (Ex. 14:21). Nevertheless, we may imagine that this strict parallelism between the action of the sea and that of the Jordan was very suggestive to later generations of worshipers singing the hymn during their ritual reenactment of the Jordan crossing.

It is little wonder that in time these worshipers would be instructing their children on the meaning of this ritual with the catechesis of Joshua 4:23. The transfer of the motif crossing dry shod from the Jordan to the Red Sea was undoubtedly aided by this psalm.

Equally important, however, are the suggestive openings to mythic connotations allowed by the psalm. The personification and pairing of the sea and the River Jordan, although perhaps originally inspired by authentic Yahwistic cultic practice at Gilgal, could not but evoke reminiscences of the Canaanite version of the Combat Myth, wherein Baal had to overcome the twin foe of Prince Sea and Judge River before he could establish his universal rule. Such mythic connotations are extremely restrained in Psalm 114, but in other passages they are given free rein.

In the old psalm preserved in Habakkuk 3, references to Israel's "salvation history" are almost completely muted, while mythic accommodations are allowed unrestrained expression. Note how in this poem the River Jordan and the (Red) Sea have been completely recast in the language of the primeval battle of the creator deity against the sea-dragon.[27]

> Is not your wrath, O Yahweh, against River,
> Your anger against River,
> Your ire against Sea,
> When you drive your horses,
> Your chariot of salvation?
> You unsheathe your bow . . .
> The mountains see you and quake;
> Abyss cries aloud . . .
> With your horses you trample Sea,
> The raging of Mighty Waters!
> (Hab. 3:8–10, 15)

The text of Habakkuk 3 is replete with textual corruptions, making it extremely difficult to translate and interpret. The historical references are vague. Distinguishing between past and present is grammatically impossible as forms slip easily between perfect and imperfect. Yahweh's movement from Mount Paran (= Sinai, cf. Deut 33:2) to the Transjordan (Midian and Cushan, v. 7) apparently refers to the exodus wilderness trek through the desert. Yahweh's anger against Sea and River would then contain allusions to the historical incidents at the sea of the exodus and the Jordan crossing. Even so, it is obvious that these "historical events" have been incorporated into Yahweh's eternal cosmic battle against the forces of chaos, even more so than in the Song of the Sea. History and myth have been thoroughly homogenized in this poem by a kind of mythopoeic speculation. The meaning of the "event" has been interpreted and extended by creatively applying old mythic concepts to new situations. In this way Israel achieved a more definitive meaning and universal applicability for its traditions and beliefs.

Once unleashed, the power of mythopoeic speculation to transform the exodus traditions achieved a life of its own. Increasingly the sea tradition would assume not only the language but also the spirit of the common Semitic Combat Myth. Of course, independently of the sea tradition, the Israelites had already long ago begun to substitute Yahweh for the West Semitic storm god Baal—as they would later for the Babylonian god Marduk—in their retelling of the battle against chaos. Thus, Psalm 29, perhaps originally a Canaanite hymn,[28] was instantly transformed into a Yahwistic hymn by replacing the name of Baal with that of Yahweh. Other measures, less blatant perhaps, were none the less effective. Partially in a polemic against the Canaanite religious threat, partially as an affirmation of the uniqueness and universality of Yahweh's rule, Israel attributed to her God the defeat of the primeval sea-dragon and the creation of the ordered cosmos. Such mythopoeic processes continued through the period of the exile and afterward, and are quite manifest in the cultic hymns of that period.

Psalm 74 implores God to regard the ruins of Jerusalem and the temple, especially, and act to restore his people. In terms reminiscent of the so-called ode to Yahweh's arm (Isa. 51:9–11), the psalmist recalls God's defeat of the primeval sea-dragon as a motive for God to act in the present threat to his universal rule.

> Why do you restrain your hand?
> your right hand remain idle inside your cloak?

> O God, my king from primeval times,
>   who works salvation in the middle of the earth,
> It was you who broke apart the sea by your might,
>   who smashed the heads of the dragon on the water.
> It was you who crushed the heads of Leviathan,
>   who gave him to the desert folk as food.
> It was you who opened springs and brooks;
>   you who turned primordial rivers into dry land.
>   (Ps. 74:11–15)[29]

It is obvious that the psalmist is indebted here to the Canaanite myth for his portrayal of Yahweh's victory over chaos and evil. Ugaritic texts depict Baal's battle with the primeval sea-dragon in almost identical terms:

> When you smote Lotan [= Leviathan] the fleeting dragon,
> Destroyed the crooked serpent,
> Shilyat with the seven heads . . . [30]

By appropriating the myth for Yahweh the psalmist affirmed his—and his community's—belief that Yahweh, and not some other power, whether in the heavens, on earth, or under the earth, is the creator and lord of the universe. In other words, myth has been found to be an appropriate medium for theologizing about the most profound issues.

Various reflexes of this conception of Yahweh's rule are found throughout the bible. Yahweh is the one who established order in the universe by stilling the raging of the sea and its destructive waves (Ps. 65:6–7), the raging sea being of course the embodiment of the chaos dragon (Ps. 89:9–10). The sea may rage all it wishes but Yahweh's rule is firmly established over it (Ps. 93:3–4). Yahweh's victory over the sea provides confidence that chaos will not overwhelm the present day (Ps. 46:2–3; 107:29).

The image of the sea as the enemy of both Creator and creature left its mark also in the exodus tradition. For the author of Psalm 77, meditation upon God's primordial deeds (vs. 6, 12–13 [E.T.: 5, 11–12]) leads him to see the exodus as an extension of the deity's battle against the sea:

> The waters saw you, O God,
>> the waters saw you and shuddered;
>> yea, the Abyss trembled.
> The clouds poured down water;
>> the darkened skies rumbled;
>> your arrows sped about.
> Your thunder resounded in the whirlwind;
>> your lightning lit up the world;
>> the earth quivered and quaked.
> Upon the Sea was your foot/dominion,
>> upon Mighty Waters your treading,
>> though no one saw your footprints.
> You led your people like a flock
>> by the hand of Moses and Aaron.
>
> (Ps. 77:17–21 [E.T.: 16–20])

The last two cola make it clear that the psalmist has the exodus in mind. Nevertheless, the description is otherwise a portrayal of the battle against chaos. Pharaoh and the Egyptians have been completely replaced here as the enemy. Only the sea remains as the object of God's wrath. This transformation is more than mere poetic license. It is rather an attempt to get at the fundamental problem. The real obstacle to Israel's freedom was not of flesh and blood but the very power of evil itself. It was through the lens of myth that the universal meaning of the exodus was revealed to Israelite believers, thereby enabling the exodus to become the primary paradigm of salvation in the Hebrew scriptures.

Thus we arrive at the Israelite understanding of the exodus in the exilic and postexilic periods, which has become the standard one in the received biblical text. Other biblical authors might seem to tell the exodus story in more historical terms, but the mythic language that allowed the universalizing of the story is never far beneath the surface. We have already observed how P used mythopoeic speculation to recast Israel's epic traditions so as to make Israel march right through the middle of the "Sea of End" and how P used Combat Myth language to portray Israel's emergence as a nation as a new creation.[31] The same is true of Psalm 106. This exilic (postexilic?) psalm emphasizes the contrast between God's steadfast love and the perennial perversity of Israel right from its very beginnings. It is as if God's saving acts failed to completely free Israel from the power of the evil one who enslaved her.

> We have sinned in our fathers . . .
> They rebelled even as they emerged[32] from the Red Sea,
> Yet he saved them for his name's sake . . .
> He rebuked the Red Sea, and it became dry.
> He caused them to walk through the Abyss
>   as through the desert.
> He saved them from the hand of the foe
> And redeemed them from the power of the enemy.
> The waters covered their adversaries;
> Not one of them remained.
> And they believed his words;
> They sang his praise.
> But they quickly forgot his deeds.
>
> (Ps. 106:6–13)

The psalmist here is clearly dependent upon the completed P recension of the Torah.[33] More so than P, however, the psalmist plays upon the personification of the "Sea of End" (*yam sûp*) as the real enemy. Pharaoh and his hosts may have been swallowed up in the Abyss, but Israel was not completely freed from the power of the real enemy. The sea continued to exercise some power over them even as they emerged from its belly, as their subsequent actions reveal. The psalmist, as the cultic spokesperson for the Israelite community, voiced the Israelites' conviction that they have sinned the sin of their forefathers. The victory over evil would have to be recapitulated in each and every one of them.

CONCLUSION

Cult, as the celebration of belief through ritual action and cultic legend (word or song), has the potential to radically transform the beliefs of a community. Cult functions not only as a vehicle through which a community passes on its traditions from generation to generation but also as a force for creating the "ideal" expression of a community's beliefs about itself, its god, and its world. In the world of religion such "ideal" expressions frequently displace the "historical." The generation of the dry shod motif as a part of the Israelite exodus tradition is a case in point.

The crossing dry shod motif belonged originally to the Gilgalite conquest tradition, which expressed the local Benjaminite community's conviction that the deity had given the former land of Canaan to "Israel," a new socioreligious group with no prior historical or legal rights to the land. The story of a miraculous crossing of the Jordan provided justification for the "Israelite" occupation of the land. Yahweh, the "lord of all the earth," himself had "split" the Jordan before them and allowed them to cross dry shod as a sign that their seizing of Canaanite territory had divine approbation.

Apparently the pre-Israelite (i.e., Canaanite) cultic traditions of Gilgal partially survived and were incorporated into the new Benjaminite and later Israelite cult legend. In the Canaanite version of the Combat Myth, the divine sovereign El enlisted the services of the storm god (Hadad/Baal) in the battle against the chaos dragon. After a series of preliminary battles the storm god eventually overcame his archenemy the chaos dragon under its twin forms as Prince Sea and Judge River. Victory songs composed for the Israelite (Benjaminite) cult at Gilgal celebrated Yahweh's sovereignty and his gift of the land to "Israel" in images drawn from this myth. The River Jordan was personified as the chaos dragon, which had turned and fled from the awesome presence of the divine sovereign. Yahweh's victory over "River" was manifested in the Jordan's being "split" and Yahweh's sovereignty established by planting his people in his land.

Over the centuries, the old Benjaminite conquest festival and the Israelite passover festival were homogenized within the Gilgalite cult. The theme of crossing dry shod was extended to apply to the exodus tradition as well, in part because of the influence of Canaanite myth in which Sea and River were linked as parallel concepts. Thus did the story of deliverance at the sea became a story of crossing dry shod through the sea, with all the mythic implications inherent in the common Semitic Combat Myth. From this stage it was but a short step to the work of the

Priestly Writer, considered in the preceding chapter. During the Babylonian exile the Priestly Writer recast the whole of the torah tradition, starting with creation, as a statement of Yahweh's divine sovereignty. Also, the Priestly Writer took his inspiration principally from the Babylonian version of the Combat Myth rather than from the Canaanite version. But no matter which stage of the biblical tradition one probes, early or late, not far from the surface one discovers cult as a force both in the transmission of the tradition and in its transformation into myth.

Chapter 6

◆

EGYPT AND GOG AS MYTHIC SYMBOLS IN EZEKIEL

◆

Thus far our investigation of myth and mythopoeic speculation in the Bible has been focused principally on the Torah, and on traditions and cultic institutions deriving from the Torah. Within the Hebrew Bible the Torah is esteemed as the primary source of divine revelation. This canonical primacy of the Torah, of course, reflects the importance attached to the priestly *torah*, or instruction, within ancient Israel. It was no coincidence, therefore, that priests' tradents have figured so prominently in our investigations up to this point. Next to the Torah, the prophets were considered to be the principal channel of divine revelation. The prophets were thought to have special knowledge of God's will, whether because they were possessed by a divine spirit (Num. 11:24–30; 1 Sam. 10:5–13; 1 Kings 22:6–23, esp. 21–22; Isa. 61:1; etc.) or because they were thought to be privy to what transpired in the heavenly council of Yahweh (1 Kings 22:19–23; Isa. 6:1–8; Jer. 23:18, 21–22; etc.). Accordingly, we must turn to the prophetic literature for examples of the use of mythopoeic speculation, if our thesis that myth is an important medium for revelation is to carry conviction.

The use of myth and mythic imagery within the prophetic literature is actually quite extensive. In previous chapters I have already called attention to a few of these. Ezekiel's likening of Tyre to the primeval human in Eden was noted (chapter 3). In conjunction with the study of the transformation of the exodus tradition (chapter 4), I observed how Deutero-Isaiah built a message of consolation to the exiles around the themes of a new exodus and a new creation, with the implication that Yahweh's battle against the chaos monster was being played out dramatically in the exiles' own experience. The assurance of Yahweh's victory over his eternal foe was presented as a motive for confidence among the exiles. According to Isaiah 27:1, the deity's victory over Leviathan, that evasive, writhing, serpentine sea-dragon, will inaugurate the eschatological "day of Yahweh" foretold by all the prophets. Behind the "covenant of peace" (Isa 54:10; Ezek. 34:25; 37:26) lies a prophetic restructuring of age-old ancient Near Eastern myths about the quelling of divine wrath against humankind and the establishment of peace and harmony between God and his creatures.[1] And the list goes on and on.

In this chapter I propose to limit consideration to one further instance of prophetic mythopoeic speculation, with the suggestion that this one example is representative of many other cases. The example I have chosen is the portrayal of Egypt and Gog in the book of Ezekiel. Ezekiel, no less than the priestly authors of the Torah, has consciously and deliberately adapted older mythic patterns and motifs to express his vision of religious realities in a highly original manner and in fact has actually extended the older mythic patterns into new mythic paradigms for his intended audience.[2]

INTERPRETING THE BOOK OF EZEKIEL
FROM ITS STRUCTURE

In no small measure the interpretation of the book of Ezekiel is bound up with its structure. The book of Ezekiel is a finely architectured book. Despite the attempts of an earlier generation of critical scholars to cast doubt about the authenticity of numerous oracles and to assign vast portions of the book to a much later period,[3] recent scholarship has rallied to defend the essential unity and structure of the book. Moshe Greenberg goes so far as to assign the actual authorship of the book to the historical prophet Ezekiel.[4] Likewise, Lawrence Boadt points to recurring phrases and themes found dispersed throughout the book as deliberate rhetorical strategies on the part of the author for linking the different parts of the book one to another.[5] Space does not permit me to elaborate this point. Suffice it to say that I am working from a thesis that the overall structure of the book must be considered deliberate and expressive of the author's intended meaning. Hence, both the content and the placement of the oracles against the nations and the Gog oracles in chapters 25–32 and 38–39, respectively, are not only authentic to the original formulation of the book but even essential to the author's message (see chart: Outline of the Book of Ezekiel). After compiling a long list of similarities between the oracles against the nations in chapters 25–32 and the oracles of judgment against Judah in chapters 1–24, Lawrence Boadt observes that the many unusual vocabulary words or expressions common to both sections can hardly be accidental, particularly since almost all of them are unique to Ezekiel in the Bible.[6] In my opinion, neither the oracles against the nations nor the Gog oracles may be deleted as secondary intrusions, as some scholars have proposed.[7]

OUTLINE OF THE BOOK OF EZEKIEL

I. Call Narrative (1:1–3:15)
Vision of Yahweh's glory enthroned upon cherubim and commissioning of the prophet.

II. Book of Judgment (3:16–32:32)
  A. Extended call
    1. Watchman to house of Israel (3:16–21)
    2. Imposition of dumbness (3:22–27)
  B. Oracles of judgment against Israel (chs. 4–24)
    Yahweh's glory departs from sinful land.
    Opening of mouth announced, suspended (24:25–27)
  C. Oracles against (historical) nations (chs. 25–32)
    1. Amon (25:2–7)
    2. Moab (25:8–11)
    3. Edom (25:12–14)
    4. Philistia (25:15–17)
    5. **Tyre** (26:1–28:19)
    6. Sidon (28:20–23)
    7. **Egypt** (29:1–32:32) [historical embodiment of evil]
      a. 29:1–16   hubris of Egypt as "creator"
      b. 29:17–21   Egypt as Nebuchadnezzar's wages

    c. 30:1–19   sword to devastate Egypt
    d. 30:20–26   Egypt's arms broken
    e. 31:1–18   Egypt as grandest tree in Eden,
                     cut down
    f. 32:1–16   Egypt as chaos monster killed by
                     Yahweh
    g. 32:17–32   Egypt buried in Sheol

III. Book of Salvation/Restoration of Israel (33:1–39:29)
    A. Renewed call
       1. Watchman (33:1–20)
       2. Removal of dumbness (33:21–22) (= able to pro-
          claim salvation).
    B. Oracles of Salvation for Israel (chs. 34–37)
       Promise of restored Israel. Yahweh's sanctuary in midst
       of his people announced, suspended (37:26–28).
    C. Oracles against Gog of Magog (chs. 38–39)
       Elimination of anti-creator/power of evil

IV. Eschatological Vision (40:1–48:35)
    Creation perfected: temple on cosmic Mount Zion with
    Yahweh dwelling in midst of his people.

The principal argument for seeing these two sections as intrusions is that in each case the oracles seem to interrupt an idea that is announced immediately prior to the oracle but that reaches its conclusion or fulfillment only in the passage following the oracle. Thus, Ezekiel 24:26 announces that the day is approaching when a fugitive will arrive to report the fall of Jerusalem and Ezekiel's dumbness will be removed. The fulfillment of this announcement is related in chapter 33. Sandwiched in between the announcement and the fulfillment are the oracles against the seven foreign nations in Ezekiel 25–32. Similarly, Ezekiel 37:26–28 contains Yahweh's announcement that he will set his sanctuary in the midst of a sanctified Israel and dwell in their midst forever. The fulfillment of this announcement is the subject of Ezekiel's vision in chapters 40–48. Again coming between announcement and fulfillment are the Gog oracles of chapters 38–39.[8]

This apparent violation of logical sequence disappears, however, when one recognizes that built into the literary structure of the book of Ezekiel is a *pattern* of suspension, resumption, and/or reversal of themes. To mention but a few examples, dumbness is first imposed upon the prophet in 3:17–27; its removal is announced in 24:25–27 but left suspended until 33:21–22 when the prophet's mouth is actually opened;[9] the oracle against the mountains of Israel announced in 6:1–14 is reversed in 36:1–15; the glory of Yahweh abandons the temple in chapters 8–11 but returns to the new temple in 43:1–12; the wild beasts sent to ravage the land in 14:15 are removed in 34:25. On a larger scale, the whole section of the oracles of judgment against Israel (chs. 4–24) are reversed in the oracles of salvation for Israel (chs. 34–37). This pattern of resumption and reversal is part of the rhetorical strategy of the author.

These structural observations give us confidence to assert that oracles against the nations (chs. 25–32) are intentionally parallel to the oracles against Gog of Magog (chs. 38–39). The former precede and lead into the restoration of the historical Israel in chapters 34–37; the latter precede and lead into the advent of the eschatological era (chs. 40–48). The author even underscores correlation between Egypt and Gog by having God say to both Pharaoh and Gog, "I will put hooks in your jaws" (RSV *wĕnātattî ḥaḥîm bilĕḥāyêkā*) (cf. Ezek. 29:4 and 38:4). This image is obviously inspired by the Combat Myth of the creator subduing the watery chaos monster, as the same image is found again in Job 40:25–26 (E.T.: 41:1–2) where Yahweh demonstrates his mastery over Leviathan. With this last point we enter directly into the question of Egypt and Gog as mythic symbols in Ezekiel.

EGYPT AND GOG AS MYTHIC SYMBOLS

The superabundance of mythic allusions within Ezekiel is well known. Perhaps the clearest example is to be found in the oracle against Tyre (Ezekiel 28), which I discussed in chapter 3. In that oracle the hubris of the king of Tyre is caricatured under the double image of a man who claimed to be a god (vs. 2–10) and of a perfect being who once inhabited the Garden of Eden (12–19). In addition, Jon Levenson[10] has called attention to the mythic allusions in chapters 40–48. The "very high mountain" (Ezek. 40:2) to which Ezekiel is transported at the beginning of his vision is at once Mount Zion and the cosmic mountain of myth, the *axis mundi*, the center of the creation. This land of the vision, with Yahweh's sanctuary in the center, is simultaneously the environs of Zion and the Garden of Eden restored, with the river of life flowing from the sanctuary at its center outward across the barren wilderness toward the Dead Sea, to produce paradisiacal conditions throughout the whole of the land (Ezekiel 47). There will be no more death because "the tree of life" is available once more in the form of the trees lining the river's banks, trees whose "fruit will be for food and their leaves for healing." Even the Dead Sea, famous for its absence of aquatic life, will teem with fish as it receives refreshment from this river of life. In a more familiar theological idiom, this is nothing short of a vision of the eschatological kingdom of God, similar to that of the book of Revelation (chs. 21–22).

The comparison with the apocalyptic book of Revelation is quite appropriate. Ezekiel, which may be fairly characterized as a proto-apocalyptic work,[11] shares with apocalyptic an expectation that the eschatological kingdom of God will come about only after divine intervention makes a definitive end, first, of the evil powers that rule this world and, second and more importantly, of the very power of evil itself.[12] Such a double elimination of evil is the purpose of linking in tandem the oracles against the nations (chs. 25–32) and the oracles against Gog of Magog (chs. 38–39). The former represents the destruction of the hostile earthly (or historical) powers who oppose the establishment of the people of God; the latter represents the metahistorical power of evil. Both powers, historical and metahistorical, oppose the designs of the creator and so must be destroyed. This two-stage destruction of evil corresponds to the program in the book of Revelation where first the beast which is Babylon-Rome, the earthly manifestation of evil, is overcome (chs. 17–19); then the dragon, Satan himself, is overcome and eliminated (ch. 20). Only after both powers are disposed of can the new creation be unveiled (21:1–22:5). Quite obviously the author of the book of Revelation is dependent upon Ezekiel, as his mention of both Gog and Magog (20:8) and of the river with the tree of life (22:1–2; cf. Ezek. 47:1–12) proves.[13] I maintain, further, that this apocalyptic author also derived from Ezekiel his program of subduing evil in both a historical and a metahistorical form prior to the advent of the new, eschatological creation—and that the author of Revelation has correctly understood Ezekiel's meaning.

If this interpretation of Ezekiel is correct, then it is pointless to try to identify Gog and Magog with known historical entities from the ancient world.[14] This is not to say that Ezekiel's description of Gog and Magog may not have been partially patterned after known or legendary ancient Near Eastern personage(s) or nation(s),[15] only that the author intended Gog and Magog with their strange names to represent a metahistorical reality.[16] The advent of the kingdom of God—albeit, primarily a hierarchical and cultic kingdom, in keeping with Ezekiel's priestly theology—necessarily involves the elimination of the very source of evil.

The mythic dimensions of this definitive battle are unmistakable in that the battle is defined as a conflict between creation and nonexistence, between "cosmos" and "chaos." Gog has assembled a horde of wicked allies for the purpose of attacking a forgiven and restored Israel. We are no longer dealing with the historical nation of Israel but with the eschatological people of God. Consequently, eschatological Israel is depicted in traditional mythic terminology as possessing the fullness of creation. Israel's populace "dwells at the center [navel] of the earth" (*ṭabbûr hā-ʾāreṣ*, 38:12) around the mountain sanctuary of the divine king and creator. They live in a "land of unwalled villages" (38:11); there is no need of fortification walls or bars or gates, since this is obviously the land living under the covenant of peace from which has been banished all hostility, whether of man or beast (34:25–31).[17]

Within this mythic context, Gog is an apt symbol of chaos. By portraying Gog as coming forth "from the farthest corners of the north" (*yarkĕtê-ṣāpôn*) (38:15; 39:2), the author seems to be portraying Gog as the very antithesis of creation. In the biblical tradition *yarkĕtê-ṣāpôn* is much more than a distant geographic region to the north; it also carries heavy mythic connotations. In Canaanite tradition Mount Zaphon is the home of El, the creator god and head of the pantheon. Thus, *yarkĕtê-ṣāpôn* can refer to the loftiest recesses of this mountain sanctuary of the creator and divine sovereign. Such is the referent in Isaiah 14:13, where Babylon is excoriated for its hubris in exalting itself as if it were the chief god:

> You said in your heart,
>   "I will ascend to heaven;
> above the stars of God
>   I will set my throne on high;
> I will sit on the mount of assembly
>   in the far north (*yarkĕtê-ṣāpôn*);
> I will ascend above the heights of the clouds,
>   I will make myself like the Most High." (RSV)

The prophet has in mind Babylon's boast that its patron god Marduk ascended to the position of king of the gods when the other deities proved incapable of mastering the chaos dragon, a claim the prophet rejects as utter nonsense because Yahweh is indisputably the divine sovereign.

A similar usage is found in Psalm 48:1–3. In this psalm also Mount Zion is equated with *yarkĕtê-ṣāpôn*, with the obvious intention of promoting Yahweh instead of the Canaanite god El as the king of the universe.

Ezekiel, however, uses the phrase *yarkĕtê-ṣāpôn* in quite a different meaning. For him *yarkĕtê-ṣāpôn* is not the cosmic mountain but rather the point on earth most removed from "the center of the earth." It is thus the antithesis of creation. In this respect it is much like *yam sûp*, that sea at the end of the world which has connotations of a place of nonexistence and even of opposition to the creator.[18]

Ezekiel's meaning is clearly related, though not identical, to Jeremiah's mysterious foe from the north who will appear suddenly and spread terror and destruction upon the land (see esp. Jer. 6:22; 25:32; 31:8; 50:41).[19] In the later stages of the Jeremian tradition this foe will be understood as Babylon. And this is the manner in which King Jehoiakim interprets Jeremiah's prophecy (Jer. 36:29). Likewise, in Jeremiah 25:26 there is mention of all the kings of the north, both near and far (*kol-malkê haṣṣāpôn haqqĕrōbîm wĕhārĕḥōqîm*), those nations who shall drink "the cup from Yahweh's hand" (v. 17). Last of all to drink is Babylon.[20] Nevertheless, the original meaning of

Jeremiah's foe from the north was at once less determinate and more mythic.[21] In Jeremiah 6–8 this foe is identified only as "a people coming from the land of the north (*ṣāpôn*), a great nation arising from the farthest recesses of the earth (*miyyarkĕtê-ʾāreṣ*)" (Jer. 6:22). For our purposes, it is important to notice the consequences of this northern foe's arrival. The earth reverts back to its state of chaos prior to creation!

> I looked on the earth, and lo, it was waste and void;
>   and to the heavens, and they had no light.
> I looked on the mountains, and lo, they were quaking,
>   and all the hills moved to and fro.
> I looked, and lo, there was no man,
>   and all the birds of the air had fled.
> I looked, and lo, the fruitful land was a desert,
>   and all its cities were laid in ruins
>   before the LORD, before his fierce anger.
>
>   (Jer. 4:23–26, RSV)

There is an intrinsic connection between chaos and this character from the extreme recesses of the north. His presence means the undoing of creation.

Similarly in Jeremiah 25:30–33, the focus has shifted from being primarily a judgment upon Israel's historical northern enemies to the more eschatological scene of the Day of Yahweh:

> The LORD will roar from on high,
>   and from his holy habitation utter his voice;
> . . . .
> The clamor will resound to the ends of the earth,
>   for the LORD has an indictment against the nations;
> he is entering into judgment with all flesh,
>   and the wicked he will put to the sword,
>   says the LORD.
> Thus says the LORD of hosts:
> Behold, evil is going forth
>   from nation to nation,
> and a great tempest is stirring
>   from the farthest recesses of the earth (*miyyarkĕtê-ʾāreṣ*).
>
>   (RSV)

In this passage, too, evil seems to originate in the *yarkĕtê-ʾāreṣ*, and only secondarily manifests itself in historical nations said to be located in the north. It was but a short step from Jeremiah's mysterious northern foe who arises "from the farthest recesses of the earth" (*yarkĕtê-ʾāreṣ*) to Ezekiel's Gog of Magog who originates in "the farthest recesses of the north" (*yarkĕtê-ṣāpôn*).

Gog of Magog, who comes forth from a region that lies at the fringes of creation, or even beyond, is thus the ultimate Ezekielian symbol of anticreation and of all that stands in opposition to the will of the divine sovereign. In apocalyptic fashion, Ezekiel envisions the establishment of the kingdom of God coming about only through a cosmic battle between Yahweh and Gog so awesome in scope that the whole world will be shaken to its very foundations (38:19–23). "The face of the land"— or should one translate, "the face of the earth"—will be "cleansed" of the evil when Gog's carcass and the carcasses of his followers are buried (39:11–16) or, alternatively, fed as carrion to the scavengers (39:17–20).

But if in the Ezekielian schema Gog is the symbol of metahistorical evil, Egypt is the personification of historical evil. Within the oracles against the seven historical enemies of Israel Egypt is the seventh and last named and presumably, therefore, the worst of the lot. Furthermore, Ezekiel directs seven oracles against Egypt alone; and these oracles take up as much space as all the oracles against the other nations combined![22] Egypt is singled out as more deserving of Yahweh's wrath than all the other nations of the earth.

A partial solution to the question of why Ezekiel portrays Egypt as the bête noire of the ancient world may be sought in the history of Egypt's involvement in Judah's disastrous politics of relying upon Egypt for aid against Babylon (17:17; 29:6–7, 16). Like Jeremiah, Ezekiel saw Babylon as Yahweh's divinely appointed instrument of punishment for Judah's sins (17:18–22; 21:18–27; cf. 26:7–14; 30:10–12). Submission to Babylon was, accordingly, submission to the divine will—which undoubtedly accounts for why there is no oracle against Babylon in either Jeremiah or Ezekiel.[23] But Ezekiel's animosity toward Egypt is more radical still.

Egypt was the source of Israel's "original sin" acquired in youth. It was in Egypt that Israel first learned idolatry and acquired an addiction to turning in apostasy from Yahweh to "go awhoring" (KJV) after other gods, an addiction that neither of the sister nations of Israel and Judah were able to overcome during their period of national existence. The allegory of the sisters, Oholah and Oholibah, in chapter 23 is the most explicit:

> . . . they played the harlot in Egypt, they played the harlot in their youth; there their breasts were pressed and their virgin bosoms handled (v. 3).
>
> [Oholibah] increased her harlotry, remembering the days of her youth, when she played the harlot in the land of Egypt (v. 19).
>
> Thus I will put an end to your lewdness and your harlotry brought from the land of Egypt; so that you shall not lift up your eyes to the Egyptians or remember them any more (v. 27, RSV).

Similarly in chapter 20, in another long diatribe against Israel because of its infidelity, Yahweh reminds the Israelites of his admonition to them when he brought them out of Egypt:

> And I said to them, Cast away the detestable things your eyes feast on, every one of you, and do not defile yourself with the idols of Egypt; I am the LORD your God. But they rebelled against me and would not listen to me; they did not every man cast away the detestable things their eyes feasted on, nor did they forsake the idols of Egypt (vs. 7–8, RSV).

Thus, while Israel may have worshiped the idols of many nations, including those of Babylon (23:14–17), Egypt was singled out as the real culprit. In Ezekiel's view, Egypt was the source of Israel's sinfulness, and as such, the historical embodiment of the power that stands in opposition to Yahweh God.

This view shapes the manner in which Ezekiel has constructed his seven oracles against Egypt. Rather obviously, there is a movement from indictment to sentencing to infliction of the death penalty to burial. Here I shall concern myself primarily with Egypt's "sin." Basically, Egypt is found guilty of being the chaos monster, and as such must be eliminated from the face of the earth. The charge is laid forth in the first oracle (29:3):

> Behold, I am against you, Pharaoh king of Egypt, the great dragon that lies in the midst of his Niles,[24] that says, "My Nile is my own; I (even) made myself![25]

The "great dragon" (*hattannîm haggādôl*) is, of course, the primeval watery chaos monster well known from the common Semitic Combat Myth. Contrary to what some have thought, this is not a paranomasia or play upon a self-image of Egyptian kings as divine, taking the zoomorphic shape of the crocodile or the like. The self-image of the pharaoh, as we are informed in 32:2, is that of a "lion among the nations." By contrast, the title "chaos monster" is a hostile label being pinned upon pharaoh and "all Egypt" by the prophet in the name of Yahweh.[26]

The introduction of the label "chaos monster" may have been partially inspired by a desire to contradict Egyptian claims that the pharaoh was the incarnation of the Egyptian chief god, frequently regarded as the creator. Pharaoh's reported statement in 29:3, "I made myself," seems to imply some sort of claim to being the creator, just as the words "The Nile is my own" may perhaps imply not only ownership but also creation of the Nile. Ezekiel's implication is, then, that Pharaoh (Egypt) is not the incarnation of the deity but of the chaos monster. Be that as it may, Ezekiel seems more interested in exploiting themes inherent in the Combat Myth, that is, of creation versus chaos, and of creator versus chaos monster. Egypt is charged with hubris in attempting to usurp the authority of the true creator. Ironically, Egypt is a creator of sorts—actually, more of an anticreator. What it created was the monster that is itself, the very opposite of authentic creation! Egypt also created "its Niles" in which it lives. In the parallel passage in 32:2, these are termed "your rivers," and in parallelism, "the seas" in which the dragon dwells. These terms clearly are to be connected with Yam and Nahar ("Prince Sea" and "Judge River"), the opponents of Baal in the Canaanite Combat Myth.[27] What Ezekiel has drawn, then, is a portrait very similar to that of

Ti'amat in the opening scenes of *Enuma elish*, wherein the chaos monster dwells in dark, watery mire and prevents authentic creation from occurring.[28]

Almost in affirmation of Egypt's anticreation stance, Yahweh in 29:10–12 sentences Egypt to become a place of noncreation, a place of absolute desolation, which neither man nor beast inhabits. After forty years as an utter wasteland, Yahweh will gather up the remnant of Egypt dispersed among the nations and return them to their land (29:13–16). But never again will Egypt challenge Yahweh's creation, for it will be merely another human kingdom, and the lowest of the low at that!

The second, third, and fourth oracles against Egypt are more like "normal" oracles against foreign nations in that principal persons and places are recognizably historical (Nebuchadrezzar, Tyre, Memphis, etc.) and the threats to be accomplished are within the normal human sphere (invasion, the sword, plunder, etc.). But beginning with the fifth oracle mythic elements again begin to dominate. The theme of Egypt's hubris is developed further. Using the metaphor of a cedar whose top towered among the clouds and whose roots reached down into the Abyss (*těhôm*), Egypt is said to be grander than all the trees in Eden. However, because of pride, Egypt will be chopped down and cast into Sheol.

With the sixth oracle Ezekiel returns to the image of Egypt as the chaos monster who, like Ti'amat, writhes in mire in its watery abode. Continuing the Combat Myth motif, Yahweh, like Marduk in battle with Ti'amat, captures the dragon in his net and slays it, apparently by severing its arteries:

> I will drench the land with your outflow,
> To the mountain-heights with your blood,
> And the watercourses will be filled with your vital
> fluids.

> (32:6)

Yahweh then casts the dead body of the monster into the open field to be devoured by scavengers (32:4–5).

The theme of anti-creation versus creation continues into this oracle as well. With the slaying of the chaos monster Yahweh has shown himself to be the sole creator. To make that point as strongly as possible, Yahweh causes the land of Egypt to revert completely into a precreation state of stygian night:[29]

> I will cover the heavens when you are snuffed out,
> And I will darken their stars.
> The sun with a cloud I will cover,
> And the moon will not give forth its light.
> All the great lamps of heaven
> I will blacken on account of you,
> And I will allow darkness over your land!
>
> (32:7–8)

It is perhaps the ultimate irony, now that Egypt has become an uninhabited and uninhabitable wasteland (32:12–13), that Egypt's "many waters" (v. 13)—an allusion to *tĕhôm*—will finally become "settled" or clear waters (v. 14), something that could never happen as long as the chaos monster kept churning the mire through its chaotic behavior. Upon the elimination of the chaos monster, the power of the authentic creator begins to appear in the land. Yahweh will cause Egypt's streams to flow with oil (v. 14)—an allusion to the motif of paradisiacal plenty known from Bible (e.g., Job 29:6) and Ugaritic literature (*CTA* 6.III.6–7).[30]

The seventh oracle against Egypt, a description of Egypt's condemnation to the deepest part of Sheol where Egypt will lie with the uncircumcised and the polluted, seems at first glance unnecessary and even awkward in view of the previous oracle, in which its cadaver was eaten by scavengers. But here I think an intentional parallel between Egypt and Gog guided Ezekiel. Just as Gog's body was both buried and consumed as carrion by scavengers, so Egypt also is made to suffer both fates. Given this close approximation between Egypt and Gog, it is hardly surprising that the prophet has specified that lying alongside of Egypt in Sheol will be Gog's closest associates: Meshech and Tubal (32:26) and all the princes of the north (32:30).

CONCLUSION

In Ezekiel meaning is determined both by structure and by content of individual oracles. The author has deliberately paired

Egypt and Gog as historical and metahistorical symbols of chaos or evil, respectively. By creatively adapting traditional mythic motifs, especially those of the Combat Myth, Ezekiel has set forth a new vision of the end of the Israelite creation story. Creation will be complete only when Israel is established under a covenant of peace around the cosmic mountain throne of Yahweh in Zion. Before this can happen, however, the nihilistic power of evil must be totally eliminated from the face of creation. In Ezekiel's apocalypticlike thinking, this meant the elimination of Egypt, that principal source of Israel's temptation to turn away from its creator and God.

Ezekiel expressed this theological message in the language of myth, the most powerful symbol known to him and his audience. Through such deliberate recasting of commonly accepted myths of that time, Ezekiel attempted at once to undermine the position of the enemy and to enrich the Yahwistic faith of his own community.[31] In this regard his method did not differ significantly from that of the priestly tradents of the Torah who reshaped the primeval myth of origins to fit their theological agenda.

CONCLUSION

The theme of this volume has been the importance of mythopo-esis, that is, of myth and mythmaking speculation within the Hebrew Bible. The extension of myth to new situations through mythopoeic speculations can be documented in biblical book after biblical book and therefore should be considered a stan-dard biblical method of "doing theology." Moreover, if the three Babylonian poet-theologians analyzed in chapter 1 may be considered typical of the ancient Near East, biblical writers em-ployed much the same techniques and even the same mythic motifs as their ancient Near Eastern neighbors. Each of the three Babylonian authors recomposed older mythic traditions to cre-ate a new myth, which in turn became the new standard for that society and the basis for still further mythopoeism in subse-quent generations.

The Old Babylonian author who composed the Akkadian *Atrahasis* as a new statement of human origins used extant Su-merian mythic texts and motifs as raw materials. At a still later period another Babylonian author created *Enuma elish* as a story about Babylon's patron deity Marduk, in which he claimed for Marduk the exalted position of divine sovereign. In effect, this author rewrote the common Semitic Combat Myth as a story of the inadequacy of the traditional high gods of Mesopotamia to meet newer challenges and of Marduk bravely stepping for-ward to rescue the situation, thereby establishing himself as the supreme ruler of the gods and the creator of the world. This Babylonian author increased his composition's appeal and credibility by interweaving familiar motifs from the by now standard Mesopotamian "creation myth" of *Atrahasis*. The result was a new primeval myth that served to undergird Babylon's hegemony over all Mesopotamia.

Similarly in Israel, the Yahwist (chapter 2) drew heavily upon the Babylonian myth of *Atrahasis*, supplementing with motifs from *Gilgamesh* and other traditional myths, to create a specifically Israelite primeval myth. Therein, very likely for the first time, an Israelite author claimed for Israel's patron deity Yahweh the status of divine sovereign and universal creator. The Yahwist's portrait of "God" may in some ways appear crude to our way of thinking, but it represented a major advance in Israel's budding theological tradition.

Allowing for the differences between the polytheism of Babylon and the Yahwism of Israel, we see that the Priestly Writer (chapter 3) did almost exactly what the author of the Babylonian myth *Enuma elish* did. Presumably unhappy with an earlier version of Israel's "national myth," the Priestly Writer used the Combat Myth to construct a new framework into which he set the stories of the older (J-E) "Israelite myth." Although most biblical allusions to the Combat Myth are closer in typology to the Canaanite Baal myth, the Priestly Writer seemingly preferred the Babylonian version of *Enuma elish*. The result was a timely reformulation of Israel's politicoreligious myth at a time when the older formulations seemed to have lost their power to speak to a community facing dissolution and loss of identity. The new priestly myth gave renewed hope to the Judahite exiles by emphasizing that Yahweh, and not the god of their Babylonian captors, was truly the divine sovereign who created and rules the universe.

Like their ancient Near Eastern counterparts, Israel's theologians were concerned with the place of humankind—and particularly of their own people—within the realm of being. Israel's faith was founded on the conviction that the Creator of all being had gratuitously entered into a covenantal union with them that was unique among the nations on the face of the earth. But how to reconcile a belief in Israel's special election with the sordid history of its infidelity to that God was a theological problem. The Yahwist found umbrage in a mythic tradition that posited that it was the very nature of humankind to rebel against its vocation of service to the Creator. Some of the blame must be laid at the feet of the Creator for having created flawed creatures. But whatever the "original" condition of humankind, the myth assures one that the Creator is now genuinely reconciled to a flawed humanity. Moreover, the Creator truly loves his creatures and watches out for their welfare. This is a universal truth of which Israel is the best and foremost exemplar.

The Priestly Writer readily accepted the part that affirmed human frailty but reacted strongly against the idea that any blame for such "sin" could be attributed to the Creator. The Creator's design was perfect. The culprit is the power of evil, which stands opposed to the creative will of God. In the Combat Myth P found a vehicle for affirming a perpetual tension between the "goodness" intended by the Creator and the fact of evil, which is endemic in the real world. The sovereignty of Yahweh guarantees that no portion of creation will be abandoned to the power of "the dragon." Creation is secured through a series of perpetual covenants that Yahweh has sworn with humankind, beginning with a universal covenant "with all flesh" (Gen. 9:1–17) and culminating in the Mosaic covenant, which joined one nation and Yahweh in the profoundest of unions (Exodus 19–40).

Despite the particularity of the Sinai covenant, Israel's theologians saw the story of Israel's deliverance from enslavement in Egypt and the establishment of her covenant with the Lord of heaven and earth as a story of universal significance. Hence they took great pains to suggest a cosmic significance for the exodus and the Mosaic covenant. Whatever historical core the exodus story may have had originally, the exodus was traditioned in canonical literature primarily as a mythic event that continued the work of creation and ordering of the universe. Obviously, an event of these proportions was not wrought by ordinary human powers. It could only have been accomplished through divine agency. P's solution was to underscore the cosmic significance of the Sinai covenant by elevating the covenant mediator Moses to near divinity.

One of the driving forces in the process of mythopoeism in

ancient Israel was the cult. We observed how at the old Benjaminite sanctuary of Gilgal the exodus tradition and the conquest tradition were celebrated together. Over time the two traditions were confused in cultic legend, causing the motif of crossing dry shod to be transferred from its original setting in the legend of the Israelites' miraculous entry into the Promised Land across a dried-up Jordan, to the legend of deliverance at the Red Sea during the Israelites' exodus from Egypt. (One may assume that similar processes were operative also at Jerusalem within the royal Davidic cult and later in the restored temple cult of postexilic Judaism.)

The earliest mythopoeisms at Gilgal were based upon the Canaanite version of the Combat Myth, which depicted the battle against chaos dragon as a conflict with the primeval ocean under its twin names, Sea and River. As the Gilgal festival grew from a conquest festival into a celebration of Israel's passover from Egypt also, so by extension the Israelite deliverance at the Red Sea took on gradually more and more the mythic overtones of the deity's battle against the sea. Later at the hand of the Priestly Writer these exodus traditions were transformed still further, this time by tilting toward the Babylonian version of the Combat Myth. Through such mythopoeisms the exodus gradually assumed the shape it has in the received text, as the core "event" in the Israelite myth of origins.

As the story of Israel's exodus out of Egypt became linked more and more with the Combat Myth, so also the "players" assumed the roles of the characters in the Combat Myth. The Egyptians' claim of divinity for their king only served to heighten the Israelite drama in which Pharaoh was cast not as a god but as the very embodiment of the dragon. Appropriately Pharaoh was submerged into the mythic "Sea of End," that ancient symbol of the very antithesis of creation and life. Reminiscent of the primeval event, the sea itself was split once more and Israel emerged from its midst as Yahweh's final and greatest act of creation.

The focus of this volume has been the various ways in which biblical writers throughout the history of the composition of the Hebrew Bible have used and reused myth—and particularly after chapter 2, the common Semitic Combat Myth—to undergird their religious and/or sociopolitical agenda. My purpose has not been to provide an exhaustive study of myth—not even the Combat Myth—in the Bible; it has been only to show through representative examples how biblical authors actually went about using mythic motifs in their writings and how they consciously manipulated these to serve their specific purposes.

The book of Ezekiel (chapter 6) is a prime example of the deliberateness with which biblical writers composed their works. Following a common biblical technique of historicizing the battle against chaos by identifying Israel's national enemies with the chaos monster, Ezekiel painted Egypt as that dragon— a menace not only to Israel but even to its own land of the Nile. Like his contemporary P, Ezekiel saw wicked humans as but the arm of a deeper menace, the metahistorical force of evil. This force Ezekiel named Gog, from the mysterious land of Magog. In the language of the original Combat Myth, the battle against the chaos dragon was depicted in the grammatical past tense. Nonetheless, implicit in myth is the recognition that mythic events stand outside of historical time. In myth primeval event and eschatological event merge; *Urzeit wird Endzeit*. Thus the myth provided assurance that the outcome of the struggle between Creator and chaos is certain, and that the power of evil has been broken. Nevertheless, to humans living in historical time the outcome of this battle often seems far from certain; its ravages are experienced as all too present. Accordingly, Ezekiel projected the outcome of the battle against evil into the future, rather than into the past. The day is imminent, the prophet assures the reader, when God and the dragon will meet for the final battle. Even now Gog is marshaling its evil forces in anticipation of victory over the Creator. In the end God will prevail and confirm his rule, symbolized in the rebuilding of the temple-palace within the eschatological Jerusalem.

Some of the most graphic references to the Combat Myth are contained in the Psalter and in the book of Job. Nevertheless, I have shunned these for the most part, since they occur within manifestly poetic contexts and therefore might be regarded merely as instances of poetic license or mere literary metaphors that neither the author nor his audience took "literally"— though such a distinction between metaphor and myth in these works is for the most part not justified. My concern has been with real mythmaking, myth that is "believed," rather than with myth used primarily for artistic effect; that is, I have been concerned with mythopoeism rather than with mythopoetry.

Examples of mythmaking speculation in the Bible could be multiplied many times over. The few studied in this volume are intended to be illustrative of a favored ancient method of "doing theology." In the past many readers of the Bible have expended considerable energy reading myth out of the Bible. Fidelity to biblical tradition would seem to demand just the opposite attitude, however. Rather than denying myth in revelation, those who seek to enter into the spirit of biblical tradition should exalt myth as a proven path by which to approach the divine *mysterium tremendum*.

EPILOGUE:
MYTHOPOEISM
IN THE NEW TESTAMENT

Although this volume is primarily about myth and mythopoeism in the Hebrew scriptures, it is worthy of note that this process did not cease with the close of the Hebrew canon but continued on into the emerging Jewish and Christian communities that took their point of departure from the Hebrew scriptures. Christians are often willing to see myth in the Hebrew scriptures but usually balk at admitting myth in the New Testament. For that reason it may be helpful to add a note about mythopoeism as one of the theological methods employed by New Testament writers.

APOCALYPTIC MYTHOPOEISM

Myth and mythopoeism based upon the Combat Myth are especially prominent in apocalyptic literature. In this volume, however, apocalyptic has not been examined because its mythic background is well known. Moreover, apocalyptic is a genre unto itself and involves a whole set of new ways of looking at the world; a full consideration of these would take us too far afield from our main topic.[1] However, a few comments about apocalypticism are necessary to set the stage for our consideration of mythopoeism in the New Testament, particularly for how New Testament evangelists used mythopoeic speculation to theologize about the authentic nature and role of Jesus.

Essentially, apocalyptic affirms that this world is threatened by an evil so radical that the creative will of God is in danger of

174

being totally nullified. Although this evil manifests itself in historical persons and events, its origin is suprahistorical and as such requires a suprahistorical power to overcome it and to restore the creative will of God. Apocalyptic looks beyond history to an eschatological resolution in which evil will be completely eliminated and the creative will of the deity definitively and eternally established. In short, the Combat Myth has been transformed from a primeval myth of origins into an eschatological myth[2] in which the archfoe of the Creator has evolved into "Satan."[3]

An early eschatologizing of the battle against chaos can be found in the book of Daniel.[4] In particular in Daniel 7 the four winds that stir up the great sea harken back to the ancient Combat Myth motif of the deity using the wind as a weapon with which to defeat primeval sea. The practice of historicizing the chaos monster as a national enemy is continued in the representation of the four kingdoms of Babylon, Media, Persia, and Greece as four beasts arising out of the sea. Particular attention is paid to the "little horn" growing out of the fourth beast's head, a cipher for Antiochus IV Epiphanes (175–164 B.C.E.). This Seleucid Greek king in the author's own day was waging a brutal persecution against those Jews who maintained fidelity to their religion. Encouragement was offered to these beleaguered religionists through the apocalyptic vision of Daniel 7 that these evil beasts will be slain in the near future. Very soon now God will ascend his throne to exercise his divine sovereignty.

The Combat Myth imagery in Daniel 7 is clear. However, in a surprising innovation for the biblical tradition, God ("the ancient of days") is said to confer his authority upon a younger divinelike figure, "one like a son of man." This latter figure very likely represents Michael, Israel's patron angel. The source of this portrayal of God transferring some of his power to Michael seems to be drawn from the Canaanite Baal myth; in this myth hoary old El, the head of the Canaanite pantheon, seated the vigorous young storm god Baal at his side as his associate. What is most interesting about this is that it shows just how persistent mythic traditions can be. Despite the proscription of Canaanite religious practice from Israel, this Canaanite mythic motif, known from a fourteenth-century B.C.E. Ugaritic text, endured outside of official Israelite religious tradition to reemerge as a fully operative mythic motif in Judaism of the second century B.C.E.[5]

Within the New Testament, the author of the book of Revelation likewise portrays the battle against the chaos monster as an event of the end times.[6] In this Christian adaptation of the common Semitic Combat Myth, as might have been expected, the divine sovereign makes the Lamb (that is, Jesus Christ) his associate in the exercise of cosmic rule. God's will is announced in the proclamation of the heavenly citizens who surround the throne of God:

> "Worthy is the Lamb who was slain, to receive power and wealth and wisdom and might and honor and glory and blessing!" And I heard every creature in heaven and on earth and under the earth and in the sea, and all therein, saying, "To him who sits upon the throne and to the Lamb be blessing and honor and glory and might for ever and ever!" (Rev. 5:12–13, RSV)*

Thus invested with divine authority, the Lamb goes forth as the "King of kings and Lord of lords" (19:16) to defeat a modernized version of the chaos monster and his confederates. "And he seized the dragon, that ancient serpent, who is the Devil and Satan, and bound him for a thousand years" (20:2). At the end of the thousand years the dragon will be temporarily freed for a definitive showdown with the Lamb. Borrowing from the imagery of Ezekiel, the dragon gathered his cohorts "which are at the four corners of the earth, that is, Gog and Magog" (20:8), to do battle with God and the Lamb. As in the ancient myth, the dragon and its confederates are completely subdued, but this time they are banished forever from the face of creation and "thrown into the lake of fire and sulphur" where "they will be tormented . . . for ever and ever" (20:10).

With the battle against chaos thus definitively ended and the

---

*Scripture quotations throughout this chapter are from the Revised Standard Version, except for instances when the original Greek or Hebrew is cited and translated or when a different emphasis is noted (nn. 12 and 13).

reign of God and of the Lamb firmly established, the author of Revelation paints a new canvas of what a cosmos fully in accord with the designs of the Creator (21:5) would look like. In this perfect "new heaven and new earth" that is to issue forth from the throne of God, there will be no pain or sorrow or lack of any kind. Even Death, recognized in Canaanite myth and the Hebrew scriptures as an associate of the chaos dragon, will be banished (20:14; 21:4) from this new creation. The author very effectively symbolizes the absence of every form of evil by informing the reader that there is no room for the sea in this new world (21:1). The sea, of course, was an ages-old ancient Near Eastern metaphor of noncreation. Sea has appeared throughout our study of the Combat Myth as the archfoe of the divine sovereign: in Mesopotamia as Ti'amat, in Canaan as Yam, in Israel as Yam or "Yam Suph." In Daniel 7 and Revelation 13 the sea is the source from which the beast(s) comes forth to attack the just. With the arrival of the reign of God, it is obvious that the sea could be no more. Not yet satisfied, the author continued to pile mythic metaphor upon mythic metaphor after the pattern of previous biblical writers, Ezekiel in particular. At the center of this new world is the cosmic mountain on which will rest the new, perfect Jerusalem (21:10; cf. Ezek. 40:2). From its midst, issuing forth from the throne of God and of the Lamb, will flow a river of the waters of life, which transforms the cosmos into that paradise of which Ezekiel and the Priestly Writer spoke (22:1–5; cf. Ezek. 47:1–12 and Genesis 2).[7]

Clearly, the author of the book of Revelation was continuing the long-standing biblical tradition of theologizing through mythopoeic speculation. The common Semitic Combat myth was revised—and not very subtly at that—to incorporate the Christian doctrine that Jesus is the Messiah sent by God into this world to inaugurate the reign of God. Given the apocalyptic spirit of Jesus' own ministry, going about preaching the imminence of reign of God and exorcising demons, it was inevitable that Jesus' disciples should interpret Jesus as the eschatological agent of God whose mission was to destroy finally the chaos monster. Moreover, a growing belief in the divinity of Jesus led to the conviction that it was impossible to think of God as exercising his rule over this world except through the Lamb, who at the same time is "King of kings and Lord of lords" (Rev. 19:16).

MYTHOPOEISM IN THE GOSPELS

As innovative as the author of the book of Revelation may have been, his mythmaking speculations may be considered somewhat superficial in comparison to those of the evangelists, especially Matthew. In the book of Revelation the structures and motifs of the ancient myth of the battle against chaos remain relatively intact; only the names and places are changed to accord with the new demands of a Christian setting and an apocalyptic outlook. But when we turn our sights to the Gospels, we find that the evangelists are much more creative in their use of the ancient Combat Myth and its motifs to undergird their new theological programs.

One of the major themes in the Synoptic Gospels of Matthew, Mark, and Luke is that the advent of Jesus means that the reign of God has begun. The corollary of this is that the reign of the Evil One, or Satan, has come to an end. Sin, sickness, and death are manifestations of the power of evil over this world, standard biblical doctrine held. Accordingly, in the Synoptic Gospels Jesus goes about forgiving sins, healing the sick, and raising the dead. But more importantly, Jesus also attacked the source of the power of evil by casting out demons, Satan's cohorts, in anticipation of the final, eschatological battle with Satan himself. This is not mere posturing. It is a battle to the death in which there can be only one victor. The demons understand this well. They cry out in alarm, "What have you to do with us, Jesus of Nazareth? Have you come to destroy us? I know who you are, the Holy One of God" (Mark 1:24). In turn, the Evil One seeks to destroy Jesus and his disciples. Luke expresses this theme most explicitly. As Jesus prepares for his own passion and death, he warns Peter, "Simon, Simon, behold, Satan demanded to have you, . . . but I have prayed for you that your faith may not fail" (Luke 22:31–32). And as he himself is being arrested, Jesus declares to his captors, "This is your hour, and the power of darkness" (Luke 22:53).

Within the context of this eschatological war between the

forces of God and Satan, the evangelists carefully shaped their individual Gospels and manipulated their materials, the better to convey each his unique message and insight. One of the methods by which they did this was mythopoeic speculation. The two stories of Jesus calming the sea and Jesus walking on the sea—particularly as Matthew tells these stories—illustrate this point well.

The story of Jesus calming the sea is found in Matthew 8:23–27, Mark 4:35–41, and Luke 8:22–25. The story of Jesus walking on the sea is found in Matthew 14:22–33, Mark 6:45–52, and John 6:16–21.[8] Both stories are found only in Matthew and Mark. If the majority of New Testament scholars are correct, Mark was written first. Then some years later, Matthew composed his own Gospel, using Mark's Gospel as one of his sources. If this historical reconstruction is correct, one may discern Matthew's purpose and message by noting how he has changed his own Gospel from Mark's. Already in the Markan formulation both stories are epiphanic, that is, they are revelatory of the true identity of Jesus as divine. In the Hebrew Bible the power both to still the raging sea[9] and to trample upon the back of the sea[10] belong to God alone. Though mediated to Mark principally through biblical tradents, these motifs derive ultimately from the common Semitic Combat Myth in which the Creator triumphs over primeval sea by quelling it and treading victoriously upon it. It is not accidental, therefore, that Mark describes Jesus' walking on the sea in the very language used to depict Yahweh trampling on the back of the sea.[11] Likewise, Jesus' calming of the sea utilizes the language of Yahweh stilling the hostile sea by rebuking it.[12]

Presumably, Jesus' stilling of the sea in Mark retains the ancient connotations of the divine sovereign battling the chaos monster (as in Job 26:11–13), rather than the "demythologized" image of the Creator merely controlling one of his creatures (as in Ps. 107:29). In Mark the sea is personified and rebuked in almost identical terms as the demon in Mark 1:25.[13] Also, in the scene immediately following that of Jesus walking on the sea, the sea and the demonic are again identified. When Jesus casts the "Legion" of demons out of the possessed Gerasene, the demons enter the swine and rush headlong over the cliff and into the sea. The appropriateness of the image is readily apparent, given the ancient symbol of the sea as the home of the anti-god and source of evil.[14]

Because of our remoteness from these ancient symbols, we have not always recognized their presence—and thus we also failed to appreciate the extent to which the evangelists were engaged in theologizing through mythopoeic speculation. The notice that Jesus was asleep in the boat on the sea, prior to his calming of that same sea, is a case in point. Elsewhere[15] I have shown that a standard motif of the Combat Myth is that, following his victory over the chaos monster, the deity rests. Upon defeating his archfoe, the deity builds a palace for himself over the dead body of his foe (the subdued sea) from which he rules as the divine sovereign. Sometimes the divine sovereign is even depicted as retiring to his private quarters to sleep. The image of the deity asleep functions as a graphic symbol of the absoluteness of the deity's sovereignty. The divine king can rest because the whole universe, including the chaos monster, is firmly in his control.

The evangelist Mark understood well the power of this symbol and used it to great effect to suggest that Jesus was divine. The image of Jesus calmly sleeping inside the boat while the sea raged futilely outside is modeled after that of the sleeping divine king. Jesus' sleep arises not from human tiredness. Neither is it a sign of the human Jesus' confidence in God's power to protect him, as some commentators have suggested. Rather, it is the evangelist's symbol that Jesus himself possesses that authority over the demonic sea that the scriptures attribute to God alone. Then to prove that he indeed has such authority, the evangelist has Jesus awaken and still the raging of the sea.

Luke seems not to have been at home in this tradition and to have played down the mythic elements. Whether this was because of a misunderstanding of the particular mythic tradition involved or because he was uncomfortable with theologizing about Jesus in this fashion is unclear. In any case, Luke seems deliberately to de-emphasize the mythic overtones of the Markan version by reinterpreting the incident as a "natural" event. He places the incident on "the lake" (i.e., Gennesaret), thus avoiding the mythic connotations associated with "the sea." Likewise, in Luke the peril seemed to consist solely of unusually large swells caused by the "windstorm," rather than some demonic force per se. After the calming of the water, in Luke 8:25 the disciples exclaim, "Who then is this, that he commands even the wind and *the water*, and they obey him?" whereas in Mark (and Matthew) reference is to "the wind and *the sea*" (RSV, italics mine).[16] Finally, the fact that of the three Synoptic Gospels only Luke omitted the similar story of Jesus walking on the sea points in the same direction.

But if Luke tried to play down the mythic in these stories, Matthew sought to magnify it. Instead of a "great windstorm" (*lailaps anemou megalē*, Mark 4:37; cf. Luke 8:23), Matthew posits a "great earthquake" (*seismos megas*, Matt. 8:24). Earthquakes in both Testaments, as well as in various extrabiblical apocalyptic texts, are associated with the end times. Since Matthew later uses earthquakes to symbolize the eschatological significance of Jesus' death and resurrection (27:51, 54; 28:2), it appears that the evangelist wished to suggest that the end time has arrived and that the definitive battle between the kingdom of God and the kingdom of Satan has begun in earnest (cf. Matt. 24:7).

That Matthew understood well the epiphanic value of the stories about Jesus calming the sea and Jesus walking on water is illustrated in the way he orchestrates these stories within his Gospel to reveal Jesus' true identity. In Matthew the theme of Jesus' identity is connected with that of his authority. That Jesus can heal every infirmity and can teach with authority is a cause for amazement (4:23–25; 7:28) but not necessarily for faith. Jesus' calming of the sea evoked the disciples' amazement (8:27) but not their faith (8:26). At this point the disciples are unable to grasp the sign value of what they have just witnessed. These "men of little faith" do address Jesus by his proper title "Lord" (*kyrie*)—the Greek translation of the name of Yahweh in the Hebrew scriptures—and call upon him to save them (8:25). Yet in the end they merely marvel and wonder uncomprehendingly, "What sort of man is this, that even winds and sea obey him?" (8:27). Thus far they perceive Jesus as only a man, albeit an extraordinary one, but a man nonetheless.

In stark contrast to the uncomprehending disciples, the demons recognize completely the significance and so in the following scene assail Jesus with the question, "What have you to do with us, O Son of God? Have you come here to torment us before the end of time?" (8:29). Not only do the demons recognize that Jesus is the Son of God, they also realize that the end time is rapidly approaching when they must face—and be defeated by—this divine representative.

The theme of Jesus' identity and authority continues in the following episodes. The Pharisees mistakenly reason that Jesus' authority over demons must derive from an association with "the prince of demons" (9:34). From his prison cell John the Baptist begins to question whether Jesus is really "he who is to come, or shall we look for another?" (11:3). The crowds ask, "Is not this the carpenter's son?" (13:55). Herod assumes that Jesus is the ghost of John the Baptist, whom he had killed, come back to haunt him (14:2).

The question asked at 8:27, Who is this that even winds and sea obey him? begins to be answered in the story of Jesus' walking on sea (14:22–33). Matthew makes Peter the vehicle of the disciples' dawning understanding that Jesus is somehow to be identified with God. This is evident from the way Matthew alters the story from his Markan source. According to Mark, the epiphanic nature of Jesus walking on the sea was missed by the disciples, just as previously they had failed to comprehend at every step of the way: "they were utterly astounded, for they did not understand about the loaves, but their hearts were hardened" (6:51–52, cf. RSV). But in Matthew this notice about noncomprehension is omitted and a quite different response inserted instead. As Mark had already suggested, the disciples should have recognized Jesus' true identity, as only God can walk on the sea. It should have been further evident from Jesus' reassurance to the disciples who think they are seeing a ghost: "Take heart, it is I (*egō eimi*); have no fear" (Mark 6:50). These are divine assurances, reminiscent of the self-revelation of Yahweh in the book of Exodus (3:14) as "I am" (LXX: *egō eimi*) and the one who prepares a way for them through the sea with the assurance, "Fear not" (14:13). Moreover, Isaiah 43:1–13 repeatedly uses similar divine reassurances in appealing to this same Exodus motif as a reason for confidence in a similar situation centuries later.[17]

In contrast to Mark, Matthew has the disciples at least begin to comprehend the epiphanic character of Jesus walking on the sea. Peter, their spokesperson, addresses Jesus by the divine title "Lord," and adds with a double entendre, "if it is you (i.e., not just not a ghost, but also truly the LORD[18]), bid me come to you on the water" (Matt. 14:28). If Jesus is the LORD, then he also has the power to make Peter walk on the sea as if on dry land, even as Yahweh did in leading his people out of Egypt. Jesus shows that he indeed has that power. When Peter begins to sink, it is not so much that he doubts his own ability to walk on water as he begins to doubt whether Jesus really is who the epiphany suggests: "O man of little faith, why did you doubt?" (14:31). Jesus in turn reaches out to save Peter and again quells the wind (and by implication, the sea also). In contrast to their uncomprehending posture in the previous epiphany, this time the disciples begin to comprehend what the demons have long since known, that one whom "even wind and sea obey" is no mere man. Accordingly, they "worshiped him, saying, 'Truly you are the Son of God' " (14:33).

That Matthew has deliberately manipulated his material to emphasize its full epiphanic value is confirmed by the way he again altered the scene at Caesarea Philippi two chapters later. In this story as narrated in Mark, to Jesus's question about his identity, Peter responded, "You are the Christ" (Mark 8:29). Matthew embellishes Peter's answer: "You are the Christ, the son of the living God" (Matt. 16:16). In addition, Matthew adds an entirely new scene in which Jesus acknowledges the correctness of Peter's answer, saying that this "revelation" is not from human insight ("flesh and blood") but from God ("my father in heaven"). Now that at last Peter understands Jesus' true identity, Jesus associates Peter with himself in his mission to destroy the kingdom of the Evil One and to establish the kingdom of God; he makes Peter the foundation of his church, against which "the powers of death [Greek: Hades] shall not prevail" (16:17–19).

This scene served as an effective conclusion to the first half of

Matthew's Gospel. The question of Jesus' true identity has been answered at last.

CONCLUSION

With this last example we have come a full circle in our investigations. What we have seen is that the evangelists consciously crafted their Gospels in much the same way that we have observed for other ancient Near Eastern "theologians," from the Old Babylonian Mesopotamia and fifteenth-century B.C.E. Canaan, through Israelite and Jewish writers right up to the close of the biblical period. A feature they all shared in composing their individual works was the use of mythmaking speculation. In each case we have observed how an author deliberately altered and expanded older mythic tradition to express a new understanding about God and the divine activity in this world. Often the myth involved was some form of the ancient Semitic myth of the battle against chaos.

Perhaps there is a salutary moral to be learned from this. One of the real advances in biblical scholarship of the last quarter century is an appreciation of the extent to which the various biblical books are true literary works, that is, that each is a unique text having its own peculiar purpose, message, and compositional techniques. We have yet to come to a like appreciation of the positive value of theologizing by mythopoeic speculation, that is, of retelling the old myths in such a way that they reach across the centuries to new audiences. Matthew is a case in point. He recognized the Combat motifs present in Mark's telling of the stories of Jesus' calming of the sea and walking on the water. But rather than play them down as did Luke, Matthew strengthened them to bring out even more clearly his belief that in Jesus the reign of God has finally come into our world in its definitive form. This meant that God is even now finishing the task of creation by bringing primeval sea (translate: Satan/Evil) under control, as promised in the Hebrew scriptures, themselves dependent upon older myth. By portraying Jesus as exercising the powers that myth and the scriptures say belong to God alone in his role as Creator and Divine Sovereign, the evangelist is clearly attempting to expand the frontiers of the readers' understanding of Jesus as divine and as the manifestation of God in the world.

Given the fact that Christianity was still in the incipient stages of formulating a Christology, that is, the doctrine of Jesus Christ as both human and divine, it is doubtful that any other form of theologizing could have been more effective. The next three or four centuries were to witness great christological debates among Christians, which relied more on philosophical theologizing than on mythopoeic speculation. Professional theologians may appreciate the precision in language and conception of the classical formulations of Christology coming out of the Councils of Nicea, Ephesus, Chalcedon, and others besides. But among the rank and file Christians such philosophical theology probably will never reveal Jesus as "the Son of the living God" as forcefully as the mythopoeic narratives of Mark and especially of Matthew.

ABBREVIATIONS

AB   Anchor Bible

AHw   W. von Soden, *Akkadisches Handwörterbuch*

AnBib   Analecta biblica

ANEP   J. B. Pritchard (ed.), *Ancient Near East in Pictures*

ANET(^{3})   J. B. Pritchard (ed.), *Ancient Near Eastern Texts* (3d ed.)

AS   Assyriological Studies

BA   *Biblical Archaeologist*

BARev   *Biblical Archaeology Review*

BASOR   *Bulletin of the American Schools of Oriental Research*

BBVO   Berliner Beiträge zum Vorderen Orient

BETL   Bibliotheca ephemeridum theologicarum louvaniensium

Bib   *Biblica*

BTB   *Biblical Theology Bulletin*

186

BWANT Beiträge zur Wissenschaft vom Alten und Neuen Testament

BZAW Beihefte zur *ZAW*

CAD The Assyrian Dictionary of the Oriental Institute of the University of Chicago

CBQ *Catholic Biblical Quarterly*

ConB Coniectanea biblica

CT *Cuneiform Texts from Babylonian Tablets in the British Museum*

CTA A. Herdner, *Corpus des tablettes en cunéiformes alphabétiques*

E.T. English translation(s)

HALAT W. Baumgartner et al., *Hebräisches und aramäisches Lexikon zum Alten Testament*

HAT Handbuch zum Alten Testament

HSM Harvard Semitic Monographs

HUCA *Hebrew Union College Annual*

IDB G. A. Buttrick (ed.), *Interpreter's Dictionary of the Bible*

IDBSup Supplementary volume to *IDB*

IEJ *Israel Exploration Journal*

JAOS *Journal of the American Oriental Society*

JBL *Journal of Biblical Literature*

JCS *Journal of Cuneiform Studies*

JNES	*Journal of Near Eastern Studies*
JPSV	Jewish Publication Society Version
JQR	*Jewish Quarterly Review*
JSOT	*Journal for the Study of the Old Testament*
JSOTSup	Journal for the Study of the Old Testament— Supplement Series
KB	L. Köhler and W. Baumgartner, *Lexicon in Veteris Testamenti libros*
LXX	Septuagint
MDOG	*Mitteilungen der deutschen Orient-Gesellschaft*
MSL	*Materialien zum sumerischen Lexikon; Materials for the Sumerian Lexicon*
MT	Masoretic Text
NAB	New American Bible
NT	New Testament
Or	*Orientalia* (Rome)
OT	Old Testament
OTL	Old Testament Library
OTS	Oudtestamentische Studiën
RA	*Revue d'assyriologie et d'archéologie orientale*
RB	*Revue biblique*
RR	*Review of Religion*
RSV	Revised Standard Version

SBLDS Society of Biblical Literature Dissertation Series

SBT Studies in Biblical Theology

VT *Vetus Testamentum*

VTS Vetus Testamentum, Supplements

ZA *Zeitschrift für Assyriologie*

ZAW *Zeitschrift für die altestamentliche Wissenschaft*

NOTES

INTRODUCTION

[1]Robert A. Oden, Jr., *The Bible Without Theology: The Theological Tradition and Alternatives to It* (San Francisco: Harper & Row, 1987), 40–91.

[2]The phrase was popularized by G. E. Wright in a widely read little volume, *God Who Acts: Biblical Theology as Recital*, SBT 8 (London: SCM Press, 1952), 13.

[3]For example, see John H. Hayes and J. Maxwell Miller, eds., *Israelite and Judean History*, OTL (London: SCM Press, 1977); and J. Maxwell Miller and John H. Hayes, *A History of Ancient Israel and Judah* (Philadelphia: Westminster Press, 1986).

[4]Darwin himself studiously avoided using the term "evolution," lest any notion of "progress" be associated with his theory of the natural selection of the species. In popular usage, however, Darwin's name has become synonymous with the concept of evolutionary progress because his writings have been frequently invoked in support of theories of evolution.

[5]So E. B. Taylor, *Primitive Culture*, 2 vols. (London: Murray, 1871).

[6]James George Frazer, *The Golden Bough: A Study in Magic and Religion*, 3rd ed., 12 vols. (London: Macmillan, 1911–1915). The first edition appeared in 1890.

[7]Lucien Lévy-Bruhl, *Primitive Mentality* (London: George Allen & Unwin, 1923) and *How Natives Think* (New York: Alfred A. Knopf, 1925). Approximately a half century earlier the philologist F. Max Müller (1823–1900) had asserted the existence of a kind of mythopoeic thought based upon his theory of the development of language, according to which myths are erroneous explanations of natural phe-

nomena, especially the sun. Müller's "solar mythology" never acquired a wide following, however.

[8]In particular the philosopher Ernst Cassirer (*Philosophie der symbolischen Formen*, 2 vols. [Berlin: B. Cassirer, 1923–1931]) championed this view. It was subsequently popularized among biblicists by Henri and H. A. Frankfort in an essay entitled "Myth and Reality" (*The Intellectual Adventure of Ancient Man*, ed. H. and H. A. Frankfort [Chicago: University of Chicago Press, 1946], 3–27), and still later by G. Ernest Wright (*The Old Testament Against Its Environment* [London: SCM Press, 1950]).

[9]See Oden, *Bible Without Theology*, 70–73.

[10]See Jaan Puhvel, *Comparative Mythology* (Baltimore/London: Johns Hopkins University Press, 1987), 12.

[11]Cited from W. Doty, *Mythography: The Study of Myths and Rituals* (Tuscaloosa, Ala.: University of Alabama Press, 1986), 136. On pp. 131–166 of *Mythography* Doty provides an excellent overview of the psychological approach to myth and to various practitioners of that method.

[12]Structuralism is associated primarily with the name of French linguistic philosopher and anthropologist Claude Lévi-Strauss. Among other of his works, see esp. "The Story of Asdiwal," in Claude Lévi-Strauss, *Structural Anthropology*, vol. 2 (New York: Basic Books, 1976), 146–197; and his four-volume work, *The Raw and the Cooked: Introduction to a Science of Mythology* (New York: Harper & Row, 1975); see also his "Structuralism and Myth," *Kenyon Review*, N.S. III 2 (Spring 1981), 64–88. For other structualist studies, particularly as applied to biblical texts, see Edmund Leach, *Genesis as Myth and Other Essays* (London: Cape, 1969); Roland Barthes et al., *Analyse Structurale et exegese biblique* (Neuchâtel: Delachaux et Niestlé, 1972); Edmund Leach and D. Alan Aycock, *Structuralist Interpretations of Biblical Myth* (Cambridge: Cambridge University Press, 1983); Robert Polzin, *Biblical Structuralism*, Semeia Studies (Missoula, Mont.: Scholars Press, 1977); Daniel Patte, *Structural Exegesis: From Theory to Practice* (Philadelphia: Fortress Press, 1978).

[13]The French sociologist Emile Durkheim (1858–1917) is often considered the founder of the sociofunctional school of myth; see his *The Elementary Forms of Religious Life* (London: George Allen & Unwin, 1915 [originally published in French in 1912]). However, anthropologist Bronislaw Malinowski (1884–1942) was perhaps the principal advocate and popularizer of this school; see his very influential essay, "Myth in Primitive Psychology," in *Magic, Science and Religion, and Other Essays by Bronislaw Malinowski*, ed. Robert

Redfield (Garden City, N.Y.: Doubleday & Co., 1954 [originally published in 1926]), 72–124.

[14]This view has been widely popularized through the writings of G. van der Leeuw (*Religion in Essence and Manifestation* [New York: Harper & Row, 1963]) and especially Mircea Eliade; of the many writings of Eliade see especially *Myth and Reality* (New York: Harper & Row, 1963) and *The Myth of the Eternal Return* (New York: Pantheon Press, 1954).

[15]For a more complete study of myth see Doty, *Mythography*. See also the shorter but very useful survey of Percy S. Cohen, "Theories of Myth," *Man*, N.S. 4 (1969), 337–353. For studies of myth in the ancient Near East and in biblical studies see G. S. Kirk, *Myth: Its Meaning and Functions in Ancient and Other Cultures* (Berkeley/Los Angeles: University of California Press, 1970); J. W. Rogerson, *Myth in Old Testament Interpretation* (Berlin/New York: Walter de Gruyter, 1974); and Oden, *Bible Without Theology*, 40–91.

[16]See B. Batto, "Myth," in *The New Dictionary of Theology* (Wilmington, Del.: Michael Glazier, 1987), 697–701.

[17]So, for example, in *Atrahasis*; see chapter 1.

[18]See Ps. 50:12–13, for example.

[19]See Isa. 1:11–17; Jer. 6:20; 7:21–22; Hos. 6:6; Amos 5:21–27; Mic. 6:6–8.

[20]Roland de Vaux, *Ancient Israel*, vol. 2 (New York: McGraw-Hill Book Co., 1965), 451.

CHAPTER 1
MYTHOPOEIC SPECULATION IN BABYLON

[1]On the importance of scribal schools in the dissemination and canonization of cuneiform literary tradition, see W. G. Lambert, "Ancestors, Authors and Canonicity," *JCS* 11 (1957), 1–14; W. W. Hallo, "New Viewpoints on Cuneiform Literature," *IEJ* 12 (1962), 13–26; id., "Toward a History of Sumerian Literature," *AS* 20 (1976), 181–203. Specifically on the concept of a literary canon in Mesopotamia see the essay of W. W. Hallo, "The Concept of Canonicity in Cuneiform and Biblical Literature: A Comparative Appraisal," in *The Biblical Canon in Comparative Perspective: Scripture in Context IV*, ed. K. Lawson Younger, Jr., W. W. Hallo, and B. Batto (Lewiston, N.Y.: Edwin Mellen Press, 1991), 1–19.

[2]See J. H. Tigay, ed., *Empirical Models for Biblical Criticism* (Philadelphia: University of Pennsylvania Press, 1985).

[3]For the history of critical scholarship regarding the Gilgamesh epic

see J. Tigay, *The Evolution of the Gilgamesh Epic* (Philadelphia: University of Pennsylvania Press, 1982), 16–22.

[4]W. L. Moran, in *The Encyclopedia of Religion*, s.v. "Gilgamesh"; see further T. Jacobsen, *Treasures of Darkness: A History of Mesopotamian Religion* (New Haven, Conn.: Yale University Press, 1976), 208–215.

[5]Moran, "Gilgamesh," 558. See also S. N. Kramer, *The Sumerians: Their History, Culture, and Character* (Chicago/London: University of Chicago Press, 1963), 185–205.

[6]A translation of this text, and of nos. 4 and 6, may be found in *ANET*, 44–52.

[7]For text and translation see M. Civil, "The Sumerian Flood Story," in W. G. Lambert and A. R. Millard, *Atrahasis: The Babylonian Story of the Flood* (Oxford: Clarendon Press, 1969), 138–145; and T. Jacobsen, "The Eridu Genesis," *JBL* 100 (1981), 513–529; for translation only see S. N. Kramer, "The Deluge," *ANET*, 42–44; T. Jacobsen, *The Harps That Once . . . : Sumerian Poetry in Translation* (New Haven, Conn.: Yale University Press, 1987), 145–150.

[8]For English translations see A. Heidel, *The Gilgamesh Epic and Old Testament Parallels*, 2nd ed. (Chicago: University of Chicago Press, 1949); E. Speiser, supplemented by A. K. Grayson, "Gilgamesh," in *ANET*[3], 72–99, 503–507; Maureen Gallery Kovacs, *The Epic of Gilgamesh* (Stanford, Calif.: Stanford University Press, 1989); Stephanie Dalley, *Myths from Mesopotamia* (Oxford/New York: Oxford University Press, 1989), 39–153.

[9]See n. 3. Much of what follows is a summary of Tigay, *Evolution of the Gilgamesh Epic*, esp. 240–250.

[10]Ibid., 42–43.

[11]Ibid., 243.

[12]This theme may have derived from the sacred marriage ritual as practiced at Uruk. As a ruler of Uruk Gilgamesh would have been the *en* priest; in the annual rite of the sacred marriage he took on the identity of Dumuzi-Amaushumgalanna and married the goddess Inanna, or Ishtar, so as to ensure fertility and plenty in the land. See Jacobsen, *Treasures of Darkness*, 209.

[13]Like immortality, the ability to do without sleep when necessary is a mark of divinity. Ps. 121 says that God never sleeps. For a full study of the motif of divine sleep and its opposite, see my article, "The Sleeping God: An Ancient Near Eastern Motif of Divine Sovereignty," *Bib* 68 (1987), 153–177.

[14]Tigay, *The Evolution of the Gilgamesh Epic*, 50–51. Jacobsen (*Treasures of Darkness*, 215–219), who works from the standard late

Assyrian recension, finds the message of the epic to be about growing up, about putting aside adolescent fantasies and accepting the responsibilities of adulthood. For Jacobsen the key to the epic is the loss of the plant of life, which is a metaphor for the loss of the illusion that one can go back to being a child. In accepting its loss Gilgamesh has at last become mature.

[15]Tigay, *Evolution of the Gilgamesh Epic*, 243.

[16]Moran, "Gilgamesh," 559.

[17]There is no consensus among scholars that the plant of life story dates to the Old Babylonian version. Moran ("Gilgamesh," 559) argues that it is a late addition: "Like the flood story, it reveals a secret of the gods. It also illustrates a wisdom theme complementing that of divine transcendence: human frailty."

[18]Tigay, *Evolution of the Gilgamesh Epic*, 240–241.

[19]Translation from Tigay, ibid., 141.

[20]See Tigay, ibid., 143, n.8, and 205–206; Lambert, "Ancestors, Authors, and Canonicity," 1–14; and A. D. Kilmer, "The Mesopotamian Counterparts of the Biblical *Nepilim*," in *Perspectives on Language and Text: Essays and Poems in Honor of Francis I. Andersen's Sixtieth Birthday July 28, 1985*, ed. E. W. Conrad and E. G. Newing (Winona Lake, Ind.: Eisenbrauns, 1987), 39–43.

[21]See W. G. Lambert, "History and the Gods: A Review Article," *Or* 39 (1970), 170–177, esp. 175.

[22]For English translations see *ANET*, 101–103; Dalley, *Myths from Mesopotamia*, 184–188.

[23]In the lexical series $L\acute{U} = \check{S}A$, the equation A-DA-AB = *a-mi-lu* is given (*MSL* XII, 93), i.e., Adapa = "man"/"human"—the same semantic content as for the Hebrew word "adam." Note that in text B, which was discovered at El-Amarna in Egypt, Adapa is addressed as "Man" (*amīlu*; line 21). In addition, to be called "man/human," Adapa, is comparable to "Adam" in other ways. Both are specially creations of the creator deity and possess uncommon wisdom. (For the motif of "Adam" eating from the wisdom tree in Eden, see chapter 2.) Both pass up the opportunity for immortality by not eating the food of life, and this in the context of divine commands about eating or not eating such food. "Adam" is commanded by Yahweh God not to eat of "the tree of knowledge of good and evil" because that would mean death; Adapa is commanded by Ea not to eat of the "bread of death" or drink of the "water of death." "Adam" is commanded to eat of all the trees of the garden, which would include "the tree of life" (Gen. 2:16), which he failed to do (cf. Gen. 3:22); Adapa is offered the "bread of life" and the "water of life" but declined it. In Eden Yah-

weh God clothed the human couple in skin garments in place of their leaf garments (Gen. 3:21); Anu gave Adapa new garments in place of his mourning garments. The human couple was driven out of Eden to die; Adapa was returned from heaven to earth (to Eridu) to die. Moreover, there is an indirect link of Adapa to "Adam" through the figure of Atrahasis. In chapter 2 I gather evidence that suggests a real correspondence between "Adam" and Atrahasis. But there is also evidence that Adapa and Atrahasis are essentially the same character. Both Adapa and Atrahasis are representative of primeval humankind and involved with humankind being denied immortality. Atrahasis saved his own and others' lives by means of a boat; Adapa's connection with a boat has already been mentioned—though here the latter scene seems an ironic reversal of the former. Both are devotees of Ea and endowed with superhuman wisdom. Finally, like Adapa, Atrahasis is a priest of Ea because he lives in the temple of Ea, according to the Sumerian flood story; see R. Borger, "Notes brèves: 10. Sur le récit de Déluge RS 22421," *RA* 64 (1970), 189.

[24]The phrase is used as the subtitle of this myth by the editors of this text, W. G. Lambert and A. R. Millard (*Atra-hasis: The Babylonian Story of the Flood*). For other (more selective, less complete) English translations of this myth see Dalley, *Myths from Mesopotamia*, 1–38; and *ANET*[3], 99–100 ("Creation of Man by the Mother Goddess"), 104–106, 512–514.

[25]See notice on Sippar in "Excavations in Iraq, 1985–86," *Iraq* 49 (1987), 248–249.

[26]For the interpretation of *Atrahasis* offered here, see my two articles, "The Covenant of Peace: A Neglected Ancient Near Eastern Motif," *CBQ* 49 (1987), 187–211; and "The Sleeping God"; additional bibliography for this myth will be found therein also.

[27]The translation and meaning of this line has been much debated. The translation adopted here follows W. Moran, "Some Considerations of Form and Interpretation in *Atra-hasis*," in *Language, Literature, and History: Philological and Historical Studies Presented to Erica Reiner*, ed. Francesca Rochberg-Halton, American Oriental Series 67 (New Haven, Conn.: American Oriental Society, 1987), 245–255, esp. 247. Moran's translation, "When gods were man," has been modified to reflect the practice in this volume of using "human" instead of "man" when the reference is generic rather than gender specific.

[28]Although Atrahasis is never called a king in the Akkadian myth, in the Sumerian version of *The Deluge* (iii.20–21) the flood hero Ziusudra is termed both "king" (**l u g a l**) and "lustration priest"

(**g u d a - a b z u**), and if Jacobsen's restoration is correct, also a "seer" (**e n s i**); see T. Jacobsen, "Eridu Genesis," 521–522.

[29]In the main recension of *Atrahasis* the original "human regulations" are lost in the break in Tablet I between lines 260 and 272, but they can be reconstructed from text S, line 14: *ú-ṣu-ra-te šá niši*[meš]*-ma ú-ṣa-ar* [d]*ma-mi*, "Mami imposed the human regulations"; see Lambert and Millard, *Atra-hasis*, 62.

[30]See Anne D. Kilmer, "The Mesopotamian Concept of Overpopulation and Its Solution as Reflected in Mythology," *Or* 41 (1972), 160–177; W. L. Moran, "Atrahasis: The Babylonian Story of the Flood," *Bib* 52 (1971), 51–61; T. Frymer-Kensky, "The Atrahasis Epic and Its Significance for Our Understanding of Genesis 1–9," *BA* 40 (1977), 147–155; V. Fritz, " 'Solange die Erde steht'—Vom Sinn der jahwistischen Fluterzählung in Gen. 6–8," *ZAW* 94 (1982), 599–614.

[31]See Robert Oden, Jr., "Divine Aspirations in Atrahasis and in Genesis 1–11," *ZAW* 93 (1981), 197–216, esp. 201–210; and G. Pettinato, "Die Bestrafung des Menschengeschlechts durch die Sintflut," *Or* 37 (1968), 165–200. See also W. von Soden ("Der Mensch bescheidet sich nicht: Überlegungen zu Schöpfungserzählungen in Babylonien und Israel," *Symbolae Biblicae et Mesopotamicae Francisco Mario Theodoro de Liagre Böhl dedicatae,* ed. M. A. Beek, A. A. Kampman, C. Nijland, and J. Rychmans [Leiden: E. J. Brill, 1973], 349–358), who maintains that the crime of humanity was to overreach the human realm and encroach upon the divine realm. The Neo-Babylonian poem of Erra provides confirmation that some sort of rebellion is implied. The poem alludes back to *Atrahasis* and the *ḫubūru* that prevented the king of the gods (here Marduk) and the Anunnaki from sleeping in primordial times as a parallel to the contemporary sin that caused the gods to bring catastrophic punishment upon the cities of Babylonia. See L. Cagni, *The Poem of Erra*, Sources from the Ancient Near East, 1/3 (Malibu, Calif.: Undena, 1977), 29, n. 12, and 41, n. 84. Although the date of *Erra* was at one time much controverted, recent scholars have followed the lead of W. von Soden, who has abandoned his earlier dating of the poem as a fourteenth-century B.C.E. composition (*MDOG* 85 [1953], 23) in favor of a Neo-Babylonian date (*Ugarit-Forschungen* 3 [1971], 255–256); on the basis of precise historical, archaeological, and astronomical arguments Soden now dates this poem to the period 765–763 B.C.E.

[32]For details see my article, "The Sleeping God" (n. 13 above).

[33]Indeed, the decree of death may have been explicitly stated, if W. G. Lambert ("The Theology of Death," in *Death in Mesopotamia*, ed.

B. Alster, Mesopotamia 8 [Copenhagen: Akademisk, 1980], 54–58) is correct in restoring *Atrahasis* III.vi.47–48, on the basis of *Gilgamesh* X.vi.28–32, as follows: [*at-ti ša-a*]*s-sú ba-ni-a-at ši-ma-ti* / [*mu-ta šu-uk-ni*] *a-na ni-ši* "(Enki opened his mouth / and addressed Nintu, the birthgoddess,) '[You, bi]rthgoddess, creatress of destinies, / [Create death] for the people."

[34]Text G may be an exception according to Lambert and Millard, *Atra-hasis*, 34; its fragmentary condition precludes firm conclusions, however.

[35]A recently published Neo-Babylonian text (VS 24, Nr. 92) from Babylon, unfortunately only partially preserved, may be a late version of *Atrahasis*. The differences are sufficiently great, however, that on the basis of present evidence it is best to regard it as a distinct composition about the creation of kingship, patterned after the creation typology of *Atrahasis*. See W. R. Mayer, "Ein Mythos von der Erschaffung des Menschen und des Königs," *Or* 56 (1987), 55–68.

[36]S. N. Kramer, *Sumerian Mythology: A Study of Spiritual and Literary Achievement in the Third Millennium B.C.*, revised ed. (New York: Harper & Row, 1961), 68ff.; for a more critical edition see C. A. Benito, *"Enki and Ninmah" and "Enki and the World Order"* (Ann Arbor, Mich.: University Microfilms, 1969). See further G. Komoróczy, "Work and Strike of the Gods: New Light on the Divine Society in the Sumero-Akkadian Mythology," *Oikumene* 1 (1976), 9–37.

[37]Jacobsen, *Harps That Once*, 151–166.

[38]See Civil, "Sumerian Flood Story," in Lambert and Millard, *Atrahasis*, 138–139.

[39]E.g., Jacobsen, "Eridu Genesis," 526–527; W. W. Hallo, "Antediluvian Cities," *JCS* 33 (1970), 57–67.

[40]For English translations of this myth see A. Heidel, *The Babylonian Genesis: The Story of Creation*, 2nd ed. (Chicago/London: University of Chicago Press, 1951); *ANET*[3], 60–72, 501–503; Dalley, *Myths from Mesopotamia*, 228–277.

[41]The name *ti'amat*, from *ti'amtum/tâmtum* ("sea, ocean"), is the absolute state without case endings and without mimation, a form frequent with common nouns used as proper names. The ancient scribes were clearly aware of the identity of Ti'amat and Sea; see T. Jacobsen, "The Battle Between Marduk and Tiamat," *JAOS* 88 (1968), 104–108.

[42]See pp. 29–31, this chapter.

[43]So W. G. Lambert, "The Reign of Nebuchadnezzar I: A Turning Point in the History of Ancient Mesopotamian Religion," in *The Seed*

of Wisdom: Essays in Honour of T. J. Meek, ed. W. S. McCullough (Toronto: University of Toronto Press, 1964), 3–13. But most recently Dalley (*Myths from Mesopotamia*, 228–230) argues that Tablets VI and VII date to the Kassite period and Tablets I–V to a still earlier period.

⁴⁴See W. G. Lambert, "The Historical Development of the Mesopotamian Pantheon: A Study in Sophisticated Polytheism," in *Unity and Diversity: Essays in the History, Literature, and Religion of the Ancient Near East*, ed. Hans Goedicke and J. J. M. Roberts (Baltimore/London: Johns Hopkins University, 1975), 191–200, esp. 193–194.

⁴⁵See W. G. Lambert, "Ninurta Mythology in the Babylonian Epic of Creation," in *Keilschriftliche Literaturen: Ausgewählte Vorträge der XXXII. Rencontre Assyriologique Internationale, Münster, 8–12.7.1985*, ed. Karl Hecker and Walter Sommerfeld (Berlin: Dietrich Reimer, 1986), 55–60.

⁴⁶See E. Speiser and A. K. Grayson, in *ANET³*, 113 and 514–517, respectively.

⁴⁷Erra I.130–162; see Cagni, *Poem of Erra*, 32–34.

⁴⁸Translation from Lambert, "Historical Development of the Mesopotamian Pantheon," 197–198.

⁴⁹Jacobsen, *Treasures of Darkness*, 163–191.

⁵⁰See also VII.90, where Marduk is praised as *ābit* DINGER.MEŠ *ša Tiāmat ēpiš* UN.MEŠ *ina mimmîšun*, "Destroyer of the gods of Ti'amat, who made humankind out of their substance."

⁵¹Another related example of motif replacement, though not in *Enuma elish*, is that in one tradition Marduk, rather than Enlil or Adad, is said to have brought on the flood; see P. F. Grössmann, *Das Era-Epos*, I.132, cited in *CAD* A I.77.

CHAPTER 2
THE YAHWIST'S PRIMEVAL MYTH

¹For a recent, revised statement of the Documentary Hypothesis, see Richard Elliott Friedman, *Who Wrote the Bible?* (New York: Summit Books, 1987).

²See, for example, Isaac M. Kikawada and Arthur Quinn, *Before Abraham Was* (Nashville: Abingdon Press, 1985); Robert Alter, *The Art of Biblical Narrative* (New York: Basic Books, 1981); Michael Fishbane, *Text and Texture* (New York: Schocken Books, 1979); K. R. R. Gros Louis in several articles on Genesis 1–11 in the two volumes by K. R. R. Gros Louis, et al., *Literary Interpretations of Biblical Narratives* (Nashville: Abingdon Press, 1974, 1982); J. P. Fokkelman,

Narrative Art in Genesis (Amsterdam: van Gorcum, 1975); Jack M. Sasson, "The 'Tower of Babel' as a Clue to the Redactional Structuring of the Primeval History [Gen. 1–11:9]," in *The Bible World: Essays in Honor of Cyrus H. Gordon*, ed. G. Rendsburg, et al. (New York: KTAV Publishing House, 1980), 211–219; Gary A. Rendsburg, *The Redaction of Genesis* (Winona Lake, Ind.: Eisenbrauns, 1986).

[3]Frank M. Cross, *Canaanite Myth and Hebrew Epic* (Cambridge, Mass.: Harvard University Press, 1973), 293–325.

[4]This composition originally would have ended with an account of the death of Moses, which was subsequently removed and spliced together with Deuteronomy 34, when at a still later date Deuteronomy was joined to the Priestly work to form the present Pentateuch.

[5]The masculine pronoun is used here on the assumption that biblical authors were men. Presumably in ancient Israel, as in the ancient Near East generally, the scribal profession rested mostly in male hands. Nevertheless, there is nothing to preclude the possibility of the Yahwist having been a woman; see Friedman, *Who Wrote the Bible?* 85–86. However, Harold Bloom (*The Book of J* [New York: Grove Weidenfeld, 1990]) exceeds the meager biblical evidence in pinpointing J as a royal woman in the court of Rehoboam, son of Solomon. In contrast, P likely was a man (or a group of men), if the common assumption is correct that P was transmitted by *priestly* tradents.

[6]A notable exception is John Van Seters (*Abraham in History and Tradition* [New Haven, Conn.: Yale University Press, 1975]) who posits J as a late pentateuchal tradition deriving from the late Neo-Babylonian period (seventh and sixth centuries B.C.E.).

[7]Gerhard von Rad, "The Form-Critical Problem of the Hexateuch," in *The Problem of the Hexateuch and Other Essays* (New York: McGraw-Hill Book Co., 1966; London: SCM Press, 1938), 1–78. Hans Walter Wolff ("The Kerygma of the Yahwist," in W. Brueggemann and H. W. Wolff, *The Vitality of Old Testament Traditions*, 2nd ed. [Atlanta: John Knox Press, 1982], 41–62) interprets J as offering to Solomon a theological program of conduct appropriate to his growing empire.

[8]Robert B. Coote and David Robert Ord, *The Bible's First History* (Philadelphia: Fortress Press, 1989), esp. 31–41. My interpretation, especially of the beginning of J, differs significantly. Coote and Ord's single-minded reading of J as a polemic against corvée labor associated with state controlled irrigation agriculture of Egypt and Mesopotamia causes them to ignore other, more prominent themes that are suggested by the typology of ancient Near Eastern myth.

[9]In 1965 W. G. Lambert and A. R. Millard published major new

portions of the myth in *CT*, part 46; four years later these same editors published a transliterated edition and English translation of the full myth in *Atra-hasis: The Babylonian Story of the Flood* (Oxford: Clarendon Press, 1969).

[10]Kikawada and Quinn (*Before Abraham Was*) likewise point to parallels between Genesis 1–11 and *Atrahasis*; however, they posit that the whole of Genesis is the work of one author. My study, done quite independently, posits two successive redactions of Genesis 1–11, and that the *Atrahasis*-like themes are to be found exclusively in those passages identified as Yahwistic.

[11]The debate outlined by C. Westermann (*Genesis 1–11: A Commentary* [Minneapolis: Augsburg, 1984], 186–190) between those scholars who argue that Genesis 2–3 constitutes a unified narrative and those who posit two or more parallel narratives within Genesis 2–3 should be fair warning that the actual process of composition of the Yahwistic epic was much more complex than this brief chapter can capture.

[12]On the Canaanite scribe in particular see Aaron Demsky, "The Education of Canaanite Scribes in the Mesopotamian Cuneiform Tradition," in *Bar-Ilan Studies in Assyriology Dedicated to Pinḥas Artzi*, ed. Jacob Klein and Aaron Skaist, Bar-Ilan Studies in Near Eastern Languages and Culture (Ramat Gan: Bar-Ilan University, 1990), 157–190. See further W. G. Lambert, "The Interchange of Ideas Between Southern Mesopotamia and Syria-Palestine as Seen in Literature," in *Mesopotamien und seine Nachbarn*, ed. Hans-Jörg Nissen and Johannes Renger (Berlin: Dietrich Reimer, 1982), 311–316; W. W. Hallo, "Towards a History of Sumerian Literature," *AS* 20 (1976), 181–203; id., "Sumerian Literature: Background to the Bible," *Bible Review*, June 1988, 28–38.

[13]The recently published texts from Emar provide an important witness to scribal practice in the western periphery at the end of the Late Bronze Age and the beginning of the Early Iron Age; see P. Hoskisson, "Emar as an Empirical Model of the Transmission of Canon," in *The Biblical Canon in Comparative Perspective: Scripture in Context IV*, ed. K. Lawson Younger, Jr., W. W. Hallo, and B. Batto (Lewiston, N.Y.: Edwin Mellen Press, 1991), 21–32.

[14]For a more detailed analysis of selected motifs and mythic themes employed by the Yahwist, see esp. the various studies by this writer and by Robert A. Oden, Jr., mentioned in this chapter.

[15]These two symbols of chaos have been frequently studied, often with different conclusions. The ground-breaking study was H. Gunkel, *Schöpfung und Chaos in Urzeit und Endzeit* (Göttingen: Vandenho-

eck & Ruprecht, 1895). G. R. Driver ("Mythical Monsters in the Old Testament," *Studi Orientalistici in onore de Giorgio Levi della Vida*, 1 [Pubblicazioni dell'istituto per l'oriente, 52; Rome: Istituto per l'Oriente, 1956], 234–249), following a long-standing tradition to naturalize the monsters, saw in Behemoth a description of the crocodile. Mary K. Wakeman (*God's Battle with the Monster* [Leiden: E. J. Brill, 1973], 106–117) argues that, in addition to the sea monster Leviathan, the Old Testament also knows of a second monster, the earth monster Eres, also called Behemoth. John Day (*God's Conflict with the Dragon and the Sea* [Cambridge: Cambridge University Press, 1985], 62–87) argues that just as Leviathan is derived from the Ugaritic dragon *ltn*, so Behemoth has its origins in an oxlike creature of the water called Arš or ʿgl ʾil ʿtk, "El's calf Atik." Richard J. Clifford in a private communication notes that a third symbol of chaos is stygian night, e.g., Gen. 1:2–5; Ps. 104, esp. vs. 20–23; Isa. 45:7, 19; 50:2–3, et passim; Jer. 4:23, 28.

[16]Some centuries after J, Deutero-Isaiah will play upon this imagery of God making the desert into Eden, alternately "the garden of Yahweh," as a symbol of Israel's restoration after the Exile (Isa. 51:3). Jer. 4:26 uses the reverse of the image to suggest that in the day of judgment Yahweh will turn fruitful land into desert.

[17]The meaning of the word ʾēd is uncertain. The translation "primeval flood" assumes that the Hebrew vocable is cognate to Akkadian *edû*, a Sumerian loanword; see E. A. Speiser, "*Ed* in the Story of Creation," *BASOR* 140 (1955), 9–11. For a discussion of other possible meanings, see Westermann, *Genesis 1–11*, 200–201. The meaning of "underworld" for ʾereṣ is well attested in biblical Hebrew; see M. Dahood, *Psalms I*, AB 16 (Garden City, N.Y.: Doubleday & Co., 1965), 106. I interpret the author to intend an allusion to the common Semitic belief that prior to the Creator's ordering of chaos, primeval floodwaters prevailed over the earth, thus making life impossible. This image of primeval flood as the symbol of chaos is found both in *Enuma elish* and in the creation account of Genesis 1.

[18]J's psychological understanding of the river phenomena is reversed from ours. E. A. Speiser (*Oriental and Biblical Studies* [Philadelphia: University of Pennsylvania Press, 1967], 23–34) notes that the "head" of a river is what we call its mouth; its course is traced upstream, not downstream; moreover, ancient Mesopotamian tradition located paradise [= Dilmun] in the vicinity of the confluence of the Tigris and the Euphrates rivers near the Persian Gulf. On the problems of interpretation of Sumerian **k a** and **k u n** as referring to the "mouth" and "tail" of a watercourse (river or canal), see F. R. Kraus,

"Provinzen des neusumerischen Reiches von Ur," *ZA* 51, 45–75, esp. 52–55; *CAD* Z, *zibbatu* 2b. Contrary to Speiser, however, Dilmun should not be equated with "paradise" because Mesopotamia lacked a true paradise motif; see my article, "Paradise Reexamined," in *The Biblical Canon in Comparative Perspective: Scripture in Context IV*, ed. K. Lawson Younger, Jr., W. W. Hallo, and B. Batto (Lewiston, N.Y.: Edwin Mellen Press, 1991), 33–66.

[19]See E. A. Speiser, "The Rivers of Paradise," *Festschrift Johannes Friedrich* (Heidelberg: Carl Winter Universitätsverlag, 1959), 473–485, reprinted in *Oriental and Biblical Studies: Collected Writings of E. A. Speiser*, ed. J. J. Finkelstein and Moshe Greenberg (Philadelphia: University of Pennsylvania Press, 1967), 23–34.

[20]See A. R. Millard, "The Etymology of Eden," *VT* 34 (1984), 103–106.

[21]The theme of Eden as a paradise for humankind is a later biblical development resulting from the juxtaposition of the P and J creation accounts in Genesis 1–3; see my article, "Paradise Reexamined" (see n. 18 above).

[22]See Ali Abou-Assaf, Pierre Bordreuil, and Alan R. Millard, *La statue de Tell Fekherye et son inscription bilingue assyro-arameénne*, Etudes assyriologiqes 7 (Paris: Editions Recherche sur les civilisations, 1982) for the *editio princeps*.

[23]W. W. Hallo suggested to me that one perhaps should compare Sumerian **a - t i - l a** and **ú - t i - l a**, "vivifying water/verdure" in Lugalbanda I.258–263 and elsewhere; see Hallo, "Lugalbanda Excavated," *JAOS* 103 (1983), 165–180.

[24]See p. 61, with n. 47.

[25]Contrast Westermann, *Genesis 1–11*, 222. Also, led by their belief that J was written as a polemic against the corvée labor policies of Egypt, Coote and Ord (*Bible's First History*, 50 and 61) mistakenly claim that J rejected the Mesopotamian tradition that humankind was created as laborers for the gods.

[26]An echo of this theme is found in the sacrifice of Noah at the conclusion of the flood. In *Atrahasis* the sacrifice of the flood hero is patently presented as the act of a faithful devotee, which is contrasted with the rebellious actions of the impious generation that brought on the flood through their refusal to carry out their function of provisioning the gods. For further discussion see B. Batto, "The Covenant of Peace: A Neglected Ancient Near Eastern Motif," *CBQ* 49 (1987), 187–211.

Recognition of this motif may also provide the explanation as to why Cain's offering was not acceptable to Yahweh (Gen. 4:3–5).

Since Cain is portrayed as continuing the sin of his parents, it was unnecessary to state that the offering that this "tiller of the soil" brought forward "from the fruit of the soil" was inherently unacceptable. Cain was rebellious in his attitude of cultivating the soil and provisioning the deity.

[27]For a good treatment of the importance of the theme of "the ground" (*hā-ʾădāmâ*) in the Yahwist's primeval story, see Patrick D. Miller, Jr., *Genesis 1–11: Studies in Structure and Theme*, JSOTSup 8 (Sheffield: University of Sheffield, 1978), 37–42.

[28]*Atrahasis* does not preserve a motif of animals being created from clay, but it was implied if not made explicit since the flood would have wiped out animalkind as well as humankind, had not the flood hero saved a remnant of both species (III.ii.32–38; text W, lines 9–10; note also Atrahasis's charge to *na-pí-iš-ta bu-ul-li-iṭ*, "save life," in III.i.24). The poem of Erra, which is dependent upon *Atrahasis* for the motif of humankind being almost destroyed because of its cries of rebellion that disturbed the deity, likewise parallels the threat of annihilation for both humankind and animalkind (Erra I.41–45); and a bit further: "Let men be frightened and may their noise subside; / May the herds (animalkind) shake and turn into clay again" (Erra I.74–75; cf. IV.150). Erra supposes that humankind and animalkind are drawn from the same matter and guilty of the same crime (I.77); see L. Cagni, *The Poem of Erra*, Sources from the Ancient Near East, 1/3 (Malibu, Calif.: Undena, 1977), 29, n. 19.

[29]The resemblances between Genesis 3 and *Gilgamesh* have long been recognized. The first "human" couple lost their chance at immortality because the serpent "tempted" them; Gilgamesh lost his chance at immortality because a snake deprived him of the plant of life. The first couple, originally naked, are clothed by Yahweh; Enkidu, originally adorned only with hair like an animal, is clothed by the harlot. In both stories an original state was "lost" but divine wisdom was acquired in the process.

[30]The term *lullû* is attested only in contexts referring to primordial humankind. Speiser (*ANET*, 38, n. 86) translates it as "savage"; but *AHw*'s "Ursprünglicher Mensch" is closer to the textual evidence. See J. Tigay, *The Evolution of the Gilgamesh Epic* (Philadelphia: University of Pennsylvania Press, 1982), 202.

[31]*HALAT* III.965. The interpretation of *ṣēlāʿ* as "side" is attested already in early Judaism (*Mishnah Rabbah*, Gen. 8.1, 17.6). The traditional interpretation of *ṣēlāʿ* as a bone ("rib") derives in large measure from the joyous exclamation of the human in 2:23,

> This one, this time, is bone from my bone
> and flesh from my flesh!
> This one shall be called "woman"
> because from "man" this one was taken.

The function of this poetic couplet, however, is to emphasize the consubstantiality of the male and the female of the human species and the mutuality of their relationship; it is not intended to define the material derivation of the female of the species. Also to be discounted is the frequently repeated theory of S. N. Kramer (*Enki and Ninhursag: A Sumerian 'Paradise' Myth*, BASOR Supplementary Studies 1 (New Haven, Conn.: American Schools of Oriental Research, 1945], 8–9) that the Genesis topos derives originally from a Sumerian pun involving cuneiform TI, which ambiguously signifies both "life" and "rib"; repeated by J. B. Pritchard, "Man's Predicament in Eden," *RR* 13 (1948/1949), 15; T. Gaster, *Myth, Legend, and Custom in the Old Testament* (New York: Harper & Row, 1969), 21–23; Westermann, *Genesis 1–11*, 230. This theory is based upon the Sumerian myth of "Enki and Ninhursag" (*ANET*, 37–41). In the concluding portion Ninhursag saves Enki, who unwittingly has impregnated himself with his own semen but as a male is unable to give birth; Ninhursag places Enki in her vulva and vicariously gives birth to the eight deities with which Enki is pregnant. The eight children are named for the various parts of Enki's body in which they developed: tooth, mouth, arm, etc. The goddess born from the rib is named Nin-ti. The pun with TI, "rib," is clear but derives solely from a similarity in sound, as it is unlikely that the corresponding syllable (TI) in the name Nin-ti is the word for life. (See T. Jacobsen, *The Harps That Once . . . : Sumerian Poetry in Translation* [New Haven, Conn.: Yale University Press, 1987], 203, n. 26.) Moreover, the myth makes no connection with "life." Whatever the correct interpretation of this myth, it has nothing to do with the creation of the female of the human species. Instead the myth seemingly speaks about the Mesopotamian concern for the generative power of water and irrigation within what would otherwise be a barren steppe; see T. Jacobsen, *The Treasures of Darkness: A History of Mesopotamian Religion* (New Haven, Conn.: Yale University Press, 1976), 112–113; G. S. Kirk, *Myth: Its Meaning and Functions in Ancient and Other Cultures* (Berkeley/Los Angeles: University of California Press, 1970), 91–99. In a different direction, Hans Goedicke's ("Adam's Rib," in *Biblical and Related Studies Presented to Samuel Iwry*, ed. Ann Kort and Scott Morschauwer [Winona Lake, Ind.: Eisenbrauns, 1985], 73–76) ingenious speculation that the Genesis tradition about Eve being created from Adam's rib may derive from a confusion *in Egyptian* of the two homophones *imw* "rib" and *imw* "clay," is unconvincing because there is no corroborating evidence that the Genesis account is in any way dependent upon Egyptian tradition, much less upon an obscure *and erroneous* conflation of homophones in that tradition.

[32]The question of whether "the human" originally was androgynous (bisexual) (so W. Doniger O'Flaherty and Mircea Eliade in *The Encyclopedia of Religion*, s.v. "Androgynes") or sexually undifferentiated (so P. Trible, *God and the Rhetoric of Sexuality* [Philadelphia: Fortress Press, 1978], 141, n. 17) need not be settled here. A bisexual interpretation is attested already in *Mishnah Rabbah* (Genesis) 8.1.

[33]To my knowledge, no one has remarked upon the fact that in *Atrahasis* at the corresponding position in the myth the institution of marriage is established, which provides additional confirmation to my thesis that the Yahwist's primeval myth is patterned on *Atrahasis*. The relevant passage in *Atrahasis* occurs in a damaged section and must be restored from several fragments (texts E, S, and R, as designated by Lambert and Millard, the latter misplaced by the editors). Improving upon the restorations by C. Wilcke ("Familiengründung im Alten Babylonien," in *Geschlechtsreife und Legitimation zur Zeugung*, Veröffentlichungen des Instituts für Historische Anthropologie e. V., 3, ed. E. W. Müller [Freiburg/München: Alber, 1985], 295–298), I read: "(When) a young woman [develops breasts on] her chest, / a beard [appea]rs [o]n the cheek on a young man, / [in gar]dens and in the streets / [let them choo]se one another the wife and her husband" (I.271–276). I treated this passage and its biblical analog in "The Institution of Marriage in Genesis 2 and in Atrahasis," a paper read at the Catholic Biblical Association meeting, Los Angeles, Aug. 10–13, 1991.

[34]Published by E. Chiera, *Sumerian Religious Texts* (Upland, Penn.: Crozier Theological Seminary, 1924), no. 25, obv. i.3–6 (= lines 18–22 of Chiera's translation, 29); also trans. S. N. Kramer, *From the Tablets of Sumer: Twenty-five Firsts in Man's Recorded History* (Indian Hills, Colo.: Falcon's Wing, 1956), 145. The text has been studied most recently by B. Alster and H. Vanstiphout, "Lahar and Ashnan: Presentation and Analysis of a Sumerian Disputation," *Acta Sumerologica* 9 (1987), 1–43. The translation given here is based upon T. Jacobsen, "The Eridu Genesis," *JBL* 100 (1981), 513–529, esp. 517, n. 7.

[35]Translation based upon the restorations proposed by Jacobsen, "Eridu Genesis," 17, n. 6. See also B. Alster, "Dilmun, Bahrain and

the Alleged Paradise in Sumerian Myth and Literature," in *Dilmun: New Studies in the Archaeology and Early History of Bahrain*, ed. Daniel T. Potts, BBVO 2 (Berlin: Dietrich Reimer, 1983), 39–74, esp. pp. 56–57.

[36]Robert A. Oden, Jr. ("Grace or Status? Yahweh's Clothing of the First Humans," in *The Bible Without Theology: The Theological Tradition and Alternatives to It* [New York: Harper & Row, 1987], 92–105) is thus wrong in arguing that nudity is a symbol of (near) divinity. His thesis is correct, however, to the extent that in Mesopotamian and Israelite myth the investiture of primeval humans with clothes does signify their full humanization.

[37]One is reminded of the biblical injunction against eating flesh containing blood, "because the life is the blood" (Deut. 12:23; similarly Gen. 9:4).

[38]In Ezek. 28:13, in a passage containing many thematic and verbal similarities to Genesis 2–3, Eden is identified as "the garden of God." Although not found in Genesis, this Ezekielian phrase is an authentic commentary on the Yahwist's intended meaning. See chapter 3. Also in Isa. 51:3, Eden and "the garden of Yahweh" are given as parallel terms.

[39]I prescind from the debate as to whether the narrative originally spoke of only one tree or whether there were originally two parallel narratives in Genesis 2–3; see above n. 11. In my reading of the text, the two trees have been consciously woven into a unified narrative.

[40]On the concept of the "sacred tree" in Mesopotamian literature and iconography, see H. York, "Heiliger Baum," in *Reallexikon der Assyriologie* 4 (Berlin/New York: Walter de Gruyter, 1972–1975), 269–282, and the literature cited there.

[41]See *ANET*[3], 101–103.

[42]The well-known reconstruction of the first part of this line as "Thou are [wi]se, Enkidu, art become like a god!" (so Speiser, *ANET*, 75) must now be given up. Maureen Gallery Kovacs (*The Epic of Gilgamesh* [Stanford, Calif.: Stanford University Press, 1989], 9) notes that "a recently published Akkadian fragment from Anatolia confirms the restoration 'beautiful' " instead of "wise." Accordingly, any dependence of Gen. 3:5, 22 upon Gilgamesh is much less than is frequently assumed by commentators.

[43]Noah is the biblical counterpart of Ziusudra/Atrahasis/Utnapishtim, the Mesopotamian pious survivor of the flood from whom the earth was repopulated. This apparently is the source of the tradition that grouped Noah with Job and Dan'el in Ezek. 14:14, 20. Job, of course, is well known as a righteous man in the wisdom tradition.

Dan'el in Ezek. 28:3 is depicted as a wise man of legendary fame. In Genesis wisdom is not ascribed to Noah, but the Ezekiel passage suggests that wisdom was indeed characteristic of Noah, like his Mesopotamian counterpart Ziusudra/Atrahasis/Utnapishtim.

[44]There are three leading theories about the meaning of the phrase, "to know good and evil": (1) sexual maturity, that is, the period from puberty until senility when one is able to enjoy sex; (2) moral independence, that is, the ability to determine for oneself what is right and wrong, which implies the possibility of going against divinely imposed standards of morality; and (3) universal knowledge, the meaning favored here. Each of these theories claims biblical grounding by appeal to different passages; indeed, they are not necessarily mutually exclusive. The author, as we argue, was almost certainly familiar with *Gilgamesh* and its story of Enkidu acquiring his humanity through sexual intercourse. Likewise, Genesis 3 suggests that moral independence is part of becoming fully human.

[45]The correctness of this interpretation is confirmed by Ezekiel 28, where the hubris of Tyre is depicted as an illegitimate aspiration to divine wisdom. The allusions to the Yahwist's creation myth are patent and can serve as a commentary in helping to understand the Yahwist's meaning. See chapter 3.

[46]See Karen Randolph Joines, "Winged Serpents in Isaish's Inaugural Vision," *JBL* 86 (1967), 410–415; and Othmar Keel, *Jahwe-Visionen und Siegelkunst*, Stuttgarter Bibelstudien 84/85 (Stuttgart: Verlag Katholisches Bibelwerk, 1977), 46–124. The serpent is here termed *nāḥāš* rather than a *śārāp*; however, the two terms are joined in the "fiery serpents" (*hannĕḥāšîm haśśĕrāpîm*) with which God punished the Israelites in the desert (Num. 21:6, 8; cf. Deut. 8:15). The terms *nāḥāš* and *śārāp* are used interchangeably throughout Num. 21:6–9; cf. 2 Kings 18:4. A flying or winged serpent (*śārāp mĕ-ʿôpēp*) is mentioned in Isa. 14:29 and 30:6. Finally, for a possible linking of cherub with serpent in the garden of god (Eden) in Ezekiel 28, see chapter 3, pp. 95–96.

[47]The use of the grammatical first-person plural form here, as in Gen. 1:26 and 11:7, is indicative of the mythical origins of this passage; see Miller, *Genesis 1–11,* 9–26.

[48]Elsewhere I have treated at length this scene in *Atrahasis* and the meaning of the various terms used to signal rebellion, viz., *rigmu* and *ḫubūru* as cries of rebellion, and depriving the king of the gods of sleep as an act of rebellion. See my article, "The Sleeping God: An Ancient Near Eastern Motif of Divine Sovereignty," *Bib* 68 (1987),

153–177; and "The Covenant of Peace: A Neglected Ancient Near Eastern Motif," *CBQ* 49 (1987), 187–211.

[49]See Isaac Kikawada, "Two Notes on Eve," *JBL* 91 (1972), 33–37. Because of the parallels to which Kikawada points and because Gen. 4:25 presents Eve operating in conjunction with God, I find it difficult to see in Eve's exclamation here any of the defiance against God suggested by Coote and Ord (*Bible's First History*, 66).

[50]As to the nature of Cain's sin, see n. 26 above.

[51]Contrary to some commentators, Gen. 6:1–4 is integral to the biblical flood story; see W. M. Clark, "The Flood and the Structure of the Pre-patriarch History," *ZAW* 83 (1971), 184–211, esp. 190.

[52]R. S. Hendel ("Of Demigods and the Deluge: Toward an Interpretation of Genesis 6:1–4," *JBL* 106 [1987], 13–26) also has seen the integral connection between this pericope and the flood narrative, based on parallels in *Atrahasis*. He correctly observes that the story concerns the definition of a proper boundary between the divine and the human realms. Unfortunately, Hendel follows the overpopulation interpretation of *Atrahasis* and consequently fails to see how rebellion motifs in the latter text inspired the Yahwist to set this pericope as the introduction to his flood narrative.

[53]Genesis 5, which attributes life spans of some eight or nine hundred years to the antediluvian generations, is from the P source. But the Yahwist had a similar conception of abnormally long lives prior to the flood, as proved by the *reduction* to one hundred and twenty years. This was a stock motif in ancient Near Eastern literature, as evident from the even longer life spans attributed to the antediluvian generations in "The Sumerian King List"; see *ANET*, 265–266.

[54]So J. Klein, "The 'Bane' of Humanity: A Lifespan of One Hundred Twenty Years," *Acta Sumerologica* 12 (1990), 57–70; I have altered Klein's "mankind" to "humankind" in keeping with the inclusive language policy of this volume. The text is No. 771, lines 19'–26', in D. Arnaud, *Recherches au pays d'Aštata, Emar VI/1–4* (Paris: Editions Recherche sur les civilisations, 1985–1987).

[55]Another name for divine Mami, the mother-goddess, the creator of humankind.

[56]The conclusion that the biblical Nephilim were antediluvian only must be tempered by the recognition that these creatures may be typologically—though not functionally—related to the Babylonian *apkallu*, a class of semidivine, semihuman creatures mentioned in certain cuneiform mythic texts. These *apkallu* are normally associated with the antediluvian period, although in a few instances they are mentioned also in postdiluvian contexts.

[57]In v. 4 the words "and also afterward" (*wĕgam 'aḥărê kēn*) are a secondary gloss, probably added by a later editor to reconcile the text with the statement in Num. 13:33 that the Israelite spies had seen Nephilim in the land in the days of Moses. But such a literal reading of Num. 13:33 is a misunderstanding of the text. Within Numbers 13 there are two statements about what the spies saw. In v. 28 the spies report *to Moses*, "we even saw the descendants of the Anakim there!" But in vs. 32–33 the spies report *to Israelites*, "All the people that we saw there were gigantic! There we saw the Nephilim (the Anakim are from the Nephilim) and in our own eyes we seemed like grasshoppers—and so we must have seemed to them!" Source critically, these two reports may be from different traditions. There is clear evidence of at least two sources present in this chapter; see S. R. Driver, *An Introduction to the Literature of the Old Testament* (Cleveland: World/Meridian, 1956), 62. Verse 32 is usually assigned to P while vs. 26–31 and 33 are assigned to J-E. It is doubtful, however, that v. 32 and v. 33 should be assigned to different sources since they form one report that parallels the report of vs. 26–31. In the present arrangement of the chapter the two reports are to be read as building to a climax. The spies, terrified by the fortifications they had seen, attempt to forestall an attack. When they fail to dissuade Moses and Caleb from the planned attack (vs. 26–31), the spies take their case directly to the people (vs. 32–33) and this time deliberately exaggerate the awesome stature of the natives by referring to them as Nephilim rather than as Anakim. The gloss in v. 33, which explains that the Anakim are descended from the Nephilim, was probably added by a literal-minded editor—perhaps the same one as in Gen. 6:4 who wished to reconcile these two seemingly contradictory statements. In any case, Num. 13:33 supports the conclusion that the Nephilim were legendary gigantic warriors from the long distant past.

[58]See *CAD*, Vol. L, 242.

[59]Robert Oden ("Divine Aspirations in Atrahasis and in Genesis 1–11," *ZAW* 93 (1981), 214–215) has suggested that the *uṣurāt nišī* of *Atrahasis* are "regulations for people," or divinely imposed laws for human conduct, and that these have their counterpart in the priestly blood laws of Gen. 9:1–7. Oden argues from the shape of the received text of Genesis. My study, however, finds counterparts to *Atrahasis* present only in the J literary strand of Genesis, not in P. Moreover, if my interpretation of *uṣurāt nišī* as limitation on the vitality of humankind is correct, then there is no need to appeal to the (later) priestly text for a biblical counterpart, since the limitation of human vitality is a prominent theme in J.

[60]The motif of the creator reconciling himself to creation after a human sin and attempted annihilation of humankind occurs in several forms and a variety of texts in the ancient Near East; see my article "The Covenant of Peace" for a full discussion.

[61]For a discussion of the oath and its token of warranty not only in the various versions of the flood story but also in Isa. 54:9–10 and the Canaanite Baal myth, see my "Covenant of Peace," 190–201. In addition, Jer. 31:35–36 contains an allusion to the permanency of the cosmos as a sign of God's fidelity to his creatures, specifically, Israel. The reference to "my [God's] covenant of day and my covenant of night" in Jer. 33:20–21 likely is to be explained similarly.

[62]See H. Gese, "The Idea of History in the Ancient Near East and the Old Testament," *Journal for Theology and the Church* 1 (1965) (translated from the German, 1958), 134f.; and Clark, "The Flood and the Structure of the Pre-patriarch History," 205.

[63]See Clark, "The Flood and the Structure of the Pre-patriarch History," 205–211.

[64]Source critics divide this chapter between J and E. In both versions the brothers conspire to kill Joseph; in J the intent of fratricide is clear from v. 26.

[65]Not all the material in these chapters of Exodus is to be assigned to J, but the basic storyline was established by this source.

CHAPTER 3
THE PRIESTLY REVISION OF THE CREATION MYTH

[1]Within Genesis 1–11 the passages that source critics identify as P include the first creation account (1:1–2:4a), the genealogies from Seth to Noah (5:1–32 [except v. 29]), a second version of the flood interwoven with the J version (6:9–22; 7:11, 13–16a, 17a, 18–21, 24; 8:1–2a, 3b–5, 14–19), the blessing and covenant with Noah (9:1–17), the conclusion of the genealogy of Noah (9:28–29), the table of nations descended from Noah and his three sons after the flood (10:1–32 [J and P materials are thoroughly interwoven here]), and the geneology of Shem (11:10–26).

[2]On the use of the masculine pronoun with reference to P, see chapter 2, n. 5.

[3]See, for example, the objections of J. A. Emerton in his two-part study, "An Examination of Some Attempts to Defend the Unity of the Flood Narrative in Genesis," *VT* 37 (1987), 401–420; and *VT* 38 (1988), 1–21. Similarly, K. Koch ("P-Kein Redaktor! Erinnerung an zwei Eckdaten der Quellenscheidung," *VT* 37 [1987], 446–467) finds

it impossible that P intended his passages as additions to the older J-E redaction.

[4]For a statement about the Deuteronomist performing a comparable task during the prior Assyrian-induced crisis, see Norbert Lohfink, "Pluralism: Theology as the Answer to Plausibility Crises in Emergent Pluralistic Situations, Taking the Deuteronomic Law as the Basis for Discussion," in *Great Themes from the Old Testament* (Edinburgh: T. & T. Clark, 1982), 17–37.

[5]Within the primeval cycle P had only to rework the Yahwistic epic. Beginning with the patriarchal cycle P had to contend with the Elohistic traditions (E) as well, although in the main he continued to follow the epic version of J.

[6]"It should be stressed . . . that any affirmation concerning God that can be made in human language is to a greater or lesser degree anthropomorphic and metaphorical. . . . In reality, the statement that 'God is spirit' (John 4:24) is not less anthropomorphic than 'the just shall behold his face' (Psalm 11:7). The difference is merely that the one has used a spiritual part of man, the other a physical, as a *primum analogatum* for a truth about God." R. McKenzie, "The Divine Soliloquies in Genesis," *CBQ* 17 (1955), 157–158.

[7]Lohfink (*Great Themes from the Old Testament*, 183–201) has argued that, in addition to a mediated dependence upon *Atrahasis* through J, P had direct knowledge of *Atrahasis* and utilized its themes in his own composition, especially in the P narratives of the book of Exodus. Lohfink based this thesis primarily upon two themes: (1) renewal of the promise of fecundity before and after the flood and (2) stability of the cosmos brought about through compromise, neither of which are convincing in my opinion. As I argued in the preceding chapter, biblical literary dependence upon *Atrahasis* can be demonstrated in the J literary strand only.

[8]Herman Gunkel, *Schöpfung und Chaos in Urzeit und Endzeit: Eine religionsgeschichtliche Untersuchung über Gen 1 und Ap Joh 12* (Göttingen: Vandenhoeck & Ruprecht, 1895), 3–120. This study has been condensed and translated as "The Influence of Babylonian Mythology Upon the Biblical Creation Story," in *Creation in the Old Testament*, Issues in Religion and Theology 6, ed. B. W. Anderson (Philadelphia: Fortress Press; London: SPCK, 1894), 25–52.

[9]Alexander Heidel, *The Babylonian Genesis*, 2nd ed. (Chicago: University of Chicago Press, 1951), 82–140, with the diagram on 129.

[10]E. Speiser, *Genesis*, AB 1 (Garden City, N.Y.: Doubleday & Co., 1964), 9–13.

[11]Representatives include the Babylonian *Enuma elish* myth, the

Ugaritic Baal myth, the Canaanite/Israelite myth reconstructed from diffuse allusions in the Bible, the Egyptian stories of "Astarte and the Sea" and "the Repulsing of the Dragon," and the Hittite Illuyanka myth.

[12]For a recent discussion and bibliography see John Day, *God's Conflict with the Dragon and the Sea* (Cambridge: Cambridge University Press, 1985).

[13]Jon D. Levenson (*Creation and the Persistence of Evil: The Jewish Drama of Divine Omnipotence* [San Francisco: Harper & Row, 1988]), whose views complement my own on a number of issues, draws attention to numerous parallel themes in Gen. 1:1–2:3 and *Enuma elish*, which suggest that the biblical author was at least indirectly aware of this Babylonian myth and at times polemicized against its religious viewpoint; see esp. 51–127. Day (*God's Conflict with the Dragon and the Sea*, 49–57) denies any connection between Genesis and *Enuma elish*, but his analysis reckons only with selected verses and vocabulary rather than with comparative typology of Gen. 1:1–2:3 as a whole.

[14]*Enuma elish* follows *Atrahasis* in positing that humankind was created from clay and the blood of the divine rebel god, so that all the gods might have rest. Gen. 1:26–28 posits that humankind was created in the likeness of God but seems deliberately to revise the purpose for humankind and the mode of its creation.

[15]Cf. El's title *bny bnwt*, "creator of creatures" (*CTA* 6.iii.5, 11, et passim).

[16]One tablet has Anat go on a bloody rampage, "smiting the people of the West, smashing the folk of the East" (*CTA* 3.ii.6–8). The episode concludes with Baal and Anat reconciled to humankind and the sowing of peace on earth. Baal created lightning as symbol of this reconciliation. See B. Batto, "The Covenant of Peace: A Neglected Ancient Near Eastern Motif," *CBQ* 49 (1987), 197–201.

[17]See my article "The Sleeping God: An Ancient Near Eastern Motif of Divine Sovereignty," *Bib* 68 (1987), 153–177.

[18]Levenson (*Creation and the Persistence of Evil*, 100–120) offers a different, but nonetheless complementary, interpretation of the theme of rest in Gen. 2:1–3 and in *Enuma elish*. In Levenson's view not only the temple but also creation itself (the world) is the deity's resting place (107).

[19]See most recently Levenson (*Creation and the Persistence of Evil*, 54–56), who claims that the sea monster has been demythologized. It is true that "the great sea monsters" (*hattannînîm haggĕdōlîm*, Gen. 1:21), including Leviathan, "are neither primordial

nor an embarrassment to God's rule" in P's telling. But this fails to reckon with "the Abyss" (*tĕhôm*) itself as P's primary symbol for the primordial archfoe of the Creator in Genesis 1.

[20]M. Dahood, *Psalms I*, AB 16 (Garden City, N.Y.: Doubleday & Co., 1965), 48–51; see further Batto, "Sleeping God," 165.

[21]See also Isa. 51:15; Job 26:12. For the mythic background of *rgᶜ*, "quelling," of the sea, see M. Pope, *Job*, AB 15 (Garden City, N.Y.: Doubleday & Co., 1965), 166.

[22]Similarly W. L. Holladay, *Jeremiah 2* (Minneapolis: Augsburg Fortress, 1989), 166.

[23]E.g., Isa. 13:1–14:23; 21:9; 40:17–20; 44:9–20; 47:1–15; Jeremiah 50–51, esp. 50:2; cf. Hab. 2:18–20.

[24]In Deutero-Isaiah *Chaoskampf* is frequently linked with creation and exodus motifs in oracles of divine assurance that Yahweh will soon act to bring his people home from exile. See C. Stuhlmueller, *Creative Redemption in Deutero-Isaiah*, AnBib 43 (Rome: Biblical Institute, 1970); B. W. Anderson, "Exodus Typology in Second Isaiah," in *Israel's Prophetic Heritage: Essays in Honor of James Muilenburg*, ed. B. W. Anderson and W. Harrelson (New York: Harper & Row, 1962), 177–195.

[25]*Bĕqereb hāʾāreṣ* is artfully ambiguous here, referring both to the inhabitable earth and to the underworld. The deity "works salvation" in both the historical realm of the author and in the mythic realm of the chaos monster.

[26]The precise meaning of *pôrartā* is disputed. Usage in cognate languages seems to require a meaning of destroying or breaking. Nevertheless, the connotation of "division" is not inappropriate either philologically (see KB, 916) or mythologically. In Canaanite texts the defeat of Sea by "splitting" is not normal, though Anat does defeat Sea's counterpart Death (Mot) by "splitting" (*bāqāᶜ*) him with a sword (*CTA* 6.ii.31–32), but in *Enuma Elish* Marduk does defeat Tiʾamat by "splitting" her in two. One may also compare Isa. 51:9, "Is it not you who cuts into pieces (*hammaḥṣebet*) Rahab?" See M. Dahood, *Psalms II,* AB 17 (Garden City, N.Y.: Doubleday & Co., 1968), 205.

[27]For this meaning of *ṣiyyîm* see Dahood, *Psalms II,* 182 and 206. "Desert inhabitants" fits the mythic typology of the psalm better than the commonly conjectured "sharks"; e.g., Day, *God's Conflict with the Dragon and the Sea*, 22, n. 57.

[28]See further Levenson, *Creation and the Persistence of Evil* (n. 13 above).

[29]See S. Morenz, *Egyptian Religion* (Ithaca, N.Y.: Cornell University Press, 1973), 167–169.

[30]Gen. 6:17 is probably not a contradiction of this statement as that verse has reference not to the proximate cause of the flood but to God as the ultimate cause of all being.

[31]Patrick D. Miller, Jr. (*Genesis 1–11: Studies in Structure and Theme*, JSOTSup 8 [Sheffield: University of Sheffield, 1978], 33–34) notes that the punishment corresponds to the crime, expressed through a sevenfold paranomasia on the root *šḥt*: God sends the flood "to destroy (*lĕšaḥēt*) all flesh" (6:17, cf. 13) because "all flesh has corrupted (*hišḥît*) its way" (6:12, cf. 11).

[32]For a fuller discussion of the symbol of the bow in Genesis 9, see my article "Covenant of Peace," 199–196. For a discussion of the symbol of the drawn and the undrawn bow in Assyrian representations and the parallels in Genesis 9, see G. E. Mendenhall, *The Tenth Generation* (Baltimore/London: Johns Hopkins University Press, 1973), 44–48. See further E. Zenger, *Gottes Bogen in den Wolken: Untersuchungen zu Komposition und Theologie der priesterschriftlichen Urgeschichte*, Stuttgarter Bibelstudien 112 (Stuttgart: Verlag Katholisches Bibelwerk, 1983), 124–131.

[33]E.g., B. Vawter, *On Genesis: A New Reading* (Garden City, N.Y.: Doubleday & Co., 1977), 50–51.

[34]See Miller, *Genesis 1–11*, 9–20.

[35]C. Westermann, *Genesis 1–11: A Commentary* (Minneapolis: Augsburg Publishing House, 1984), 143, 156–157.

[36]Vestiges of the divine council of Yahweh God may still be observed in numerous other passages in the Bible; some of the more explicit are 1 Kings 22:19–23 (= 2 Chron. 18:18–21); Job 1:6–12; 2:1–7; Isa. 6:1–8; 40:13–14; Jer. 23:18, 22; Zech. 3:1–2. See Day, *God's Conflict with the Dragon and the Sea*, 54–57; R. N. Whybray, *The Heavenly Counsellor in Isaiah xl 13–14* (Cambridge: Cambridge University Press, 1971); Miller, *Genesis 1–11*, 9–20.

[37]For a survey of interpretations and critical discussion see D. J. A. Clines, "The Image of God in Man," *Tyndale Bulletin* 19 (1968), 53–103; and Westermann, *Genesis 1–11*, 148–158. My interpretation follows more closely the latter than the former.

[38]Westermann, *Genesis 1–11*, 156.

[39]Contrary to an opinion frequently encountered, *'ādām* is not a proper noun or name (Adam) here. True, it lacks the definite article. However, in this passage, as in Gen. 1:26, the further specification of *'ādām* as "male and female," the interchangeability of singular and plural pronouns ("his" and "them"/"their"), and especially the

statement "and he called *their* name *'ādām*," all show that *'ādām* still refers to the primeval humankind, which included both the male and the female of the species.

[40]Contrary to Clines, "Image of God in Man," 99–101. Gen. 9:6 need not be seen as an objection to the thesis of a diminution of the image of God, as the original premise for the creation of humankind continues. The prohibition of murder remains equally valid whether the image of God in man is once or twice removed from the being of the deity.

[41]For example, "The Sumerian King List," *ANET*, 265–267. There is no direct dependence of P upon this king list, however.

[42]Frank M. Cross, *Canaanite Myth and Hebrew Epic* (Cambridge, Mass.: Harvard University Press, 1973), 299.

[43]The Hebrew vocable *'ēl* here and in the third line is artfully ambiguous; it can be read as either a common noun "god" (like *'ĕlōhîm* in the parallel in v. 9) or as the proper name of the head of the Canaanite pantheon, El. See M. Pope, *El in the Ugaritic Texts*, VTS 2 (Leiden: E. J. Brill, 1955), 98–99. For a defense of the traditional translation, "I am a god," see H. J. van Dijk, *Ezekiel's Prophecy on Tyre (Ez. 26,1–28,19)*, Biblica et Orientalia 20 (Rome: Biblical Institute, 1968), 95–96.

[44]I.e., like Ea in Apsu or Baal enthroned over the flood; see chapter 1. The biblical reflexes of this mythic motif will be discussed further in chapter 4. Here, instead of MT *yammîm* "seas," I read singular *yām* + enclitic mem.

[45]On Daniel/Dan'el, see above, chapter 2, n. 43.

[46]See van Dijk, *Ezekiel's Prophecy on Tyre*, 100–101.

[47]Levenson, *Creation and the Persistence of Evil*, 78–99.

[48]The silver and gold that fills Tyre's storehouses (Ezek. 28:5) is a paraphrastic allusion to the "excellent gold" and precious stones associated with Eden in Gen. 2:11–12.

[49]The Hebrew is obscure. The reading adopted here emends MT *ḥôtēm* to *ḥawat* ("serpent") + enclitic mem. The word "serpent" is attested in early Aramaic in Sefire I.A.30–31 as *ḥwh* and in later Aramaic as *ḥewyā*, pl. *ḥiwwayyā*, apparently from an original form *ḥiwyatu*. The name "Eve" (*ḥawwâ*) may be etymologically derived from this root, rather than from the word *ḥay*, "life," as the pun in Gen. 3:20 suggests; for the possibility of a paranomasia involving both words, "life" and "serpent," see Howard N. Wallace, *The Eden Narrative*, HSM 32 (Atlanta: Scholars Press, 1985), 147–161. Note, further, that Genesis 2 has a serpent in the garden, though in that text the word for serpent is *nāḥāš*; see chapter 2, n. 46.

[50]This translation follows in the main van Dijk, *Ezekiel's Prophecy on Tyre*, 92–93 and 113–121; see there for translation notes.

[51]See chapter 6.

[52]See chapter 2, pp. 59–60.

[53]Thus I find Mieke Bal's modernistic reading of Genesis 1–3 out of keeping with the spirit of its ancient authors; she regards Yahweh, the man, the woman, and the serpent as mere characters in the narrative. "Sexuality, Sin, and Sorrow: The Emergence of Female Character (A Reading of Genesis 1–3)," in *The Female Body in Western Culture*, ed. Susan Rubin Suleiman (Cambridge, Mass./London: Harvard University Press, 1986), 317–338.

CHAPTER 4
THE EXODUS AS MYTH

[1]So G. E. Wright, *God Who Acts: Biblical Theology as Recital*, SBT 8 (London: SCM Press, 1952), 13.

[2]So Dorothy Irvin, "The Joseph and Moses Narratives," in *Israelite and Judaean History*, ed. John H. Hayes and J. Maxwell Miller, OTL (London: SCM Press, 1977), 180–212. See also J. J. M. Roberts, "Myth Versus History," *CBQ* 38 (1976), 1–13; and P. Machinist, "Literature as Politics: The Tikulti-Ninurta Epic and the Bible," *CBQ* 38 (1976), 455–482.

[3]So J. Maxwell Miller and John H. Hayes, *A History of Ancient Israel and Judah* (Philadelphia: Westminster Press, 1986), 74–79.

[4]*Understanding the Old Testament*, 3rd ed. (Englewood Cliffs, N.J.: Prentice-Hall, 1975), 8.

[5]*A History of Pentateuchal Traditions*, trans. B. W. Anderson (Englewood Cliffs, N.J.: Prentice-Hall, 1972), 49.

[6]This writer is in substantial agreement with the source analysis of B. S. Childs, *The Book of Exodus*, OTL (Philadelphia: Westminster Press, 1974), 218–224 and 243–248.

[7]To J, I assign the following verses: 13:21–22; 14:5b–6, 9a, 10b, 11–14, 19b, 20, 21b, 24, 25b, 27b, 30–31.

[8]To E, I assign the following: 13:17–19; 14:5a, 7, 19a, 25a.

[9]Ex. 14:25a, an allusion to God's clogging the chariot wheels so that the Egyptians could not drive, may stem from a setting in a dried sea bed. However, the action is equally appropriate to a "flight" story. Furthermore, it is controverted whether this fragment is truly E or not.

[10]To P, I assign the following: Ex. 13:20, 14:1–4, 8, 9b–10a, 10c, 15–18, 21a, 21c–23, 26–27a, 28–29.

[11]The patent references to Zion as Yahweh's mountain of abode

establish that this poem in its present form cannot be earlier than the tenth century B.C.E., contra F. M. Cross, Jr., and D. N. Freedman, "The Song of Miriam," *JNES* 14 (1955), 237–250; F. M. Cross, *Canaanite Myth and Hebrew Epic* (Cambridge, Mass.: Harvard University Press, 1973), 121–124; D. N. Freedman, "Strophe and Meter in Exodus 15," in *A Light Unto My Path: Old Testament Studies in Honor of Jacob M. Myers*, ed. Howard N. Bream et al. (Philadelphia: Temple University Press, 1974), 163–205, esp. 153–156. See further David A. Robertson, *Linguistic Evidence in Dating Early Hebrew Poetry*, SBLDS 3 (Missoula, Mont.: Society of Biblical Literature, 1972), 153–156. Others date the song to the exilic period or later. However, Martin L. Brenner's (*The Song of the Sea: Ex 15:1–21*, BZAW 195 [Berlin/New York: Walter de Gruyter, 1991], esp. 19) thesis that the Song is "wholly the product of Levitical cult personnel of the second temple" is untenable. Although the Song may have undergone subsequent development, it likely originated within the cult of Gilgal prior to the seventh century B.C.E. for reasons discussed in chapter 5.

[12]See chapter 5.

[13]See Cross, *Canaanite Myth and Hebrew Epic*, 112–144.

[14]See ch. 3, pp. 86–87.

[15]See further A. Lauha, "Das Schilfmeermotif im Alten Testament," VTS 9 (1963), 32–46.

[16]Carroll Stuhlmueller, *Creative Redemption in Deutero-Isaiah*, AnBib 45 (Rome: Biblical Institute, 1970), 143–162.

[17]Ibid., esp. chs. 4 and 9.

[18]Ibid., 41–56 and 110.

[19]Another name for the watery chaos-monster.

[20]See Stuhlmueller, *Creative Redemption*, 41–56.

[21]The portrayal of Egypt as the embodiment of the Sea-dragon of chaos was not uncommon in the Hebrew Bible. In a most obvious reference to the Combat Myth, the uselessness of Egypt's opposition to Yahweh is underscored by her name "Rahab the Quelled" [reading *rahab hammōšbāt* for MT *rahab hēm šābet*] (Isa. 30:7; cf. 27:1; 51:9–11; Job 41). Egypt is apparently mentioned again under the cipher of Rahab in Ps. 87:4. The theme of the struggle between Yahweh and Egypt, that "great dragon (*tannîn*) who crouches in the midst of the Nile, is continued in Ezekiel 29; Yahweh promises certain destruction for the king of Egypt, who arrogantly boasts of his own creative powers (vs. 3–5). The implied rival claim to divinity in this last passage is treated more explicitly in Isa. 31:1–3, where Egypt's "help"— help (*'ezer*) is usually a divine attribute in the Old Testament—is said to be worthless because "the Egyptians are human and no God!" In

other passages Pharaoh, who is nourished by the waters of the cosmic Abyss (*tĕhôm*) (Ezek. 31:4), is likened to the Sea-dragon whom Yahweh will catch in his net and kill, amid images of creation in reverse (Ezek. 32:2–8; cf. Ps. 74:12–17); the parallels to the Babylonian *Enuma elish*, where Marduk netted Ti'amat prior to cleaving her in two during the creation of the world, are patent. See further in chapter 6.

[22]See, for example, B. W. Anderson, *Creation Versus Chaos: The Reinterpretation of Mythical Symbolism in the Bible* (New York: Association Press, 1967), 106; earlier in the same work (p. 37) Anderson does acknowledge that in the Song of the Sea "the deliverance at the Reed Sea is understood to be an act of the creation of Israel."

[23]See Cross, *Canaanite Myth and Hebrew Epic*, 138–144; S. Norin, *Er Spaltete das Meer: Die Auszugsüberlieferung in Psalmen und Kult des Alten Israel,* ConB, OT Series 9 (Lund: CWK Gleerup, 1977), 94 and 105.

[24]See Cross and Freedman, "Song of Miriam," 249; Anderson, *Creation Versus Chaos*, 37. The reluctance of P. Humbert ("Qānā en hébreu biblique," in *Opuscles d'un Hébraïsant* [Neuchâtel: Université de Neuchâtel, 1958], 166–174, esp. 167) to admit a meaning of "to create" for *qānâ* in Ex. 15:16 because of the parallel *'am zû gă'āltā* (v. 13) seems unwarranted; *gă'al* is paralleled elsewhere by verbs of "creation" (Deut. 32:6, Isa. 43:1; 44:24; 54:5). The concept of God creating Israel as a people is elsewhere attested in Mal. 2:10 and frequently in Second Isaiah; see Stuhlmueller, *Creative Redemption*, 193–229. The attempt of B. Vawter ("Prov 8:22: Wisdom and Creation," *JBL* 99 [1980], 205–216, esp. 208–214) to deny altogether "to the verb *qānâ* in any of its forms the sense 'create' " is not compelling in light of the Ugarit titles of "El, creator of the earth," *'l qny 'rs,* and of Asherah, "creator of the gods," *qnyt 'ilm*; with the latter compare the analogous Akkadian titles of the mother-goddess, "creator of gods and kings," [d]NIN.MAḪ *banât ili u šarri*, and "creator of humankind," *baniat awēlūtim*. Akkadian *banû* is regularly applied to the creative activity of the gods; see *CAD* **banû** A3.

[25]For a different assessment of the tense usage in the Song, see Cross, *Canaanite Myth and Hebrew Epic*, 125.

[26]"The Reed Sea: *Requiescat in Pace*," *JBL* 102/1 (1983), 27–35.

[27]For an indisputable example see 1 Kings 9:26.

[28]Cross, *Canaanite Myth and Hebrew Epic*, 293–325, esp. 317 and 320–321.

[29]For a lucid statement of this thesis see James A. Sanders, *Torah and Canon* (Philadelphia: Fortress Press, 1972), 1–30.

[30] See Mircea Eliade, *Myth and Reality* (New York: Harper & Row, 1963).

[31] See chapter 3, esp. pp. 85–88.

[32] See further Wisd. Sol. 9:8; Heb. 8:2, 5; 9:23; Rev. 13:6; 14:18; 15:5.

[33] Levenson (*Creation and the Persistence of Evil*, 74–75) speaks of the story of the exodus from Egypt as a charter myth for Passover. In addition, Tabernacles and Passover manifest strong cosmogonic features, very much like cosmogonic patterns found in the Ugaritic Baal myth and the Babylonian *Enuma elish*.

[34] H. Gunkel, *The Legends of Genesis* (New York: Schocken Books, 1964), 14.

[35] Eliade, *Myth and Reality*, 5–6.

[36] G. Mendenhall, "The Mask of Yahweh," in *The Tenth Generation* (Baltimore/London: Johns Hopkins University Press, 1973), 32–66.

[37] R. Wilson, "The Hardening of Pharaoh's Heart," *CBQ* 41 (1979), 18–36, esp. 29–35.

[38] For a definition of legend see R. M. Hals, "Legend: A Case Study in OT Form-Critical Terminology," *CBQ* 34 (1972), 166–176.

[39] See George W. Coats ("Legendary Motifs in the Moses Death Reports," *CBQ* 39 [1977], 34–44). Coats, however, does not go far enough; he restricts the figure of Moses to the category of legend, although admitting that "it is easy to shift from legend to myth" (p. 42). Given the cumulative evidence assembled here, one cannot avoid the conclusion that the biblical tradition did make that shift.

[40] See L. Bailey, "Horns of Moses," *IDBSup*, 419–420. W. H. Propp's ("The Skin of Moses' Face—Transfigured or Disfigured?" *CBQ* 49 [1987], 375–386; and "Did Moses Have Horns?" *Bible Review* 4/1 [Feb. 1988], 30–37) recent proposal, that Moses' skin was thickened and deformed ("horny") through exposure to the intense divine radiance emanating from God, is unlikely, principally because evidence for the existence of such an ancient Near Eastern motif is lacking in ancient Near Eastern literature and iconography.

[41] Representative examples may be seen in *ANEP*; for Syria nos. 490, 491, 493, 826, 829; for Mesopotamia nos. 502, 505, 513, 514, 515, 516, 529, 535, 537, 538, 651; for Anatolia no. 540; for Egypt nos. 542, 544, 556, 567, 569, 573, and for Egyptian style deities in Canaan (Beth-Shan) nos. 475, 487. Semidivine figures such as "cherubs" (nos. 644, 646, 647, 654, 655) and monsters (no. 651) are also portrayed with horns. Occasionally even Mesopotamian kings were given horns to portray their quasidivine status, e.g., Naram-Sin of Agade (*ANEP* no. 309) and Puzur-Ishtar of Mari (*ANEP* no. 433).

[42]See A. L. Oppenheim, "Akkadian *pul(u)h(t)u* and *melammū*," *JAOS* 63 (1943), 31–35; M. Dahood, *Psalms* I, AB 16 (Garden City, N.Y.: Doubleday & Co., 1965), 132. A similar theme would appear to lie behind Num. 27:18–21 (P). Yahweh commanded Moses to transfer to Joshua through a laying on of hands "some of your splendor" (*mēhôdĕkā*). The term *hôd* primarily seems to have reference to the awesome splendor of the deity which is also bestowed upon kings and others invested with divine authority. The use of the partitive *min* in v. 20 is significant because it suggests that Joshua is incapable of bearing all of Moses' aura and function; see Coats, "Legendary Motifs," 37.

[43]See chapter 2, p. 65.

[44]This account of Moses' death (Deut. 34:6–7) is commonly acknowledged to belong to the P strata of the Pentateuch; so, for example, S. R. Driver (*An Introduction to the Literature of the Old Testament*, rev. ed. [New York: Charles Scribner's Sons, 1913; Meridian Books, 1956], 72), G. von Rad (*Deuteronomy* [London: SCM Press, 1966], 209), and O. Eissfeldt (*The Old Testament: An Introduction* [Oxford: Basil Blackwell Publisher, 1965], 230). More specifically, Cross (*Canaanite Myth and Hebrew Epic*, 308–321) argues that the account of the death of Moses (Deuteronomy 34), originally part of the J-E epic, was expanded by P to form the conclusion to the Priestly edition of the Tetrateuch. In any case, Deut. 34:7 stands in stark contrast to the Deuteronomic view of Moses as a feeble old man at the time of his death: "I am a hundred and twenty years old this day; I am no longer able to go out and come in" (Deut. 31:2, RSV).

[45]See also Coats, "Legendary Motifs," 35–56.

[46]Compare E. Auerbach, *Moses*, trans. Robert A. Barclay and Israel O. Lehman (Detroit: Wayne State University, 1975), 170–171: "Moses died, not because the enormous vitality of this giant was exhausted; he appeared to be almost immortal. He died a special death: the deity summoned the loved one to it. God ordered him to die, and die he did in full vigor. The narrator has in great simplicity molded this into a powerful image."

[47]The Talmud (b. Sotah 13b) records a tradition that "some declare that Moses never died." Other traditions acknowledged that Moses did indeed die as the biblical texts say, but that his body did not suffer the corruption of ordinary mortals because God gave Moses in death unique treatment. To this category belong the now lost Semitic story of the "Assumption of Moses" and the New Testament allusion to the struggle between the archangel Michael and the devil for the body of Moses (Jude 9, apparently citing the "Assumption of Moses"); see J. Priest, "Testament of Moses," in *The Old Testament Pseudepigrapha*,

vol. 1, ed. James H. Charlesworth (Garden City, N.Y.: Doubleday & Co., 1983), 924–925. The Midrash Rabbah on Deuteronomy (XI.6–11) relates a similar tradition that Moses in death besought God not to allow "Sammael the wicked [one]" to take charge of his soul; in answer "God came down from the highest heavens to take away the soul of Moses, and with Him were three ministering angels, Michael, Gabriel, and Zagzagel"; trans. J. Rabbinowitz, *Midrash Rabbah: Deuteronomy*, ed. H. Freedman and M. Simon (London: Soncino, 1939), 186. For Philo, Moses was a "divine man" or even, in a properly qualified sense, an incarnate deity who at death abandoned his body to return to the divinity; Josephus clearly regarded Moses as the greatest of the great and purposely left the description of Moses' death ambiguous; see James D. Tabor, " 'Returning to the Divinity': Josephus's Portrayal of the Disappearances of Enoch, Elijah, and Moses," *JBL* 108 (1989), 225–238.

[48]John J. Collins ("The 'Historical Character' of the Old Testament in Recent Biblical Theology," *CBQ* 41 [1979], 185–204) says that Old Testament narratives serve as stories of "anti-structure," that is, they point to the possibility of change in the world, rather than to unchanging order and permanence. While perhaps true of the Hebrew Bible generally, Collins's analysis is inadequate as a description of the viewpoint of P specifically.

[49]Frequently in the psalms appeal is made to God's saving deeds on behalf of "our fathers" in "the days of old (*qedem*)"—which can be translated equally well as "primordial age"—as the motive for confidence in the present age; see Pss. 44:1, 74:2, 12; 77:5, 11; 78:2; 119:152; 143:5; cf. Isa. 43:18; 51:9–10; Micah 7:20.

CHAPTER 5
CROSSING DRY SHOD:
MYTHOPOEIC SPECULATION IN CULT

[1]This position was first articulated by William Robertson Smith toward the end of the nineteenth century. Under his influence there developed the "Cambridge School" of myth-ritualists, which included anthropologist Sir James George Frazer, the well-known author of *The Golden Bough*, and classicists Jane Harrison, F. M. Cornford, A. B. Cook, and Gilbert Murray. Among biblicists this position has been adopted by Sigmund Mowinckel, Ivan Engnell, A. R. Johnson, S. H. Hooke, and T. H. Gaster, among others. For a critical assessment of the myth-ritual theory see Robert A. Oden, Jr., *The Bible Without Theol-*

ogy: The Theological Tradition and Alternatives to It (New York: Harper & Row, 1987), 64–70.

[2]W. Doty, *Mythography: The Study of Myths and Rituals* (Tuscaloosa, Ala.: University of Alabama Press, 1986), 72–106.

[3]The knowledgeable reader will recognize my heavy indebtedness to F. Cross (*Canaanite Myth and Hebrew Epic* [Cambridge, Mass.: Harvard University Press, 1973], esp. sec. II, "The Cultus of the Israelite League," 77–144) for the thesis developed in this chapter.

[4]From a somewhat different avenue Jon D. Levenson (*Creation and the Persistence of Evil: The Jewish Drama of Divine Omnipotence* [San Francisco: Harper & Row, 1988], 51–127) has demonstrated a close connection between Gen. 1:1–2:3 and Israelite cult. In Israelite cosmogony the Zion temple, like its ancient Near Eastern counterparts in Ugarit and Babylon, functioned as a microcosm of the ideal world of creation portrayed in the creation myth (pp. 78–99).

[5]The designations used here are those of Andrée Herdner, *Corpus des tablettes en cunéiformes alphabétiques* (Mission de Ras Shamra 10 (Paris: Imprimerie Nationale, 1963) (= *CTA*). Other widely used designations are those of C. H. Gordon, *Ugaritic Textbook*, Analecta Orientalia 38 (Rome: Biblical Institute, 1965) (= *UT*); and M. Dietrich, O. Loretz, and J. Sanmartin, *Die keilalphabetischen Texte aus Ugarit*, Alter Orient und Altes Testament 24 (Neukirchen-Vluyn; Neukirchener V., 1976) (= *KTU*). The equivalents for tablets 1–6 are:

CTA	1	=	*UT*	'nt, pl. IX, X	=	*KTU*	1.1
	2			68, 129			1.2
	3			'nt			1.3
	4			51			1.4
	5			67			1.5
	6			49+62			1.6

[6]In particular, Clifford argues that *CTA* 3 is a variant of *CTA* 4. Although the plot is virtually identical in both tablets, the protagonists are different: Baal and Yam in *CTA* 3, and Baal and Mot in *CTA* 4. Moreover, while *CTA* 4 belongs to the same cycle as *CTA* 5–6, the latter does not necessarily follow directly upon the former. Finally, the relationship of *CTA* 2 to either *CTA* 3 or *CTA* 4+5–6 cannot now be determined. See Richard J. Clifford, "Cosmogonies in the Ugaritic Texts and in the Bible," *Or* 53 (1984), 183–201.

[7]Convenient English translations may be found in *ANET*[3], pp. 129–

142 (by H. L. Ginsberg); and Michael D. Coogan, *Stories from Ancient Canaan* (Philadelphia: Westminster Press, 1978). Note, however, that in Ginsberg's translation the tablets are arranged in a very differ order from the one assumed here. Coogan's ordering of the tablets is closer to my understanding, except that Coogan assumes all tablets to derive from a single tale. In the terminology used here, Coogan's secs. I and II (pp. 86–96; = *CTA* 2 and 3) correspond to the Yam version, secs. III–V (pp. 96–115; = *CTA* 4 + 5–6) to the Mot version.

[8]*CTA* 2 and 3 are here treated as a connected text since Baal's opponent in both is Yam. Note the caution of Clifford (see above n. 6), however, that the relationship of *CTA* 2 to the other tablets in the Baal cycle cannot now be determined.

[9]Translation of Coogan, *Stories from Ancient Canaan*, 89.

[10]See B. Batto, "The Covenant of Peace," *CBQ* 49, 196–201.

[11]So Coogan, *Stories from Ancient Canaan*, 11.

[12]See my articles "The Reed Sea: *Requiescat in Pace*," *JBL* 102 (1983), 27–35, esp. 30–31; and "Red Sea or Reed Sea?" *BARev* 10/4 (July/August 1984), 57–63, esp. 60–63.

[13]The following discussion is based in part upon the five phrases of Gilgal postulated by J. Alberto Soggin, "Gilgal, Passah und Landnahme," VTS 15 (1966), 263–277, esp. 268–269.

[14]H. J. Kraus, "Gilgal: Ein Beitrag zur Kultusgeschichte Israels," *VT* 1 (1951), 181–199, esp. 193.

[15]In this process of assimilation and historicization a certain amount of inconsistency was inevitable. Thus the Old Testament is ambivalent in attaching the same traditions to Gilgal in one text and to Shechem in another. The recitation of the blessings and the curses attached to the covenant, once pronounced on Mount Gerizim and Mount Ebal in the region of Shechem, was later ritually reenacted in the vicinity of Gilgal, as evidenced by an editorial gloss at Deut. 11:29–30: "And when the LORD your God brings you into the land which you are entering to take possession of it, you shall set the blessing on Mount Gerizim and the curse on Mount Ebal. *Are they not beyond the Jordan, west of the road, toward the going down of the sun, beside the oak of Moreh?*" (RSV, emphasis added). See Otto Eissfeldt, "Gilgal or Shechem?" in *Proclamation and Presence: Old Testament Essays in Honour of G. H. Davies*, ed. John I. Durham and J. R. Porter (Richmond: John Knox Press, 1970), 90–101.

[16]A convenient and recent summary of the biblical data and scholarly debate is given by J. Maxwell Miller, "The Israelite Occupation of

Canaan," in *Israelite and Judaean History*, ed. John H. Hayes and J. Maxwell Miller (Philadelphia: Westminster Press, 1977), 213–284.

[17]The ritual background of these chapters in Joshua was first recognized by H. J. Kraus (see above n. 14) and reaffirmed by J. A. Soggin (see above n. 13); see also Cross's description of "Ritual Conquest" at Gilgal in *Canaanite Myth and Hebrew Epic*, 99–105.

[18]The epithet "lord of all the earth" (*'dn kl 'rṣ*) would appear to be a distinctively Gilgalite cultic formula; see Cross, *Canaanite Myth and Hebrew Epic*, 138–139.

[19]The Deuteronomistic History consists of the biblical books of Joshua, Judges, 1 and 2 Samuel, and 1 and 2 Kings. According to Martin Noth, who first proposed the theory (*Überlieferungsgeschichtliche Studien* [1943]; E. T.: *The Deuteronomistic History*, JSOTSup 15 [Sheffield: JSOT, 1981]), the Deuteronomistic History was composed by a single author during the Babylonian exile (about 550 B.C.E.) in order to explain the catastrophes of the Assyrian destruction of the Northern Kingdom in 721 B.C.E. and esp. the Babylonian destruction of the Southern Kingdom in 597 B.C.E. Subsequent studies have expanded upon Noth's original thesis and have demonstrated that there were likely two editions of the Deuteronomistic History: the original composition (Dtr[1]) completed prior to the collapse of the Southern Kingdom, likely during the heyday of King Josiah's reforms (c. 620–610 B.C.E., and a revision of the work (Dtr[2]) written from an exilic perspective some fifty years later. See Cross, *Canaanite Myth and Hebrew Epic*, 274–289. See further R. E. Friedman, *The Exile and Biblical Narrative: The Formation of the Deuteronomistic and Priestly Works*, HSM 22 (Chico, Calif.: Scholars Press, 1981), 1–43; R. D. Nelson, *The Double Redaction of the Deuteronomistic History*, JSOTSup 18 (Sheffield: JSOT, 1981).

[20]See J. A. Soggin, *Joshua: A Commentary*, OTL (Philadelphia: Westminster Press, 1972), 50–54.

[21]See Brian Peckham ("The Composition of Joshua 3–4," *CBQ* 46 [1984], 413–431), who includes a review of previous scholarship; Peckham's own idiosyncratic solution does not inspire confidence, however.

[22]Contrary to Peckham ("Composition of Joshua," 430), who posits that the original version (Dtr[1]) had an ordinary crossing by a fording of the Jordan, but that in the later (Dtr[2]) edition the fords were eliminated in favor of the miraculous crossing.

[23]M. Noth, *Das Buch Josua*, 2nd ed., HAT I/7 (Tübingen: J. C. B. Mohr [Paul Siebeck], 1953), 9; P. Langlamet, "La Traversée du Jourdain et les documents de l'Hexateuque," *RB* 79 (1972), 7–38.

Even though these verses occur in passages heavily redacted by the Deuteronomist, they did not originate with Deuteronomist, contrary to Peckham, "Composition of Joshua," 413–431. The Deuteronomist was not especially fond of the motif of crossing the Red Sea dry shod, as he failed to introduce it in passages dealing with the Red Sea (Deut. 11:3–4; Josh. 24:5–7). Elsewhere he refers to the exodus with vague, stereotyped phrases about the gracious God "who brought you/your fathers out of Egypt" (Judg. 6:8; 1 Sam. 10:18, 12:6, 8; 1 Kings 8:9, 51, 53; 9:9; 2 Kings 17:7; and secondarily in Deut. 4:20, 37; Josh. 24:17; Judg. 2:1; 2 Kings 17:36) or even less specifically, the renown of Yahweh, which spreads awe among those who hear "of all that he did to Egypt" (Josh. 9:9). See M. Noth, *A History of Pentateuchal Traditions* (Englewood Cliffs, N.J.: Prentice-Hall, 1972), 48–49.

[24]Although problematic in a number of points, the links between the deuteronomic traditions and Gilgal noted by J. N. Wijngaards cannot be ignored; see her *Dramatization of Salvific History in the Deuteronomic Schools*, OTS 16 (Leiden: E. J. Brill, 1969), 58–63 and 117–123.

[25]See esp. S. Mowinckel, *The Psalms in Israel's Worship*, I (Nashville: Abingdon Press, 1962), 1–41. H. Gunkel (*The Psalms: A Form Critical-Introduction* [Philadelphia: Fortress Press, 1967], 26–29) posited a cultic origin for many psalms, but claimed that subsequently many of these were privatized for personal use.

[26]Cross, *Canaanite Myth and Hebrew Epic*, 140–144.

[27]The premier study on Habakkuk 3 is that of W. F. Albright, "The Psalm of Habakkuk," in *Studies in Old Testament Prophecy Presented to Professor Theodore H. Robinson*, ed. H. H. Rowley (Edinburgh: T. & T. Clark, 1950), 1–18; see further Cross, *Canaanite Myth and Hebrew Epic*, 140; T. Hiebert, *God of My Victory: The Ancient Hymn in Habakkuk 3*, HSM 38 (Atlanta: Scholars Press, 1986).

[28]So first H. L. Ginsberg, "A Phoenician Hymn in the Psalter," in *Atti del XIX Congresso Internazionale degli Orientalisti* (Rome: Tipografia del Senato, G. Bardi, 1935), 472–476; followed by T. H. Gaster, "Psalm 29," *JQR* 37 (1946/47), 55–65; F. M. Cross, "Notes on a Canaanite Psalm in the Old Testament," *BASOR* 117 (1950), 19–21; and others.

[29]For additional consideration of this passage see chapter 3.

[30]*CTA* 5.i.1–3; cf. 3.iii.35–39. Biblical reflexes are found elsewhere in Job 26:12–13; Isa. 27:1; Rev. 12:3, 9. See further Cross, *Canaanite Myth and Hebrew Epic*, 112–120.

[31]See chapter 3.

[32]Repointing MT ʿal yām to ʿōlîm, with LXX, eliminates any need to

change the consonantal text; it also further emphasizes the contrast between Yahweh's grace and Israel's sin, so obvious in the psalmist's intention.

[33]Dependency upon the received text of Ex. 13:17–15:21 is observable in numerous verbal correspondences: the sea is *yam sûp*; "walk" (*hālak*) rather than "cross" (*'ābār*) in v. 9, cf. Ex. 14:29; Abyss (*tĕhōmôt*) in v. 9, cf. Ex. 15:5, 8; "redeemed" v. 10, cf. Ex. 15:13; v. 11 echoes Ex. 14:28; vs. 12a and 12b are dependent upon Ex. 14:31c and 15:1–21, respectively.

CHAPTER 6
EGYPT AND GOG AS MYTHIC SYMBOLS IN EZEKIEL

[1]See my article "The Covenant of Peace: A Neglected Ancient Near Eastern Motif," *CBQ* 49 (1987), 187–211.

[2]A. Williams ("The Mythological Background of Ezekiel 28:12–19?" *BTB* 6 [1976], 49–61) has reached similar conclusions in his study concerning the mythic character of Ezekiel's oracle against Tyre.

[3]G. Hölscher (*Hesekiel: Der Dichter und das Buch*, BZAW 39 [Giessen: Töpelmann, 1924]) argued that only one-seventh of the book came from historical Ezekiel; the remainder was the work of an unimaginative fifth-century redactor who radically transformed the nature of the original composition, including the adding of the whole proclamation of salvation in chs. 33–48. S. Herrmann (*Die prophetischen Heilserwartungen im Alten Testament*, BWANT 85 [Stuttgart: Kohlhammer, 1965], 241ff.) similarly claimed that every expectation of salvation in the book must be regarded as the work of a later hand. C. C. Torrey (*Pseudo-Ezekiel and the Original Prophecy*, Yale Oriental Studies 18 [New Haven, Conn.: Yale University Press, 1930]) maintained that the whole book was a pseudepigraph originating c. 230 B.C.E. V. Herntrich (*Ezechielprobleme*, BZAW 61 [Giessen: Töpelmann, 1933]) assigned the basic form of chs. 1–39 to an Ezekiel active in Jerusalem before 587, the remainder (including the restoration program of chs. 40–48) to a redactor living in exile c. 573. See further the convenient summaries of critical Ezekielian scholarship by O. Kaiser, *Introduction to the Old Testament: A Presentation of Its Result and Problems* (Minneapolis: Augsburg Publishing House, 1975), 248–257; and B. Childs, *Introduction to the Old Testament as Scripture* (Philadelphia: Fortress Press, 1979), 353–372.

[4]Moshe Greenberg (*Ezekiel, 1–20*, AB 22 [Garden City, N.Y.: Doubleday & Co., 1983], 26–27) states:

The various operations undertaken in this commentary test the working assumption that the present Book of Ezekiel is the product of art and intelligent design. . . . A consistent trend of thought expressed in a distinctive style has emerged, giving the impression of an individual mind of powerful and passionate proclivities. The chronology of the oracles and the historical circumstances reflected in them assign them to a narrow temporal range well within the span of a single life. The persuasion grows on one as piece after piece falls into the established patterns and ideas that a coherent world of vision is emerging, contemporary with the sixth-century prophet and decisively shaped by him, if not the very words of Ezekiel himself.

[5]L. Boadt, "Rhetorical Strategies in Ezekiel's Oracles of Judgment," in *Ezekiel and His Book: Textual and Literary Criticism and Their Interrelation*, BETL 74, ed. J. Lust (Leuven: Leuven University Press, 1986), 182–200.

[6]Boadt, "Rhetorical Strategies," 196–199.

[7]I prescind here from the question of whether the historical prophet Ezekiel or some "disciple" actually composed the book of Ezekiel; I am arguing only that the shape and contents of the canonical book derive substantially from the genius of the original author, whoever that may have been. Contrast, for example, W. Eichrodt (*Ezekiel: A Commentary*, OTL [Philadelphia: Westminster Press, 1970], 352), who, even while conceding that certain of the oracles against the nations derive from the prophet Ezekiel, argues that this "little book against foreign nations" once existed independently and that "its insertion into the midst of the text of the prophetic book has all the appearance of a foreign body pushing its way into an organic whole, and in the process tearing apart things originally connected together." Likewise concerning the Gog oracles, Eichrodt (p. 519) finds them intrusive and "contrary to the prophet's intentions." Similarly R. Ahroni, "The Gog Prophecy and the Book of Ezekiel," *HUCA* 1 (1977), 1–27.

[8]Ezek. 39:25–29 is frequently regarded as still later. On the assumption that the Gog prophecy once circulated independently, R. Ahroni ("Gog Prophecy," esp. 4–5, 24) claims that the redactor who inserted the Gog oracles into Ezekiel added these verses "as a literary artifice to form a link between ch. 37 and ch. 40"; similarly Eichrodt, *Ezekiel*, 521. P. Hanson (*The Dawn of Apocalyptic: The Historical and Sociological Roots of Jewish Apocalyptic Eschatology*

[Philadelphia: Fortress Press, 1975], 234n) discounts the Gog oracles as a late attempt to explain why the original restoration program envisioned by the prophets had not occurred.

[9]M. Greenberg, *Ezekiel, 1–20*, 102–103, 120–121; Robert Wilson, "An Interpretation of Ezekiel's Dumbness," *VT* 22 (1972), 91–104.

[10]Jon Levenson, *Theology of the Program of Restoration of Ezekiel 40–48*, HSM 10 (Missoula, Mont.: Scholars Press, 1975).

[11]D. S. Russell (*The Method and Message of Jewish Apocalyptic*, OTL [London: SCM Press, 1964], 88–91) observes that while Ezekiel 38–39, Zechariah 9–14, and Isaiah 24–27 cannot properly be called apocalyptic, these passages contain the seeds from which apocalyptic developed; Ahroni ("Gog Prophecy," 15–18) sees Ezekiel 38–39 as pure apocalyptic. For a contrary view see Hanson, *Dawn of Apocalyptic*, 228–240.

[12]Compare Joel 3 and Zachariah 14, where the advent of the eschatological reign of God is linked with a prior destruction of the foreign nations.

[13]See further A. Vanhoye, "L'utilization du livre d'Ezechiel dans l'Apocalypse," *Bib* 43 (1962), 436–476.

[14]For a summary of attempts to identify Gog and Magog and the various countries associated with Gog in these oracles, see Walther Zimmerli, *Ezekiel 2* (Philadelphia: Fortress Press, 1983), 299–302; and M. Astour, "Ezekiel's Prophecy of Gog and the Cuthean Legend of Naram-Sin," *JBL* 94 (1976), 567–579, esp. 569–571.

[15]Astour ("Ezekiel's Prophecy," 572–579) posits the origins of the Gog prophecy in the Babylonian didactic poem known as the Cuthean Legend of Naram-Sin, in which the legendary northern hordes known as the Umman-manda were repulsed by divine intervention. But even if Ezekiel knew and was influenced by such mythic literature, the Gog pericope was very likely an original composition created by Ezekiel out of prior mythic elements, just as he did in the case of Tyre; see Williams, "Mythical Background of Ezekiel 28:12–19?" 49–61.

[16]Two considerations strengthen this interpretation. First, Gog of Magog is said to come from "the fartherest corners of the North" (*yarkĕtê-ṣāpôn*), i.e., from the regions most removed from the center of the earth; cf. "the Sea of End" (*yam sûp*) for a comparable symbol of chaos/evil located at the edge of creation; see chapter 3, and my articles "The Reed Sea: *Requiescat in Pace*," *JBL* 102/1 (1983), 27–35, and "Red Sea or Reed Sea?" *BARev* 10/4 (July/August 1984), 57–63. Second, that this is the interpretation of the ancients is confirmed by the fact that the author of Revelation (20:8) associated Gog and

Magog with defeat of Satan himself, rather than with the earlier destruction of the beast (Babylon-Rome).

[17]For a full discussion of this motif see my article, "Covenant of Peace," 187–211.

[18]See above n. 16.

[19]See Zimmerli, *Ezekiel 2*, 299–300.

[20]In MT "Sheshak," a cipher for Babylon; cf. Jer. 51:41.

[21]Although ostensibly arguing for a "this-worldly" identification of the foe from the north, D. J. Reimer ("The 'Foe' and the 'North' in Jeremiah," *ZAW* 101 [1989], 223–232) arrives at a comparable conclusion: in Jeremiah ṣāpôn has reference not to a point on the compass but to the dwelling place of Yahweh from whence judgment is dispatched, which judgment may take the form of historical foes.

[22]Four, that is, one-half, of the eight chapters of oracles against the nations are devoted to Egypt. Or to count another way, of the 197 verses in these eight chapters, 97 are devoted to Egypt.

[23]See Zimmerli, *Ezekiel 2*, 3–4.

[24]The plural "Niles" is a reference to the several branches of the Nile in the delta region of lower Egypt.

[25]Reading with MT as the *lectio difficilior*. The versions read a different personal prononinal suffix after the verb; LXX: *autous* ("them"), also in v. 9; Syriac: -*h* ("it").

[26]Egypt is similarly caricatured elsewhere in the Bible. In Ps. 87:4 and Isa. 30:7 Egypt is referred to as Rahab, another name for the primeval foe of the creator; see Mary K. Wakeman, *God's Battle with the Monster: A Study in Biblical Imagery* (Leiden: E. J. Brill, 1973), 56–62. However, in Isa. 27:1 the image of chaos monster ("Leviathan that twisting serpent" *liwĕyātān nāḥaš bārīaḥ* / "Leviathan that writhing·serpent" *liwĕyātān nāḥaš ʿaqallātôn* / "the dragon which is in the sea" *ḥattannîn ʾăšer bayyām*) may apply to Assyria and Babylon as well as to Egypt (see 27:12–13).

[27]Cf. Psalm 114; Hab. 3:8–10, 15; see chapter 5, pp. 132–133.

[28]In the Ugaritic Baal myth, Mot too lives in the underworld in similar conditions; when Baal is forced to descend in the underworld:

> They left; they did not turn back;
>   then they headed toward El's son Death,
> to the midst of his city, the Swamp,
>   Muck, his royal house,
>   Phlegm, the land of his inheritance.

(trans. M. D. Coogan, *Stories from Ancient Canaan* [Philadelphia: Westminster Press, 1978], p. 107).

[29]On stygian night as a symbol of chaos see chapter 2, n. 15.

[30]See Boadt, "Rhetorical Strategies," 148.

[31]Similar conclusions are drawn by Boadt, "Rhetorical Strategies," 199–200; and Marco Nobile, "Beziehung zwischen Ez 32,17–32 und der Gog-Perikope (Ez 38–39) im Lichte der Endredaktion," in *Ezekiel and His Book: Textual and Literary Criticism and their Interrelation*, BETL 74, ed. J. Lust (Leuven: Leuven University Press, 1986), 255–259.

EPILOGUE:
MYTHOPOEISM IN THE NEW TESTAMENT

[1]On apocalypticism and related literature see D. Hellholm, ed., *Apocalypticism in the Mediterranean World and the Near East* (Tübingen: Mohr [Paul Siebeck], 1983); C. Rowland, *The Open Heaven* (New York: Crossroad, 1982); J. J. Collins, *The Apocalyptic Imagination* (New York: Crossroad, 1984); idem, *Daniel, with an Introduction to Apocalyptic Literature* (Grand Rapids: Wm. B. Eerdmans Publishing Co., 1984), esp. 2–24; M. E. Stone, "Apocalyptic Literature," in *Jewish Writings of the Second Temple Period*, Compendia Rerum Iudaicarum ad Novum Testamentum 2/2 (Philadelphia: Fortress Press/Assen: van Gorcum, 1984); and the two articles of P. D. Hanson, "Apocalypse, Genre" and "Apocalypticism," in *IDBSup*, 27–34.

[2]Already in the prophets, primeval myth has been recast as eschatological hope; see my article "The Covenant of Peace," *CBQ* 49 (1987), 187–211.

[3]On the evolution of the figure of Satan, see Neil Forsyth, *The Old Enemy: Satan and the Combat Myth* (Princeton, N.J.: Princeton University Press, 1987).

[4]See John Day, *God's Conflict with the Dragon and the Sea* (Cambridge: Cambridge University Press, 1985), 141–178; J. J. Collins, *The Apocalyptic Vision of the Book of Daniel* (Missoula, Mont.: Scholars Press, 1977), 95–147.

[5]J. Collins (*The Apocalyptic Vision of the Book of Daniel*, 101–104) points to examples of the mythic traditions in the ancient world over the period of a millennium or more through the learned circles of scribes. This is certainly one important channel of transmission, as the biblical tradition itself bears witness. But such traditions would

lose their vitality should they not continue to be operative as myth among the community that preserved them.

[6]See H. Gunkel, *Schöpfung und Chaos in Urzeit und Endzeit. Eine religionsgeschichtliche Untersuchung über Gen 1 und Ap Joh 12* (Göttingen: Vandenhoeck & Ruprecht, 1895), 171–398; A. Y. Collins, *The Combat Myth in the Book of Revelation* (Missoula, Mont.: Scholars Press, 1976); idem, *The Apocalypse*, New Testament Message 22 (Wilmington, Del.: Michael Glazier, 1979), esp. 84–98.

[7]See chapter 3.

[8]In the following treatment of these pericopes I am in large part dependent upon John Paul Heil, *Jesus Walking on the Sea: Meaning and Gospel Functions of Matt 14:23–33, Mark 6:45–52 and John 6:15b–21*, AnBib 87 (Rome: Biblical Institute, 1981).

[9]Job 26:12; Isa. 51:15; Jer. 31:35; cf. Pss. 89:9[ET 10]; 107:29.

[10]Job 9:8; Hab. 3:15; Ps. 77:19.

[11]Cf. *peripatōn epi tēs thalassēs* "(he came to them) walking upon the sea" (Mark 6:48d; cf. Matt. 14:25b and John 6:19b) with esp. the Septuagint Greek of Job 9:8b, *kai peripatōn hōs ep' edaphous epi thalassēs* "and (who) walked on sea as if (walking) on ground." See Heil, *Jesus Walking on the Sea*, 37–56.

[12]Compare especially Mark 4:39 ("And he awoke and rebuked [*epitimân*] the wind, and said to the sea, 'Keep silent! Be stilled!' " [my translation]) with Job 26:11–12 ("The pillars of heaven tremble, and are astounded at his rebuke [Hebrew: *gāʿar*; LXX: *epitimân*]. By his power he stilled the sea; by his understanding he smote Rahab."). The sea is also rebuked by God in Pss. 18:15 (= 2 Sam. 22:16); 104:7; 106:9; and Isa. 50:2. Satan is similarly rebuked in Zech. 3:2.

[13]Compare *siōpa, pephimōso*, "Quiet! Be silent!" (4:39) with *phimōthēti*, "Be silenced!" (1:25) (my translations). The similar reaction of the bystanders is further evidence that Mark intended to equate these two events (cf. 4:41 with 1:27).

[14]Cf. Dan. 7:2–3; Rev. 13:1; contrast Rev. 21:1.

[15]B. Batto, "The Sleeping God: An Ancient Near Eastern Motif of Divine Sovereignty," *Bib* 68 (1987), 153–177; or in a more popular version, "When God Sleeps," *Bible Review* 3/4 (Winter 1987), 16–23.

[16]Nonetheless, the demonic element has not been completely eliminated, for Luke retained the verb "rebuked" (*epitimân*). In Luke (4:35, 39) as in Mark this verb often is used in a technical sense of solemnly commanding demons; see J. Fitzmyer, *The Gospel According to Luke I–IX*, AB 28 (Garden City, N.Y.: Doubleday & Co., 1981), 546 and 730.

[17]The words "fear not" (*'al tîrā'*, LXX *mē phobou*) and "I am" (*'anî hû'*, LXX *egō eimi*) occur repeatedly in Isa. 43:1–13 (all RSV, emphasis added): "*Fear not*, for I have redeemed you" (v. 1c); "When you pass through the waters I will be with you" (v. 2a); "For *I am* the LORD your God" (v. 3a); "*Fear not*, for I am with you" (v. 5a); "that you may know and believe me and understand that *I am He*" (v. 10b); "*I, I am* the LORD, and besides me there is no savior" (v. 11); "*I am* God, and also henceforth *I am He*; there is none who can deliver from my hand: I work and who can hinder it?" (v. 13). See Heil, *Jesus Walking on the Sea*, 59. For a discussion of *egō eimi* as a formula of divine revelation, particularly in conjunction with the incident of Jesus walking on the sea in John 6:20, see R. Brown, *The Gospel According to John (i–xii)*, AB 29 (Garden City, N.Y.: Doubleday & Co., 1966), 533–538.

[18]There is not here a simple identification of God and Jesus. In the Hebrew Bible the LORD often manifests himself through a messenger (*mal'āk*). Moreover as noted earlier, in Daniel 7 and in the book of Revelation the deity exercises his divine rule through an associate, the Son of man and the Lamb, respectively. On the complex question of whether Jesus is ever called God in the New Testament, see R. Brown, *Jesus God and Man* (New York: Macmillan, 1967).

INDEX OF SCRIPTURE REFERENCES

INDEX OF FOREIGN WORDS

INDEX OF AUTHORS

240

INDEX OF SUBJECTS